GREAT PERSONAL LETTERS FOR BUSY PEOPLE

GREAT PERSONAL LETTERS FOR BUSY PEOPLE

501 READY-TO-USE LETTERS FOR EVERY OCCASION

Revised and Expanded Edition

Dianna Booher

McGraw-Hill
New York   San Francisco   Washington, D.C.   Auckland   Bogotá
Caracas   Lisbon   London   Madrid   Mexico City   Milan
Montreal   New Delhi   San Juan   Singapore
Sydney   Tokyo   Toronto

2 3 4 5 6 7 8 9 0 DOC/DOC 0 9 8 7 6

ISBN 0-07-146498-0

McGraw-Hill books are available at special quantity discounts to use as premiums and sales promotions, or for use in corporate training programs. For more information, please write to the Director of Special Sales, McGraw-Hill, 2 Penn Plaza, New York, NY 10121-2298. Or contact your local bookstore.

Library of Congress Cataloging-in-Publication Data

Booher, Dianna Daniels.
   Great personal letters for busy people : 501 ready-to-use letters for every occasion / by Dianna Booher.—Rev. and expanded ed.
      p. cm.
   Includes bibliographical references.
   ISBN 0-07-146498-0 (alk. paper)
  1. Letter writing. 2. Interpersonal communication. I. Title.
   BJ2101.B66 2005
   808.6—dc22   2005029381

CONTENTS

CHARITIES, VOLUNTEER WORK, AND FUND-RAISING   47

CLERGY AND SUPPORT ORGANIZATIONS   87

COLLEGE   107

CONGRATULATIONS   131

CONSUMER ISSUES AND CONCERNS   153

DECLINING INVITATIONS OR REQUESTS   237

FRIENDS AND RELATIVES   257

GOVERNMENT PROGRAMS   279

HOME CONCERNS   305

JOB REFERENCES AND INTRODUCTIONS   381

LETTERS TO YOUNG CHILDREN   393

MEDIA: ISSUES, CONCERNS, POSITIONS   409

OPINIONS AND POLITICS   435

PHYSICIANS AND MEDICAL ISSUES   485

SYMPATHY AND CONDOLENCES   511

GREAT PERSONAL LETTERS FOR BUSY PEOPLE

SO WHY WRITE WHEN I CAN PHONE?

Who's got time to write a letter or note these days? Why not just pick up the phone and call? Several reasons: speed and efficiency, impact, tact, and courtesy.

SPEED AND EFFICIENCY

Yes, writing a letter, an e-mail, or a note can be faster than making a phone call. Let me explain: How often do you dial someone at an organization and get a live person—the *right* live person—on the first try? More routinely, you receive a recorded message and a beep. Then the person returns your call and leaves you a message. Telephone tag can waste hours and days. It is not atypical that when conducting your personal business you may have to make three or four calls over a period of three to ten days to resolve a matter.

Consider this scenario. Let's say you have a problem with your checking account. The bank fails to credit your account with a deposit, returns a check to someone marked "insufficient funds," and then charges you a $20 fee for the returned check. You could call the customer service department at the bank to discuss the problem—if you have three to five minutes to wade through the phone recordings and menus to get to the right person. Then suppose that person says she'll take care of it. But she doesn't.

You call a second time and get another person on the line, who'll "have to research it" and call you back. You get a call back two days later from the bank agent saying she has corrected the error. You ask if she'll notify the merchant involved to explain that the bounced check was the bank's error rather than yours. The agent doesn't know if the bank can do that. She'll "check on it" with her supervisor. She calls you back a couple of days later to say, yes, she'll write the merchant to restore your good name. So you finally have the problem corrected—four phone calls, 20 minutes' talking time, and six days later.

And that's *if things go well*. The more likely scenario is that the bank rep asks you to bring in or mail a copy of the deposit slip for the deposit that you say you made but never got credited to your account. You'll have to write a letter when mailing the deposit slip, explaining again everything you told the bank rep over the phone. Or, worse, you'll have to go into the bank to explain it all again in person. And then that person you phone or talk to at the bank often asks for written documentation of the situation before action can be taken!

I repeat: It's often much faster and more efficient to write a letter (fax it if you're in a hurry) with all the details and supporting documentation, and let the reader do the walking and researching and conferring to take the action you want. Calling can become a long, drawn-out process of telephone tag and frustration.

IMPACT

A personal letter or note has greater impact on the recipient than a phone call. A message in black and white always looks more objective, factual, and firm. In other words, because writing is more formal than talking, your message takes on more importance and punch.

When do you need that increased impact in personal situations? Demanding that your landlord make repairs in your apartment. Insisting that the medical clinic has overcharged you. Telling the insurance company you expect a larger settlement for the damage to your car or house. Persuading the university to readmit you after you've withdrawn with failing grades and unexplained absences. Urging your congressional representative to vote no on the new tax bill. Asking a clergy member for a job reference. Hitting up your relative for a loan. Breaking a relationship for good. Demanding that the auto mechanic treat you fairly. Soliciting money for a charity that must have funds to survive. Demanding that the manufacturer refund your money on a defective product.

A letter demands more attention and a more serious response than angry words in person or on the phone.

For the same reasons, personal letters to express *positive* sentiments sound more heartfelt and purposeful. How? Expressing appreciation to a teacher for his contribution to your life. Thanking a friend for encouragement or help during a difficulty. Expressing your love to a spouse, parents, friends, or other relatives.

Letters and notes have impact—both positive and negative. They have staying power.

TACT

Most people think better on their seat than on their feet. That is, if they can take a few moments to collect their thoughts in a sensitive situation, their words are less apt to hurt someone's feelings and are more prone to protect the sensitivities of all concerned.

When do you need such tactful wording? Declining to write a job reference for a friend's son, who you think is a jerk. Turning down a friend or relative who wants you to lend money. Reminding members of your social club that they still haven't paid you their share for the going-away gift. Telling your friend you're sorry about the divorce. Reminding your neighbor that she still hasn't paid for the damaged sofa. Declining an invitation to a boring event.

You can be more tactful when you have the time to linger over appropriate phrasing for touchy situations.

COURTESY

Have you noticed that fewer and fewer people follow the accepted norms of etiquette in business and social situations? It's as if our lives move at such a fast pace that we can't be bothered with "little things"—like accepting or declining a party invitation, thanking people for gifts, or responding to someone's congratulatory message. But the well-educated, cosmopolitan, cultured few do still incorporate courtesy into their lives. That's why they stand above the crowd as people with "class."

The more technical our world becomes, the more acute the need for the human touch: Building rapport with coworkers, community leaders, and friends demands that you pay attention to what's going on in their lives and respond in a socially acceptable way. Recognize achievements in their lives. Express appreciation for volunteer work. Wish them well on anniversaries and birthdays. Express gratitude for help and encouragement. Congratulate them on happy occasions such as birthdays and graduations. Express sorrow at their losses. In a high-tech world, the human touch through written words builds strong relationships.

So for all these reasons—speed and efficiency, impact, tact, and courtesy—personal letters and notes can:

- Solve problems with businesses and government organizations
- Build goodwill in the community
- Improve relationships with family and friends
- Handle sensitive issues with tact
- Solicit charitable contributions of time and money
- Add power to potentially threatening or dangerous situations
- Clarify actions in routine personal business transactions
- Strengthen positions on moral, social, and political issues that need attention

In short, when you have a problem or situation that needs action, these model letters, e-mail messages, and notes can help you express yourself with passion, power, and speed.

ANNOUNCEMENTS

An announcement implies immediacy. The first rule of thumb about announcing an event such as an engagement or a wedding, divorce, birth, graduation, or retirement is that *your* announcement reaches the reader before the news travels by other means. If your announcement is old news, it has arrived too late.

Then put yourself in the place of the reader: What key details would you want to know? Most likely the names, places, locations, and dates. After these details, you'll want to address specific concerns or issues that will likely flood the reader's mind. If it's an engagement, what's the time frame on the wedding? If it's a wedding, will you be moving to live elsewhere? Will you be changing jobs? Is the family thrilled? If it's a retirement, what is the effective date and what are your plans? Are you in good health? What do you plan to do with yourself between 9 and 5?

Friends and family also appreciate knowing how you feel about the event, occasion, or situation. Are you proud, sad, hopeful, excited, expectant, or happy about the future? Of course, you do want to be sensitive about special circumstances, such as announcing a divorce. You'll want to avoid saying things that might reflect negatively on others involved or might make you appear to be bitter, angry, or insensitive. Generally, prefer to save the juicy, specific details for personal conversations.

Finally, use a personal, warm tone. Your announcement takes the place of a glowing smile, warm handshake, or loving hug that you would deliver in person.

• BIRTH OF CHILD •

Example 1

Dear Karen and Charles,

If you could see my face now, you'd say it was beaming. We have a new baby boy, born Wednesday, January 13, at 10 P.M. Franklin Augustus weighed in at 8 pounds; by all indications, he's happy so far with his station in life.

Jack and I are so thrilled that he's healthy and raring to get on with living. As you know, we have waited so long for this happy change in our lives that we couldn't wait to share the news with everyone. We feel very blessed.

Sincerely,

• BIRTH OF CHILD •

Example 2

Dear Warren and Ava,

Evan and Janice Beck are pleased to announce the birth of their second daughter, Britney Elizabeth Beck. Both mother and daughter are doing well. (Evan seems a bit shaken, however.)

Janice and Britney are scheduled to be released from the hospital tomorrow morning. Please feel free to phone or stop in at any time thereafter.

Britney was born at 12:43 in the morning at St. Joseph's Hospital in Phoenix. She weighs 7 pounds, 6 ounces, and has a tuft of black hair right in the middle of her forehead. She looks just like her father.

We look forward to hearing from you soon.

Sincerely,

• ADOPTION OF A CHILD •

Dear Mark and Jenny,

Well, the wait is finally over. Last week, Candace and I returned from China with a new addition to our family, Wen Nian Zhan, who'll turn four on March 5.

After Wen's mother passed away during childbirth, Wen was sent to the Zhanjiang City Children's Welfare Institute in Guangdong Province. Though she misses her friends back in China, she seems to be taking quickly to her new life and is already picking up some English (including, much to Candace's delight, the word "Mama"). She has silky black hair and a smile that lights up the room—not to mention our hearts. We can't wait for you to meet her.

Sincerely,

• ENGAGEMENT •

For those of you doubters who thought that after five years it was never going to happen: The question has been asked, and an affirmative answer given. Daniel Cedeno and I are thrilled to announce our engagement to be married.

We haven't yet set a date for the wedding, but are looking at the last week in April as the most workable option so far. We'll let you know as soon as we do.

Daniel's parents, Pete and Stephanie Cedeno, have planned an engagement party in our honor. Enclosed is your invitation.

We hope to see you there.

Sincerely,

• GRADUATION OF SON OR DAUGHTER •

Lucy and Derek Wolford are thrilled to announce the graduation of their son Matthew Arnold from Texas State University.

Commencement exercises will be held Saturday, May 14, at Stratton Coliseum on the TSU campus in San Madrid. The ceremony begins at 9 in the morning. Your formal invitation is enclosed.

To celebrate the beginning of his postgraduate life, we are planning a graduation party in his honor. It will be held at our house, at 7 on the evening of the commencement ceremony. A map to the party is enclosed.

Matthew will graduate cum laude with a bachelor of science in biochemistry. He plans to attend graduate school to continue his research in that field, but he will take a year off first to get some real-world experience in the workforce.

We look forward to seeing you on Graduation Day!

• MILITARY SERVICE •

Dear Friends and Family,

As long as I can remember, I've wanted to be a Marine, just like my dad. Now my wish is finally coming true. Next month I'll be reporting to Camp Lejeune, North Carolina, for basic training.

I'm very excited to serve my country. My goal is to one day become a Green Beret. I hear the training is brutal and the competition fierce, but I'd like to think I have what it takes. Time will tell.

Meanwhile, the recruiter says I'll be able to check my Yahoo account for e-mail, but for those of you who'd like to send a letter or a care package (hint, hint), please use the address above.

Love,

• WEDDING OF SON OR DAUGHTER •

Dear Gabe,

We are extremely proud and happy to announce the upcoming wedding of our daughter, Alana Diego Ruiz, to Arturo P. Alou. They'll be married August 6 at our ranch at Route 202, San Antonio, Texas. The ceremony will begin at 6:30 in the evening and a reception will immediately follow.

We have been anticipating this happy day since Alana was born 26 years ago. And now we can barely control our excitement, knowing that she and Arturo will begin their new life together. We have already grown to love and appreciate Arturo as one of the family.

We'd love to have you attend the wedding and reception to celebrate with us. Please let us know if you will be attending by returning the enclosed reply card.

Sincerest regards,

• BIRTH OF A GRANDCHILD •

Dear Charlene,

What could be grander than a bouncing baby grandson? I'm so happy to announce the birth of my first grandchild, Owen Lincoln Pritchett, who arrived on July 23 at Riverside Hospital in Memphis.

My daughter Ellen and her husband Tim will be visiting us with Owen at Christmastime. If you're in the neighborhood then, I hope you'll drop by to meet the newest member of the Knox clan. They tell me he has my blue eyes and my hair—which is to say, not much.

Sincerely,

Richard Knox

• RETIREMENT •

Dear Friends and Family,

I'm sure that you'll be surprised to learn that I have finally decided to take the proverbial engraved gold watch and retire. After having been with R&R Associates for 15 years, I'm ready to take some time for other, more personal pursuits.

I plan to take two weeks for a celebration vacation, August 29 through September 11. So effectively, my last day as a member of the workforce will be August 26.

My career as an editor with R&R has been a fulfilling experience for me. I now look forward to facing new (postcorporate) challenges in my life. An art class, for example, at the local junior college. A cruise to the Caribbean. More importantly, I hope to spend more time with my family, particularly my grandchildren. And perhaps a trip to Spain?

Best wishes,

• DIVORCE •

Dear Uncle Paul and Aunt Dargan,

I am truly sorry to have to inform you that Mitch and I have come to the conclusion that divorce is our only viable option.

We are expecting a quick settlement and harbor no ill feelings toward each other. We hope that you will try to understand and accept our decision, because we could both use your support right now.

For the time being, I am staying at the house, while Mitch has moved in with a friend of his, John Hawthorne. You can reach him at 555-5555.

Thank you for your prayers and good wishes as we adjust to our new separate lives.

Sincerely,

• DEATH OF A FAMILY MEMBER •

Dear Steve,

I wish I could be there to share this sad news in person. Aunt Clara passed away earlier this week, on the evening of November 11, at Methodist Memorial Hospital in Andersonville.

She died of complications related to a heart bypass. Before the operation, she told us she understood the risks but felt the surgery was necessary. Mom and I were with her until the end, and I know you would have been too if you weren't stationed overseas.

The funeral is tomorrow afternoon at Trinity Episcopal Church. I'll pass along your love to the rest of the family, and we'll all look forward to your return at Christmas.

Sincerely,

• CLASS REUNION •

Dear Class of 19—,

Ten years just flashed before our eyes, and it's now time for our 10-Year Class Reunion! It's hard to believe it has been so long since we sat in English class together. It seems like yesterday…well, on second thought, it seems like a lifetime ago.

I hope you'll be free to attend the gathering of old friends. The reunion will be held Saturday, May 30, in the Matisse Ballroom of the Carlisle Grand Hotel. It's scheduled to begin at 7 P.M. and go until 2 in the morning. (We'll see who still has that youthful spirit!)

Advance tickets are $35 for alumni and $40 for guests. At the door, all tickets will be $50.

Please indicate on the enclosed RSVP card whether you plan to attend, and check the appropriate box if you're enclosing a check to purchase tickets in advance. If you'd like to pay by credit card, call 555-5555.

See you at the reunion!

P.S. The reunion committee has been working in earnest to locate everyone. But if some people you know haven't received an invitation yet, be sure to tell them about it or notify us so we can send them their own invitation.

• MOVE TO A NEW LOCATION •

Dear Family and Friends,

I've done it! I finally moved into my new home. It took my "movers," to whom I am eternally grateful, an entire Saturday, but the task is complete. The house is newly organized and swept, stuff put away, furniture rearranged for a third time, and at last it's all livable. I really enjoyed the experience, but am glad it's over!

New address: 3412 Cordial Lane, Remington, IL 23857
New phone number: (555) 555-5555

I'd like to have an open house in the near future, but haven't firmed up those plans yet. I'll be sure to keep you updated.

Regards,

P.S. Many thanks to my "movers"—Uncle Josh, Uncle Bob, Uncle Jared, and Uncle Samuel. You made a whole lot of work seem easier.

• CHANGE OF NAME •

Dear Friends and Family,

If you don't recognize the name at the end of this letter, don't worry. It's me, Richard Spitznogle—only now I'm Rick Sprint. That's right: Last month, I legally changed my name.

As many of you know, my agent has been encouraging me to either adopt a stage name or change my name. To make things less confusing in the long run, I chose the latter. And wouldn't you know, I've already gotten two callbacks this month.

I'll be sure to let you know if I end up landing a part. In the meantime, please keep those letters and phone calls coming. The name may be different, but it's still the same old me.

Yours,

• NEW BUSINESS •

Dear Neighbors,

After ten years as an agent at F. C. Thompson, the city's largest seller of homes, I've decided to start my own realty company, one designed to meet the unique needs of downtown home buyers and sellers. I'm happy to announce the grand opening of Circle City Realty.

Over the past decade, I've personally owned and rehabbed more than a dozen homes in the city's historic preservation districts. I've also lived downtown for almost twenty years. When it comes to historic homes (and condos in historic buildings), I can provide expertise and experience that is unmatched by other realtors in town, most of whom deal primarily in newer suburban homes.

Finding the right realtor is the first—and possibly most important—step in buying or selling a house. I hope you'll stop by my new office at the corner of Pennsylvania Avenue and Sixteenth Street and give me the opportunity to serve you.

Sincerely,

• CHANGE OF EMPLOYER •

Dear Ms. Peterson,

On January 15, I'll be leaving McDowell Investment Group for a similar position at Alliance Financial, a move that will allow me to offer a broader range of investment products. I've very much enjoyed managing your portfolio these past six years and would welcome the chance to continue doing so at Alliance.

If you feel more comfortable keeping your account at McDowell, I understand completely. But if you'd like to join me in making the move, I'd be happy to send along the necessary forms, which will require only your signature.

Regards,

• LAUNCH OF WEBSITE (PERSONAL) •

Dear Friends and Family,

Mary and I have finally decided to do our part to save trees—not to mention join the twenty-first century. I'm writing to let you know about our family's new website, www.gehrigfamily.com, which should be up and running by the time you read this.

For fifteen years we've been sending our annual holiday letter to friends and family as a way of keeping you up to date on our lives. Writing the letter was always fun, but the photocopying, envelope stuffing, and stamp licking wasn't. More than that, though, we always wished we could stay in closer touch. Now that we've established our modest outpost in cyberspace, we can.

Please visit the site when you get a chance and drop us an e-mail to let us know what's happening in your life. We've already posted some pictures from our trip to Disney World, and we're sure you'll enjoy them more than the grainy snapshots in our last holiday letter.

Sincerely,

• LAUNCH OF WEBSITE (BUSINESS) •

Dear Customer,

Beginning in January, you'll no longer have to wait for our quarterly catalog of vintage baseball cards. Sluggo's Sportscards is excited to announce the launch of its new website, www.sluggosports.com. Updated daily, the site will feature our complete inventory, including high-resolution scans of many cards.

Thanks to a fully searchable database, you'll quickly be able to find the cards you're looking for, pay online using your credit cards, and even track the shipment of your order via links to our shipping partners.

Our goal, as always, is to be your one-stop store for high-grade prewar stars and commons. Please visit our site and sign up for e-mail bulletins so we can keep you up to date on our latest acquisitions.

Regards,

APOLOGIES

Have you ever tried to apologize to someone and realized that your apology made things worse? It happens. Apologies are difficult because you're already dealing with a negative situation; the other person hears you from a negative state of mind.

Your challenge with an apology, therefore, is to disarm the other person as quickly as possible. In other words, you need to acknowledge the error or insensitivity immediately and focus on making things right. The first words out of your mouth should acknowledge your inappropriate or insensitive action, behavior, words, or circumstance.

And be specific with your wording. Not: "Look, I apologize, ok?" Not: "I'm sorry that I made you angry." Not: "I couldn't help it; I'm sorry." Instead, use specific statements that let your reader know you accept full responsibility:

"I am so sorry that I failed to include you on the guest list."

"Can you ever forgive me for being so careless with your jewelry?"

"I don't know what I must have been thinking when I said such an insensitive thing."

"I regret very much the embarrassment I caused by showing up so late for the party."

"My actions were totally inappropriate and thoughtless."

"Would you please forgive me for giving your phone number to those people?"

"I'd very much like to apologize for taking your car without asking."

"Would you accept my apology for not phoning you personally about the situation and asking your preferences before making the final plans?"

"I owe you an apology for not responding to your invitation sooner."

"I offer my apology for neglecting to tell you I would not be in town over the weekend after I had promised to house-sit."

After you acknowledge your responsibility, make an empathetic statement to let your reader know you understand the damage, pain, or embarrassment caused. For example:

"You have every right to be upset with the way this was handled."

"I understand your feelings in this case."

"I know you must have been so disappointed."

If you try to minimize the situation or repercussions, the other person will feel compelled to repeat over and over what difficulties or pain you caused. If, on the other hand, your comments demonstrate that you understand the consequences, the reader will more likely forgive and forget. But do keep your tone consistent with the circumstances. Profuse apologies over minor issues sound patronizing. And flippant apologies over major issues sound unempathetic and insincere.

Above all, avoid statements that sound like excuses. Stand up straight and take your lumps!

"You are quite right."

"I was totally out of line."

"I should have been more careful in my investigation."

"I made far too many assumptions in this case."

"It was my responsibility to inform everyone concerned and I failed to do that."

Finally, offer to make things right, if possible, or demonstrate your intention to do so in the future.

• FOR MAKING AN EMBARRASSING REMARK •

Dear Ms. Cartwright,

I owe you an apology. I know how much I embarrassed you a few days ago with my impulsive statement at the conference. I should have been more aware of and sensitive to your feelings.

If you could, please forgive me. Sometimes a spontaneous comment will get away from me before I've had time to think about what I'm saying. It's not an excuse; it's just an explanation for my insensitivity. I am genuinely sorry for the thoughtless remark.

Sincerely,

• FOR AN ARGUMENT WITH A FRIEND •

Dear Dave,

I can't help cringing when I think about our argument at the ball game last weekend, about what a self-righteous blowhard I was. I just wanted to apologize for raising my voice and letting my emotions get the best of me. You are certainly entitled to your opinions on the election, and I should have shown more respect for them.

I suppose we've been friends long enough that I might expect you to overlook my behavior, to know I didn't really mean the things I said, but that's not good enough. Real friends don't speak to each other the way I spoke to you.

Please know, then, that next time we talk politics, I'll mind my manners. And know, too—notwithstanding last weekend—what great respect and admiration I have for you.

Regards,

• FOR BEHAVING INAPPROPRIATELY •

Dear Mr. Jernigan,

I wish to offer you my most sincere apology. My late arrival and surly attitude at the meeting were both uncalled for and unacceptable.

I allowed my emotions to dictate my actions, even though I am well aware that is not the protocol for business interactions. Please accept my apology for my inappropriate behavior and know that it will never happen again.

Sincerely,

• FOR DISTURBING NEIGHBORS •

Dear Mr. Turpin,

I assume it was you who called the police last night, seeing as how you're our closest neighbor and no doubt bore the brunt of our late-night noise. It was totally inconsiderate of me to have let the party go so late and to have the stereo on the deck out back. Had I been in your shoes, I'd have done the same thing, and probably sooner.

Next time we host a party, I'll be sure to let you know in advance; I'll keep the music inside; and I'll close it down no later than midnight. You have always been a good neighbor, and I want you to feel the same about me. Again, I'm terribly sorry for disturbing you and for putting you in the awkward position of having to file a complaint.

Sincerely,

• FOR FRIEND BEHAVING INAPPROPRIATELY •

Dear Mr. Sadat:

I want to apologize for my friend's behavior at the cocktail party Thursday afternoon. He doesn't often drink alcohol and hadn't eaten lunch that day, but that's no excuse for his intoxicated condition.

We are both embarrassed about the incident, and hope that you can forgive his behavior.

Generally speaking, Jake is a well-mannered and likable person. Unfortunately, he exercised poor judgment when he chose to drink the other day.

If there is anything that either of us can do to make amends, please let me know.

My sincerest apologies,

• FOR PET'S POOR BEHAVIOR •

Dear Jean,

I owe you an apology. I'm so sorry about Ringo tearing your dress at the party. We've been training him not to jump on people, but apparently we've been doing a lousy job. On top of that, it was careless of me to let him run free with so many people in the house.

Your dress, by the way, was stunning. I'd like to take you shopping for a new one, and I won't take no for an answer. Are you free on Saturday afternoon?

Sincerely,

• FOR BOUNCING CHECK TO FRIEND OR RELATIVE •

Dear Uncle Michel,

I am so embarrassed about the bad check that I gave you last week. Obviously, I had made an accounting error in my check register.

Enclosed is a new check for the $560, plus the $20 administrative fee that your bank charges for depositing a check that doesn't clear.

Don't be afraid to cash it. This one will clear!

Sincerely,

• FOR FAILING TO INVITE A FRIEND TO A PARTY •

Dear Christy,

By now you've no doubt heard about Chandra's surprise party and are probably wondering why you weren't invited. Chandra certainly was; as soon as she arrived, she asked me, "Where's Christy?"

Your absence from the guest list is entirely my fault, and I'm truly sorry for my thoughtlessness. I know how much Chandra values your friendship, and I certainly meant no offense. Even now, I still don't understand how I could have overlooked your name. It's a case, I suppose, of missing the obvious, of not seeing what's right before your eyes. Can you ever forgive me?

Sincerely,

• FOR FAILING TO PROVIDE INFORMATION •

Dear Paco,

How could I have been so careless as not to have told you about the new client's specifications for his audiences in San Francisco? I don't know how, but it completely slipped my mind.

I apologize for neglecting to supply you with that valuable information. Today, I mailed a letter of apology to the client as well, explaining that your failure to meet his expectations was entirely due to my error.

To ensure that we are now clear on the matter, his specifications for future demonstrations are as follows:

- Use no slides.
- Keep the lights on at all times.
- Be as informal as possible.

In the future, I will be more diligent about providing you with such preferences up front.

Sincerely,

• FOR DAMAGING NEIGHBOR'S PROPERTY •

Dear Paolo and Mina,

I think you'll be interested to discover who the culprits are who knocked over and then flattened your mailbox this morning. I saw the whole event because I, myself, was one of them.

I am so sorry for the incident. Please know that I take full responsibility for the damage and will be happy to reimburse you for a new mailbox. If you'd prefer, I can take the damaged one, order a replacement myself, and deliver it to your door. Please phone me at 555-8434 (my work number) and let me know whether you'd prefer to get the replacement installed yourself or have me do it.

I was giving my son a driving lesson this morning. Apparently, I was not doing a very good job, because he managed to take out your mailbox in the course of the lesson. Next time, we'll have the driving lesson in an empty parking lot.

Again, I apologize for the trouble we've caused.

Sincerely,

• FOR MISSING BIRTHDAY •

Dear Aunt Clarice,

Happy belated birthday!

It is now 17 days since the day, and I, being the punctual person that I am, am finally expressing my wish that you experience all the happiness you deserve in your sixty-second year.

I am truly sorry that I missed the day with the rest of the family. Mother tells me that you had a wonderful time, despite my absentmindedness about the event.

You are still so special to me. Have a wonderful year, and I'll be in touch again shortly.

Sincerely,

• FOR MISSING ANNIVERSARY •

Mike,

I've never felt like such a jerk as I did when I woke this morning and realized I'd forgotten our anniversary. After four wonderful years, you'd think the date would never slip my mind, but somehow it did.

I don't blame you for being upset with me—you have every right. But if you can find it in your heart to forgive, I'd like to make it up to you tomorrow night. How does dinner at Morton's sound? I could meet you at the park after work. I'll be the one with roses and a bottle of wine.

Love,

• FOR MISSING FRIENDS' ANNIVERSARY •

Dear Taylor and Tammy,

Guess what we forgot?! I hope your anniversary celebrations were very happy despite our absence. And even though I'm sure they were (happy), we'd still like to make it up to you.

How does dinner at Hedari's sound? Washington and I would love to treat you on Saturday evening, May 4. I know it's been one of your favorite restaurants for years, and we've been dying to try it.

If you don't already have plans, why don't you meet us at our place around 6:30? We'll have cocktails on the patio before we head for the restaurant.

If you can't make it, just let me know and we'll reschedule for another night. We're both still traveling, so please phone and leave your answer on the recorder. Looking forward to celebrating with you—even if belatedly.

Regards,

• FOR MISSING DINNER DATE •

Dear Rob,

It was totally inconsiderate of me to have missed our dinner date last evening. No doubt, you are furious with me.

Please accept my apology. I'd like to make it up to you. Would you please allow me to treat you to dinner at the same restaurant next week?

I didn't have a chance to give you the details on the phone, but I had to work late because of some computer billing errors that have been accumulating for a month without anyone's knowledge. I kept thinking I could break away at any minute, but, obviously, not so. My secretary and I were at the office until 9:20 trying to solve the problem.

Agree to meet me next week, and I promise that I'll show up this time. Forgiven?

Sincerely,

• FOR A CHANGE OF PLANS •

Dear Mrs. Rabinowitz,

It was very kind of you to offer to provide refreshments at this month's council meeting. Unfortunately, due to a conflict at the community center, we've had to reschedule the meeting for September 17.

I realize you've probably started baking some of your famous pies already, and I wanted to offer my sincerest apologies for the late notice of our cancellation. Your contributions to the meetings are always much appreciated, and I feel terrible for the change of date and the inconvenience we've caused you.

If you'd still like to provide refreshments for the meeting, great. If not, I understand completely and will be happy to call on another neighbor.

Regards,

• FOR BEING UNABLE TO ATTEND FUNCTION •

Dear Dr. Blackburn:

As reluctant as I am to have to tell you, I will be unable to attend the Scholarship Ball on Saturday, March 20.

Please accept my apologies and pass them along to the other Scholarship Committee members and to the ball coordinators.

I have been looking forward to the ball with anticipation for several months, but when the date was finally settled, I found myself in a quandary. I have a prior commitment that I just cannot break.

Please keep me posted on future committee functions. I would very much like to help with other upcoming events.

Sincerely,

• FOR MISSING A FUNERAL •

Dear Uncle Carlos,

I wanted to tell you how truly sorry I am that I won't be able to attend Aunt Lola's funeral. I am on the road in Vancouver this week, and there's simply no way I can make it back in time.

I know how important it is to have family close by at times like this, and it breaks my heart to think I won't be there with you. I promise to visit as soon as I get home. Meanwhile, my thoughts are with you.

Love,

• FOR MISSING A DEADLINE •

Dear Mr. Pfledderer,

I wish to offer my sincerest apologies for failing to complete the MacDowell project by Friday's deadline. I know the MacDowell account is important to your firm, and the last thing I want to do is jeopardize your relationship with the company.

I take full responsibility for the delay. We almost had the job wrapped up by Thursday afternoon, but during an electrical storm two of our hard drives were damaged. There's not much I can do about Mother Nature, but I should have been more conscientious about backing up the files, especially with the deadline so close at hand.

My entire staff will be working on the job this weekend, and I guarantee delivery by noon on Monday. Also, I will be reducing our fee by half. I value your business very much and hope we can continue to enjoy the strong working relationship we've built over the past five years.

Regards,

• FOR NOT HAVING WRITTEN •

Dear Hyunhee,

I apologize for not having responded to you sooner. I know that the important plans you have been contemplating depend on my answers, and I'm truly sorry that I haven't been more helpful and responsive.

In your letter you mentioned that you were considering expanding your business into South Korea. In answer to your question, I would be happy to offer whatever advice I can with regard to customs procedures, government policies on foreign investments, market predictions, cultural barriers, and the like. My previous experiences dealing with South Korea have left me with such a wealth of knowledge on the subject that I hardly know where to begin in a brief letter.

I'm enclosing a packet of information available from the embassy, along with various other leaflets and flyers I've collected in my travels and business dealings.

Why don't you call me (555-7746) to set up a lunch so we can go into greater detail?

Warmest regards,

• FOR FORGETTING SOMEONE'S NAME •

Dear Mr. Payne,

I wanted to apologize for mistakenly introducing you by the wrong name at the fundraiser last weekend and assure you that my lapse in memory was just that and nothing more. I hadn't forgotten *you*, of course: working with you and your organization has been a high point for me during the completion of this project.

I've always had trouble with names, especially in social situations, but that's no excuse. If someone is important to you, you get their name right, simple as that. Next time I will.

Sincerely,

CHARITIES, VOLUNTEER WORK, AND FUND-RAISING

Soliciting volunteer help, sponsorship, or money for charities has become almost as competitive as commercial endeavors. So your challenge in writing such a letter is to grab attention immediately. Open with a thought-provoking statement, startling question, or meaningful anecdote to entice the reader to stay with you rather than toss the request aside "to think it over."

Ask specifically for the action you want.

> *"Can you spend at least two days a month on the telephone to our membership?"*
>
> *"We would like to collect $200 from each family. Would that be possible on this short notice?"*
>
> *"Would you write your legislative representative to urge her support on this bill?"*

In most situations, avoid vague generalities such as "we need your support." Your effort has been wasted if readers finish your letter still wondering what *specific action* you want from them.

And because you don't have a captive audience, you must make responses easy. Give your readers all the details they need to take action: phone numbers, forms, locations, maps, or models to follow.

Remember also that people have to be assured that they are making a wise decision to devote their time or money to your cause. You can help reassure them by providing testimonials from well-known people or organizations about their enthusiasm for the cause.

Likewise, will you put your *own* money (or time) where your mouth is? Your personal commitment is always a thought in the back of a reader's mind. So don't forget to comment about your own enthusiastic support and affiliation with the charity.

As for reluctant participants, it never hurts to mention any benefits that will come to readers for responding. Will they gain publicity and recognition? Will their own family or friends benefit in some way? Will they feel fulfilled and proud of their efforts? People tune in to the WIIFM (What's in it for me?) radio station quite often these days.

COMMUNITY EVENTS

• REQUESTING RECIPIENT TO CHAIR FUND-RAISER •

Dear Mrs. Aguayo:

The Keenan Jeffries Tutorial Program desperately needs your help. Taking into consideration all your previous fund-raising experience, we are turning to you for your expertise. Mrs. Aguayo, would you please do us the honor of chairing our fund-raiser?

The K. J. Tutorial Program offers inner-city children a future by providing them with access to small-group learning that reaches beyond the standard public school curriculum. Our tutorial sessions include remedial, intermediate, and advanced education for all grade levels at no cost to the children.

We employ only certified teachers, a practice which can be expensive. Until last year, we have managed to stay solvent with contributions from parents and local businesses. However, the K. J. Tutorial Program has proved so successful that we are in danger of outgrowing our funds. Over 430 students citywide now participate in the program. We simply must hire more teachers, yet we can't afford to do so. Your positive response in chairing the effort will be our first step toward that goal.

The fund-raiser is scheduled for the entire month of September. I will contact you later in the week to discuss the drive further. If you'd like to speak with me sooner about any details, you can reach me at my office (344-588-8866) or my home (344-666-4343).

Thank you for considering the opportunity to help our kids by chairing the fund-raiser. May we count on you?

Sincerely,

• INVITING RECIPIENT TO BE GUEST SPEAKER AT FUND-RAISER •

Dear Dr. Kilpatrick:

As you may have heard by now, the Keenan Jeffries Tutorial Program is planning a formal dinner to kick off a full month of fund-raising events. The K. J. Tutorial Program is a cause worthy of this city's fullest attention; its first-ever formal dinner merits the finest of guest speakers.

Would you, Dr. Kilpatrick, do the K. J. Tutorial Program the honor of speaking at the dinner this September 1 at 7 P.M.? We prefer that the subject be centered on the message that education is invaluable, but within that broad guideline the subject matter is your choice. Someone of your stature in the community will lend the appropriate importance to this event.

The K. J. Tutorial Program employs only certified, degreed teachers to tutor small classes of children in any subject, at any level. The tutoring is available to those students who need help with remedial skills as well as to those who just want to learn more than is being taught during regular school hours. All tutoring is free to any student who wishes to attend. And therein lies the need for fund-raising.

Both the K. J. Tutorial Program and I would be grateful if you could help us in this endeavor. The children, too, will be grateful, and will show their appreciation by completing high school someday and continuing their academic pursuits in college. Please contact me at the phone number or address on the letterhead. We'll look forward to your positive answer.

Sincerely,

• REQUESTING RECIPIENT TO SPONSOR EVENT •

Dear Mr. Toppinger:

The city of Carrera is celebrating its cultural diversity during Cultural Awareness Week, July 11–18. This is your opportunity to get some inexpensive advertising with a large audience!

One of the highlights of the weeklong celebration is the *Dance Around the Planet* performance scheduled for Wednesday, July 13, at the Carrera High School auditorium. In order to supply props, decorations, programs, and other equipment, we need businesses willing to sponsor the event.

If you will send your donation with the completed business information form enclosed with this letter, you will receive some terrific advertising in return.

Sponsorship of $100 or more earns you a 2″ × 3″ advertisement in the *Dance Around the Planet* program. Sponsorship of less than $100 reserves you a place in the alphabetical listing of sponsors on the back page.

Thank you for your continuing support of our community.

Sincerely,

• SOLICITING USE OF SPACE FOR A COMMUNITY EVENT •

Dear Ms. Taylor,

I've always enjoyed the wonderful exhibits, concerts, and classes offered through the Johnson Center for the Arts, so when we here at the Writer's Club decided to launch a new reading series, HCA was at the top of our list of possible venues.

Would you be willing to donate use of Gallery 3 for readings to be held on the second Wednesday of each month from 7 to 9 P.M.?

The readings will feature published authors, including poets and novelists from the greater Brownsburg area as well as out-of-towners. Primarily we will focus on new and emerging writers.

Though we don't yet have the money to rent space, we plan to apply for local and state grants once the series is established, at which time we'd gladly compensate HCA for use of the gallery. In the meantime, with a membership of more than 200 writers, we believe we'll attract a sizable audience of arts-minded people—including many potential patrons of HCA.

If you're able to offer us the gallery, I assure you we won't be a burden to you or your staff. Our members will manage the readings, operate the PA system, take care of setup and cleanup, and so forth.

I'm excited about the prospect of partnering with HCA and look forward to hearing from you soon.

All the best,

• REQUESTING RECIPIENT TO SERVE ON COMMITTEE •

Example 1

Dear Mr. Delrossa:

The World Watching Club is sponsoring the annual UN Day open forum discussion on October 23. We would be honored if you would consent to participate as a panelist for the discussion.

The discussion begins at 7:30 P.M. in Kendall Hall, Room 101. This year, the topic is U.S. participation in UN functions. Your extensive knowledge of peace studies would make you a distinguished addition to the panel.

Our purpose is to include as many different viewpoints as possible. We plan to form a panel with one professor from the department of economics, one from the anthropology department, one from geography, one from history, and two with differing areas of expertise from the political science department.

I will phone your office this week to confirm your participation.

Thank you,

• REQUESTING RECIPIENT TO SERVE ON COMMITTEE •

Example 2

Dear Ms. al Matar:

The Keep San Miguel Clean Committee provides the invaluable service of corralling volunteer participation from the community for local beautification projects. We are currently hoping to fill three committee-member openings.

Given your record of community involvement, we think you are the perfect choice to serve on this committee. Please consider joining us as we try to keep San Miguel beautiful.

The KSMCC heads up such projects as the semiannual San Miguel River Cleanup, in which organizations, individual citizens, and local businesses volunteer their time to pick up trash along a 6-mile stretch of the San Miguel river bank. We also work hand in hand with the city council on such beautification projects as flower- and tree-planting events, park trash-receptacle painting parties, and similar activities.

Your responsibilities would fall into the category of marketing. We need someone who can design fliers, write commercial spots for the college radio station, and write three- to four-line ads for the city newspaper.

Please respond as soon as possible. We can't wait to hear from you!

Warmest regards,

• INVITATION TO JOIN A NEIGHBORHOOD GROUP •

Dear Neighbor,

Are you tired of cars speeding down Jillian Avenue at all hours of the night? Do you want to put an end to the vandalism that plagues our block every summer? Have you had enough of the graffiti that keeps turning up on our garages?

If you answered yes to any of these questions, I'd like to invite you to join our Crime Watch block club. Studies show that such organizations are highly effective at reducing crime and creating safer, more close-knit neighborhoods.

Interested neighbors are encouraged to attend an informational meeting at the Irvingwood Presbyterian Church on January 13 at 7 P.M. IPD Crime Watch coordinator Jane Westman will make a presentation.

In order to become an official, active block club, we must then have a second meeting with a crime prevention officer, Detective Arnold Shyman of the South District. At this meeting, we'll receive Crime Watch signs to be posted at each end of the block. After that, all we need to do is hold at least one meeting per year to stay active.

It's that simple—no dues and no major time commitments, just a willingness to work together to make our block a safer, more pleasant place to live.

I look forward to seeing you at the informational meeting. In the meantime, please feel free to contact me with any questions or concerns. My phone number is 555-5555, but you're welcome to just stop by, too.

Sincerely,

• SOLICITING BIDS FROM VENDORS •

Dear Mr. Stevens:

Our local square dance club, the Four-Squares, is sponsoring a community fund-raiser for the Turner-Selby Shelter in June. Therefore, we are soliciting bids for the print components of our campaign: a direct-mail piece, a program brochure for the closing dance, and paper placemats imprinted with information about the shelter.

If you are interested in bidding on the three projects outlined below, please submit your bid to the above address no later than April 12. An artist member of our club has prepared mock-ups of the three print pieces (enclosed) for your review in preparing your bid. We will provide camera-ready copy, but will need you to prepare the photo separations.

We've selected the paper stock and color, as noted in red ink on each mock-up. The quantities needed for each piece are also noted. Please bid the jobs separately so that we can understand what each piece is costing us, and then give us a total bid for all three jobs, including any discount that you offer if we award the contract to a single printer. If you provide any discount on such nonprofit jobs, we would appreciate knowing that also.

Because each deadline is crucial when working toward a community-announced event, we'll expect the fee to be discounted 5 percent for each day the project goes uncompleted after the agreed-upon deadline for the finished products.

Thank you for providing us with your quotation on these projects.

Sincerely,

• ACCEPTING BIDS FROM VENDORS •

Dear Mr. Wu:

We're pleased to let you know that we have selected your firm for the three printing projects involving the fund-raiser for the Turner-Selby Shelter, sponsored by the Four-Square Club.

We have accepted your total bid of $5300 and have agreed upon a completion date of April 12 for delivery of the print pieces to my home at 478 Weedon Street. You have agreed to a 3 percent discount on the total price if the print jobs are not completed by that date. We will have the camera-ready copy and all artwork/photos to you by April 1.

I've signed your quotation, with the stipulations noted above, and am enclosing a copy for your files.

We'll look forward to working with you on this project and to a successful June fund-raiser for those dependent on the Turner-Selby Shelter in their difficult times.

Sincerely,

• Reminding Participants of Upcoming Event •

Dear Friends,

Just a reminder about the upcoming Neighborhood Safety Watch meeting next Tuesday, March 4, at 7:30 P.M. at Trisha and Blan Butterworth's home: 44900 Brentcroff (next to the park pavilion on the southwest corner). Miles Frick, of the Weston Police Academy, will be speaking to our group about ways to mark and protect our property.

If you have questions about the upcoming meeting or the overall purpose of our organization, please give me a call (543-9984) so that I can give you more details.

This program to help us protect our children, ourselves, and our property deserves our full support. Can we count on you to attend the March 4 meeting?

Sincerely,

• INVITING RECIPIENTS TO ATTEND BENEFIT •

Dear Colleague:

Are you ready for an elegant evening out—complete with formal attire, gourmet food, delightful music, and an easy opportunity to help a disadvantaged youth to boot? That's right! It's time again for the annual Sundance Gala, benefiting inner-city youth.

Saturday, October 7
Hayworth Luxury Hotel
Dinner served from 7:00 to 8:30, followed by dancing

You may be wondering whose pocket will be lined with the proceeds. Each year the Sundance Gala Recipient Committee researches a number of inner-city youth programs to discover the most deserving. This year's Recipient Committee has agreed upon the Keenan Jeffries Tutorial Program. The program employs degreed teachers to tutor small classes of children in any subject, at any grade level. The tutoring is available to those students who need help with remedial skills as well as to those who just want to learn more than is being taught during regular school hours. All tutoring is free to any student who wishes to attend.

This year's fund-raising goal is $25,000. We have yet to fail to meet a fund-raising goal, and with tickets at $200 a pop ($150 without dinner), this year's goal should be a snap.

All tickets *must be purchased no later than October 1,* and may be charged by dialing (555) 555-5555. Or send a check or money order to the Sundance Gala, c/o Tickets, P.O. Box 76434, Phoenix, AZ 67544.

The weight of the world is upon us. So don your best evening wear, come hungry, and bring your checkbooks. The kids need all the help you can offer.

Sincerely,

• ANNOUNCING UPCOMING EVENT •

Example 1

Dear Friend:

The Cherry Blossom Art Gallery is delighted to have this opportunity to invite you to the Second Annual Art for Hearts Festival. This year's showing, entitled *A Wing and a Prayer*, will showcase 12 artists and their most prominent pieces.

The more than 50 works of art range in content from the purest aesthetic simplicity to the most powerful artistic intensity. The art media range from oil and acrylic to wire and tin cans.

No admission will be charged. However, if you'd like to make a contribution, a Collector's Corner will be taking donations. All proceeds are to be donated to the St. Louis Heart Disease Research Fund.

Please return the enclosed response card indicating whether you plan to attend. We, at the Cherry Blossom Art Gallery, look forward to seeing you there.

Sincerely,

• ANNOUNCING UPCOMING EVENT •

Example 2

What could be more fun than a romp
in the cool creek on a hot spring day?

Spring Arbor DAZE
April 6–8

Snyder Park on the Square

Tickets at the Gate: Adults: $8; Children under 6: $4

We'll have—
Food: *smoked turkey legs, cotton candy, hot dogs, sundaes—
donated by local merchants*
Fun: *pony rides, cake walks, Wacky-Wack Man, roller coasters,
video games*
Fanfare: *a surprise visit from the governor, dunking booths for
council members*

**All proceeds go to the "Let's Rebuild" fund!
Call 456-9999 for details.**

• POSTPONING OR CANCELING EVENT •

Spring Arbor DAZE Postponed!

Because of the ongoing inclement weather and continued flooding, we have indefinitely postponed the April 6–8 Spring Arbor DAZE scheduled to be held on the square.

We suggest that any contributions to the "Let's Rebuild" fund be sent directly to BankFirst's account set up for that purpose: BankFirst, P.O. Box 3489, Hillsboro, OK 43711.

SOLICITING CONTRIBUTIONS

• FOR RUNAWAY CHILDREN •

Dear Mr. and Mrs. Moreau:

Every year, 10,000 children are reported missing. Of these, a high proportion are runaways. STORC, the Shelby Trenton Organization for Runaway Children, provides vital services to both runaways and their frightened parents. But we need your help to keep those resources available.

As a nonprofit organization, STORC is always seeking donations from caring people like you. If you would like to be part of the solution, send your check or money order to the address on the letterhead.

Nationwide tracking of runaways, family counseling, construction of runaway shelters, and of course reuniting families are only a few of the resources provided by STORC. Every year we bring home hundreds of kids, and then provide them and their families with a professional counselor to help ensure lasting harmony in the home.

If you wait until tomorrow to write your check, you might forget. Do it today, and your donation may help bring a lost child home tomorrow.

Sincerely,

• FOR HOMELESS SHELTER •

Dear Concerned Resident Who Wants to Give Something Back to the Community:

The Charlotte Street Homeless Shelter needs more people! It's not more occupants we need (although our door is always open). What we need is more volunteers to help run the place!

If you think you want to engage in some tough but rewarding work, helping those who need it desperately, come join our team of volunteers. Call us any time, day or night, at 555-5555. Someone will always be available to talk with you.

We currently need volunteers to prepare meals, wash dishes, clean the bathrooms (don't worry, there are only two!), answer the phone, and be all-in-one administrators. You can work 1 hour per week—or 40 hours per week. We'll accommodate your every scheduling need.

The Charlotte Street Homeless Shelter has been in operation since 1962, when founder Kevin Leithouser converted his five-bedroom home into a rent-free boardinghouse for the needy. The CSHS has since been expanded and now offers shelter to more than 3500 people each year. If you can spare the time, we can use the help.

For more information, ask for Molly at 555-5555.

Thank you,

• FOR UNITED WAY •

Dear Concerned Citizen,

I know how valuable your time is, so I'll jump right to the point. United Way is seeking your contribution (it's tax-deductible!) to fund the huge number of volunteer and philanthropic organizations that so urgently need your help.

You may be thinking that if you decide not to contribute, your dollars won't be missed. But imagine what would become of nonprofit groups such as the American Cancer Society, Head Start, the Salvation Army, Habitat for Humanity, and others if everyone thought his or her sole contribution wouldn't make a difference. Every donation—no matter how small—counts toward putting someone's life back together.

United Way is a clearinghouse for charitable contributions. What that means is that you don't have to research different philanthropic agencies to determine which ones most merit your aid. Send your contribution to United Way and we will add it to a pool of funds that we then distribute to various nonprofit groups. With one check to United Way, you can contribute to dozens of agencies!

Enclosed is a listing of the groups that United Way serves both nationally and in our local area. Also included is a contribution form. Simply fill it out, enclose your check or money order, and return it to us. Remember to fill out and keep the bottom half for your tax records. Then give yourself a satisfactory pat on the back. You've done a good deed today.

On behalf of all our organizations, thank you for your contribution.

Sincerely,

• FOR SPONSORSHIP IN A CHARITY RUN •

Dear Ms. Guinness,

Each year, more than two hundred cats are put to death by the Johnson County animal shelter. As a fellow cat lover, I'm sure you'd prefer to see these animals housed in a no-kill facility until they're adopted.

On Saturday, March 3, I'll be participating in Run for the Cats, a 10-kilometer race to raise money for a new, privately funded no-kill shelter. In addition to providing a home for stray cats, Cat Space will also offer low-cost spaying and neutering to help reduce the feline population in Johnson County.

Would you be willing to sponsor me in the race? A pledge of five dollars per mile would be fantastic, but I'm grateful for your support at any level. A pledge card is enclosed. Together, we can help prevent cats from needlessly being euthanized and ensure that fewer strays are born in our community.

Sincerely,

• FOR ATHLETIC LEAGUE •

Dear Parent,

Ever wonder where your teenager is at 10:00 on a Saturday night? If your son or daughter is a participant in the Kuwame Center's Night Hoops program, the answer is no.

Every summer, the Kuwame Center hosts boys' and girls' basketball leagues from 8 P.M. until midnight on Saturdays. Not only does the program keep kids off the street, it offers a supervised yet fun environment for them to develop their athletic skills and learn the values of teamwork and sportsmanship.

But in order to continue offering this program free of charge, the Kuwame Center needs an assist from you. Won't you help us help our city's kids by making a donation? Please send your check or money order to The Kuwame Center, P.O. Box 102, Indianapolis, IN 46202. And thanks on behalf of the 300 All-Star teens who rely on the support of involved parents like yourself.

Sincerely,

• FOR GOODS IN A CHARITY AUCTION •

Dear Mr. Rasmussen,

We need your help. For more than a decade, the O'Neill Center has provided a unique showcase for Beckwood-area visual artists such as you. In August, we'll be holding our tenth annual charity auction. Would you be willing to donate a piece of your artwork to be sold in the auction?

Last year, more than thirty area artists donated everything from paintings to sculptures to photographs. Thanks to their help, we were able to raise enough money to expand our hours and add an additional show to our lineup.

If you're willing to donate a painting, we'll need it by July 15. Along with other donated items, your piece will be displayed in the main gallery until the auction, which will take place at 7 P.M. on Friday, August 10. As a contributor, you will receive complimentary admission to the preview and wine reception preceding the auction at 6 P.M.

Artworks can be dropped off at our office Monday through Friday between 10 A.M. and 5 P.M., or we'll be happy to arrange pickup.

The O'Neill Center strives to reflect the incredible diversity of Beckwood's arts community. Won't you help us ensure its continued vitality?

All the best,

• FOR ELEMENTARY SCHOOL LIBRARY •

Dear Parent,

Think of the one locale where you'd most like to see your child today. The Blanton Elementary School library is one of the most important places in your child's day at this stage of his or her life. Unfortunately, district funding doesn't cover all the costs of library upkeep.

The PTA has established a library fund to which you may send your contributions. Please mail your check or money order to P.O. Box 3828, Regefield, CO 80934.

If the Blanton library is to purchase more books, have old ones re-bound, acquire new chairs to replace the broken ones, install new software, and provide on-line research options, we must find another source of revenue. That source is you, the parents of the children who need to have access to the best resources possible.

Thank you for your concern and for your contribution.

Sincerely,

• FOR POLITICAL CANDIDATE •

Dear Waldon School District Resident,

Have you heard often enough from Superintendent Rhodes that his hands are tied? Does it seem to you that the Waldon school system has far more potential than is currently being displayed? Minh Pham could very well embody the solution for which you've been searching.

In order to develop her plans for a school system in which the actual students become the number-one priority, Minh will seek election to the school board this June. To do so, she needs not only your vote, but your campaign contribution.

Minh has planned specific projects to turn waste into productivity—to channel unnecessary cost overruns into better programs with the students' needs at heart. In the last year alone, she's authored seven pragmatic proposals designed to maximize the wealth of teacher talent in the district and the commitment of parents for volunteer time in the classroom. Five of those proposals have been adopted by the Waldon school board. The other two have been amended and are now pending passages at the next board session.

To help Waldon's schoolchildren by contributing to Minh Pham's election fund, send your contribution to P.O. Box 350, Waldon, DE 90034. You will quickly see the difference your donation makes in the future education of your children.

Thank you,

• PUBLIC SERVICE ANNOUNCEMENT •

A Public Service Announcement

Contact Fanny Farnsworth at 555-5555

Did you know that broccoli can actually be dangerous to your health? So can oranges, lettuce, grapes, and any other fruit or vegetable that grows on a farm. The reason? Throughout the growing season, U.S. farmers use a total of 650,000 tons of pesticides on all sorts of crops.

Please take precautions. Prepare fruits and vegetables by washing them thoroughly. Use a mild soap whenever possible. A cornsilk brush can also be helpful and is soft enough that it won't bruise food. Even frozen produce should be rinsed.

Pesticides have been known to cause birth defects and have been linked to a number of cancers. They can also aggravate allergies and contribute to a breakdown of the immune system.

If you're buying fruits and vegetables, you're probably trying to eat healthy. So don't allow the overabundance of pesticides to harm you or your family. Wash all fruits and vegetables thoroughly before you enjoy them.

Sincerely,

RESPONDING TO SOLICITATIONS

• OFFER OF SERVICES RATHER THAN MONEY •

Dear Mr. Baxter,

Thanks for your recent letter regarding the renovation of the Morton Community Theater. Though I'm unable to make a donation at this time, I would be happy to help with the actual work. Are you accepting the services of volunteers?

I have experience working with drywall, refinishing floors, and painting (both interior and exterior). I'm available on weekday afternoons, but Saturday and Sunday are best.

If you're able to make use of my services, please contact me at the number below so we can work out the details. And thanks for spearheading the effort to preserve one of our town's greatest treasures.

Sincerely,

• DECLINING SOLICITATION •

Disagree with Cause

Dear Stan,

Without concerned citizens and volunteers, where would America be? I sincerely appreciate your efforts to beautify the city and the endless hours you have spent on various projects with that end result in mind.

However, I must disagree with your latest effort. Although installing holiday decorations along the streets and in the public parks would add cheer to the city and possibly, as you say, become a tourist attraction for the surrounding residents in smaller towns, I think our charitable contributions could be much better spent in other ways—for example, supporting our museums and libraries.

In fact, I think the holiday decorations could become a safety hazard and a cause for traffic congestion in the downtown area. For all these reasons, I will not be actively supporting this project with a contribution.

Sincerely,

• DECLINING SOLICITATION •

Insufficient Funds

Dear Mrs. Wang:

Our literary group was so pleased to learn of your plans to campaign for the Waldon school board seat becoming available next month. Your contributions to the district thus far during your brief two years as a resident have been invaluable.

Although our literary group supports you wholeheartedly in your attempt to gain a seat on the board, our financial committee has decided to donate all available funds to the city's public library drive for its renovation next fall.

We do wish you success in your campaign and in your ultimate efforts to ensure high-quality education for our children.

Sincerely,

• MAKING DONATION WITH STIPULATION •

Dear Ms. McGrady,

I just received your letter regarding the Cedar School's annual capital campaign, and I welcome the opportunity to help. However, I'd like for my contribution to be used only for the music club.

As you know, my daughter, Mabel Tinsley, has been an active participant in the club for two years. When she first joined, she was told that the Cedar School would be able to support a full marching band by the time she graduated. I'd like to see the administration do everything in its power to make this dream a reality. It would mean a great deal to Mabel and all of the other members who devote so much of their time to the club.

If this arrangement is satisfactory, please keep the enclosed check and provide me with a signed receipt indicating that the funds will be used only as specified above. If you're unable to accept donations with stipulations, please return the check at your earliest convenience.

Thank you,

VOLUNTEERING AND WORKING WITH VOLUNTEERS

• ANNOUNCING NEW SPECIAL-INTEREST GROUP •

Breast cancer is the second-leading cause of death for women over the age of 35. In order to devote special attention to this disease, I am in the process of forming ABC, Act on Breast Cancer. I'd like to enlist your help.

We need people who can volunteer their time and/or donate money. Currently, we could use your help in the following ways:

- Researching and writing articles for the newsletter
- Stuffing envelopes
- Building our database
- Raising funds from corporate sponsors

Please contact me or my cofounder, Natalie Little, at 555-5555. Or write us at the address on our letterhead. Even if you can't help right now but want to be added to our mailing list, I'd like to hear from you.

ABC is a nonprofit organization in its beginning stages of operation. The idea behind ABC is to empower people to fight the disease. To this end, we hope eventually to meet three goals. The first is to keep both men and women informed about the disease through a monthly newsletter. ABC's second objective is to raise awareness in the general community through publicity campaigns. Finally, we hope that ABC will eventually grow into a special-interest group that can lobby Congress for additional funding for breast cancer research.

(Continued)

I have enclosed an informative leaflet that includes some breast cancer statistics and preventive measures. Whether or not you decide to participate in ABC, please read the information and then pass it along to a friend.

Appreciatively,

• SEEKING VOLUNTEERS •

Dear Member of St. Matthew's Congregation:

The Carnival Committee in charge of organizing St. Matthew's Annual Fall Carnival is seeking volunteers. We need ticket sellers and ticket takers, people to staff the stalls, and people to deck the halls!

If you want to have a festive time in the name of a worthy cause, call Lorraine Bascombe (457-4499) to volunteer your services.

The Fall Carnival is St. Matt's most important source of revenue, outside of the weekly tithes and offerings of its faithful attendees. All proceeds go toward financing the winter and summer retreats, as well as minor parish repairs.

Anyone and everyone can participate in one way or another. So roll up your sleeves and get busy. Won't you put your commitment into action?

Sincerely,

• REQUESTING PARTICIPATION IN SURVEY •

Dear Neighbor,

Residents of the Old Northside have come to rely on the *Northside Gazette* to provide the latest coverage of news and events in our neighborhood. But in order to make our newsletter the best it can be, we need your help.

Don't worry. We're not asking for a donation. We're asking only that you take a few minutes to complete the attached survey and return it in the enclosed SASE.

With your input, we'll be able to provide more of the information *you* want, whether it's detailed listings of area estate sales, longer features on the neighborhood's history, or anything else that strikes your fancy.

And if you'd like to become involved with the *Gazette*, please be sure to check the box at the end of the survey. We're always looking for additional carriers to help distribute the newsletter, not to mention knowledgeable editors and staff writers.

Best,

• THANKING VOLUNTEERS •

Dear Nicole,

I want to express my most heartfelt gratitude to you for all your help during the MJM Scholarship fund-raising campaign. Your tireless efforts as liaison between the contributors and the university really made the difference. Your enthusiastic and thorough handling of all the details left me free to plan and manage each eventuality as it surfaced.

As for this last project, we as a team have been successful in raising more than $10,000 and are now in the final stages of receiving a presidential endowment. In addition, the university is planning a gala to kick off the scholarship. Enclosed is your personal invitation.

I hope that your services will be available to me for future projects, because I would really like to have you on my team again. Thanks again, Nicole, for all the time and effort you put into this project. I sincerely appreciate your can-do attitude and your dedication.

With warmest regards,

• RENEWING COMMITMENT OF PROJECT LEADERS •

Dear Project Leaders,

We're looking for a few good men, er, uh, women, that is. Never mind, make that ideas. We're short on plans and long on dreams. We're dreaming of achieving all those objectives set out in our first organizational meeting, but as yet we don't have specific plans from all of you, our project leaders.

Successful corporations have elaborate plans; successful individuals have elaborate plans; successful associations have elaborate plans. Concrete. Practical. Measurable. We need your input before completing our agenda for the year and setting our fee structure and budget. Success comes from the many, not the few.

Let me remind you of the issues you agreed to address as you submit your plans for your own chapter: dues, budget, charitable activities, program topics, methods for surveying potential members, and database management.

Will you let us hear from you by March 1? We're all counting on you!

Sincerely,

• VOLUNTEERING FOR SPECIAL PROGRAM OR COMMITTEE •

Dear Mr. Reeves,

I heard a public service announcement on the radio today, asking for volunteers for your remedial-reading tutorials. I would very much like to offer my services but am a bit unsure about my skills in this area.

Please send me some information regarding the program in general and volunteer duties in particular.

I have plenty of questions: Do you train the volunteers? During which hours would I be needed? Of what ages and grade levels are your students? Is there a minimum time requirement for volunteers?

I am really excited about this opportunity, both for myself and for the children your tutoring program reaches. I look forward to hearing from you.

Sincerely,

• DECLINING REQUEST FOR VOLUNTEERS •

Dear Aileen:

The children said you phoned last night, asking about my availability to work at one of the polling sites for the school board elections at the end of the month. With the sporadic voter turnout in off-election years, I can imagine how difficult it must be to anticipate how many volunteers you will actually need on election day.

Because of the unpredictability of my children's soccer games on Saturday, I've decided to reduce our family frustration level by not taking on any additional Saturday commitments of my time this year. I think it would be easier for all concerned to say no up front rather than have to cancel at the last minute.

Thank you for your own efforts on behalf of the school district. I'll be hoping for good weather and a good voter turnout.

Cordially,

• DECLINING OFFER OF A VOLUNTEER'S SERVICE •

Dear Mr. Chang,

Thanks for offering to host a course at this year's Sherwood progressive dinner. Without the generosity and hospitality of neighbors like you, this popular event would not be possible.

Unfortunately, all of the host slots have already been filled. In fact, so many people volunteered that we even added an additional course to this year's menu!

Would you be willing to serve as a backup in case one of our other hosts drops out? Or could we put you down as a host for next year's dinner? (No one else has signed up yet, so you'd have your pick of courses.)

Whatever you decide, just let me know. Meanwhile, we on the programming committee appreciate your interest, and we're looking forward to seeing you at the dinner.

Sincerely,

• RESIGNING FROM VOLUNTEER POSITION •

Dear Askold,

As you know, I have been the volunteer Spanish-English media liaison for the Soccer Cup for four years running. I have enjoyed the work immensely, and I consider this an important role to the Soccer Cup organization. For those reasons, I regret to tell you that I must resign my post.

I am giving you two months' notice with the hope that you will have time to find another bilingual sports aficionado to handle the job. I suggest that you begin your search for a replacement in the communications department of the local college.

Having begun a new job this year, I find that the demands of my travel and work schedule simply prohibit my spending the time necessary to your organization. If circumstances permit, perhaps I will be able to volunteer for the Soccer Cup organization again in the future. You have my very best wishes for another exciting year.

Best regards,

CLERGY AND SUPPORT ORGANIZATIONS

Members of the clergy and support organizations often are overlooked for their efforts because their help is perceived to be "just their job." Nevertheless, these people deserve our thanks for actions and attitudes that extend beyond what's expected.

So take every occasion to express your appreciation for the clergy and support services available to you and the community.

"I want to express my gratitude for..."

"Thank you for your expression of concern when you visited my mother in the hospital before her death."

"You have made a meaningful contribution to my life, and I wanted to let you know how much I appreciate your time."

Often, people think they are giving a stronger commendation when they are global in their comments, such as "You are always so supportive." Actually, just the opposite is true. A specific, rather than global, commendation sounds more sincere. Comment specifically on what the person has done that was so meaningful or special to you or your family or the community.

Remember, also, that individuals—not institutions—do meaningful, sacrificial work. So comment on the individual's personal dedication to the service he or she provides and the people served. For example:

"You have demonstrated remarkable commitment."

"Your personal sacrifice is very evident to observers."

"Your personal warmth shines through the community role you play."

"Your genuine goodwill and personal concern are evident."

If you are writing to ask for help, be sure to make your request for any action specific. And provide all details to make the requested action easy to take (for example, copies of past correspondence or phone numbers and addresses of people you wish to be contacted on your behalf).

Finally, remember that members of the clergy have the same need for emotional support and recognition and the same family and individual concerns as other members of society. Show your appreciation accordingly and often.

• WELCOMING NEW CLERGY TO CONGREGATION •

Dear Reverend Soloman,

My family and I are so happy that you've come to settle in the Guiding Light Parish at Clearwoods, Virginia. Although I plan to introduce myself to you in person after the worship services this weekend, I didn't want you to spend a whole week in your new town without receiving a welcome from someone.

We've all heard such wonderful things about you from Reverend Gabe. He speaks very highly of your academic credentials as well as your commitment to establish programs in the parish that benefit the whole family. Even though we are sad to see him go, I think we all consider ourselves fortunate to have you join us here to serve God in our little corner of the world.

I look forward to meeting you in person.

Sincerely,

• WELCOMING NEW SERVICE ORGANIZATION •

Dear Mr. and Mrs. Soretti,

Welcome to Greenburgh. My wife and I are overjoyed that you have decided to establish a chapter of Kid-Tracker here. Your presence will relieve part of our fear that one day the worst could happen—that not only could we lose our child, but we would then have nowhere to turn for help and comfort.

As soon as the local chapter of Kid-Tracker is up and running, we plan to bring in our two sons and one daughter for finger-printing and photo records. Everything we as parents and ministers can do to protect our children certainly merits our time and attention.

We are aware of the success that you've had in other communities, and I'm sure that that will be the case here as well. You two must be very caring individuals to have committed all your spare time to this important support service.

Sincerely,

• EXPRESSING SUPPORT FOR CLERGY POSITION •

Dear Reverend O'Callahan,

I just wanted to tell you how heartened I was by your recent remarks in support of allowing women to serve in leadership positions on the International Council. The idea that women would not be accepted in leadership roles in some countries around the world is, frankly, beside the point. The Council has been founded and funded to advance our specific humanitarian goals, and, as such, needs both genders represented as they work toward solutions.

I understand how difficult it is for someone in your position to take a controversial stand, and I appreciate and applaud your courage.

Given the current political climate in the church, you will no doubt take some heat in the coming months as the Council seeks additional direction and funding. Please don't hesitate to call on me if there's anything specifically I can do in this regard.

Sincerely,

• EXPRESSING DISAPPROVAL FOR CLERGY POSITION •

Dear Reverend O'Callahan,

I've always had great respect for your opinions and views, but I have to admit to being disturbed by your recent remarks advocating openly gay and lesbian clergy.

As I and many others interpret the Bible, homosexuality is a sin. I understand that some people disagree, but I would be remiss if I did not express my views on the subject as I read the strong Biblical statements on the subject.

Please keep in mind that you are Trinity Episcopal's chief spokesman. I would ask that in the future your public statements more closely reflect the views and values of the great majority of your congregation.

Respectfully,

• EXPRESSING APPRECIATION TO CLERGY •

For Sermon

Dear Father Talbot:

I want to be the first to tell you what a wonderful sermon you preached last Sunday. I was touched by your message, and am deeply grateful for the hope and faith that you inspired in me.

This last year has been a difficult one for me, and I sometimes find myself questioning God's wisdom, if not His existence. Some comments that you made the other day about trying to hang on to one's faith really hit home. So did your advice on how to maintain and strengthen one's relationship with God. Your words encouraged me to see the world, my purpose, and my life in a different light.

It's important to me that you know that you did reach someone. I am deeply appreciative for your hours of study and your capable delivery of God's word.

All my thanks,

• EXPRESSING APPRECIATION TO CLERGY •

For Baptism

Dear Minister Cavanaugh:

The baptismal ceremony in which you baptized our granddaughter, Elinor McCrady, last week was both meaningful and inspiring. Thank you for marking the beginning of my granddaughter's walk with God such a memorable event for her and the family.

Your comments during the ceremony fully explained to all present the significance of such a symbolic act. I especially appreciate your time spent in visiting with Elinor both before and after the ceremony to help her understand fully that commitment at this time in her life. In keeping with your message, my husband and I will do our best to further her growth as she applies her knowledge of the scripture to her daily life.

When Elinor was born, we promised that we'd dedicate her to the Lord's service, and we intend to continue with that commitment. We feel fortunate that our family has you as leader and counselor in our church and community.

Sincerely,

• EXPRESSING APPRECIATION TO CLERGY •

For Sympathy and Support

Dear Pastor Allison,

As you know, this last month has been a very difficult time for my family and me. Billy's sudden diagnosis and hospitalization took us all by surprise. Your comfort in our time of need was greatly appreciated then, as it is now.

Thank you so much for visiting Billy and us at the hospital. Your frequent presence there was a constant reminder of God's care and the congregation's concern, even when times seemed hopeless.

You'll be happy to know that Billy has been released from the hospital and is resting comfortably at home. If he maintains his regimen, the doctors predict a slow but full recovery. Thank you for giving so freely of your time in our time of need.

Warmest regards,

• EXPRESSING APPRECIATION TO CLERGY •

For Funeral Service

Dear Pastor Hollins,

My mother's death was a terrible blow for everyone in our family, but your heartfelt eulogy during her memorial service helped us all begin to move past our grief and toward an appreciation of who she was and where she is now.

I wanted to offer my deepest gratitude for the compassion and sensitivity you showed during your remarks. It's no easy task putting into words what such a woman meant to her family, her friends, and her congregation. You nevertheless managed to articulate how so many of us were feeling that day.

Your words were a rare comfort in what has been the one of the most difficult times of my life, and for that I will always be indebted to you.

All my thanks,

• EXPRESSING APPRECIATION TO CLERGY •

For Holiday Service

Dear Pastor Fenwick:

I want to commend you on a job well done. Last Sunday's Easter service was beautiful to observers, inspiring to the participants, and meaningful to all of us as a reminder of the historical event and religious significance we celebrate.

Obviously, you and your staff spent long hours in planning the service, selecting the appropriate music, coordinating the visuals and media support, and preparing the message. After 40 to 60 hours in the world of work every week, we members of the congregation appreciate a chance to get away from the hustle and bustle and reflect on our higher purpose in life. You provided that opportunity once again Sunday, and I thank you.

Sincerely,

• EXPRESSING APPRECIATION TO CLERGY •

For Counseling

Dear Reverend Jameson,

When Martha and I first came to you last year, we were on the verge of divorce. Despite four years together, despite the kids, we just couldn't see a way to make it work. Today, our marriage isn't perfect, but it's definitely back on track, thanks in large part to our sessions with you.

I just wanted to thank you for helping us to see the light, helping us get our priorities in order, and helping us recommit to our life together. Though divorce once seemed like the solution for us, looking back, we both agree it would have been a mistake.

We initially hesitated to come to you because we weren't comfortable sharing our problems with somebody else, but you immediately put us at ease with your nonjudgmental approach and calm demeanor. We never felt like we were getting "instructions" or "recommendations" from you, just carefully considered advice from a close friend.

I hope that in the coming years Martha and I can find some way to repay your friendship. Until then, you have our steadfast appreciation.

All the best,

• REQUESTING SERVICE OF CLERGY •

Counseling for Friend

Dear Pastor Sanchez,

A very good friend of mine is in trouble. He is depressed, and I no longer feel as though I can handle the problem on my own. He has agreed (with much prodding on my part) to seek counseling, and I recommended you to him.

Could you please work him into your busy schedule as soon as possible? If so, please let me know your available appointment times and I'll arrange for him to be there. It's not that he is unwilling to come for counseling; it's that his depression has left him in a very lethargic mood and I fear he'll not take the initiative to call himself.

His name is Roberto Colon, and he lost his wife about a year ago. She had had a lengthy disease, and needless to say, Roberto was devastated by her death. Six months later, however, he began dating an old acquaintance (who incidentally just lost her father). They are planning to marry and I'm afraid that, in their vulnerable, grief-stricken states, they are rushing into something they are not ready for.

Neither of them appears to be really happy with their wedding plans, but I don't think that they have the strength of will to change or postpone them either. It seems that they both need something positive to cling to. I hope that you can help them.

You can reach me during the day at 415-7849 or in the evenings at 899-9944 about available appointment times. Thanks so much for making your expertise open to the community.

Sincerely,

• REQUESTING SERVICE OF CLERGY •

Counseling for Yourself

Dear Father Ngwenya:

Lately things have been difficult for me. Although I don't feel acute depression, I simply have trouble finding meaning and keeping interested in activities that I used to find enjoyable.

Being rather unfamiliar with the working of the church behind the scenes, I'm unsure if you offer counseling to nonmembers of your congregation. (I attend, but am not a member.) If so, how do I go about scheduling an appointment? Do you charge for such personal counseling? Or could you recommend someone who might offer me some advice and/or peace of mind?

Let me give you a little background: A little over a year ago, I lost a very good friend in a car accident. She was the mother of three beautiful girls and the wife of a loving husband. Since the accident, I have seen the remainder of the family fall apart over their grief. I myself am consumed with the idea that the same thing will happen to our family someday. It seems ridiculous that I should be so concerned with such notions; nevertheless, I am beside myself with these thoughts.

I don't know where else to turn, because our financial situation is such that I cannot afford counseling from a private clinic or counselor. Having attended your church for so long, I have come to trust your judgment. I'd appreciate your call (477-3349), suggesting the next step in dealing with this issue.

Sincerely,

• REQUESTING SERVICE OF CLERGY •

Wedding

Dear Minister Flaherty,

Two years ago, when I first laid eyes on Karen Kozar, I knew she was the woman I wanted to marry. Now I'm happy to tell you she's accepted my proposal.

Since Karen and I met in your Bible study class, it only seems right that you be there for the wedding, too. Would you marry us, Minister Flaherty? Your participation would mean the world to us.

We'd like to get married on a Saturday in June, but we were waiting to set a date until we found out if you're available. You can reach me during the day at 333-3333, or we can talk after the service on Sunday morning.

Sincerely,

• REQUESTING PERSONAL CHARACTER REFERENCE •

Dear Reverend Haskell,

I am in the process of updating my résumé and would like to include some new reference letters as I begin my job search. Would you be willing to provide a character reference letter for me? If so, you can simply address it "To Whom It May Concern" and send it to me at my home address listed on the church records.

As you are probably aware, corporations have become increasingly concerned about the character and temperament of their potential employees. With violence in the workplace growing and unethical behavior a blot on any company's record, prospective employers want to know that those they're considering for hire are honest, trustworthy, and stable individuals.

Just as a reminder of my work in the church, I began attending the Eternal Light Church in 1994. During my time here, I have involved myself in a number of church activities, including volunteering for the monthly brunch for newcomers, working during the clothing drive, and sponsoring several youth events and trips.

For your convenience, I am enclosing a copy of my résumé so that you have a better idea about the kind of position I'm seeking and can tailor your comments accordingly. Thank you for taking the time to provide this reference.

Sincerely,

• INVITING CLERGY TO DINNER •

Dear Pastor Murphy,

It's been such a pleasure listening to your sermons these past few months. I can't tell you how delighted I am that you chose to settle in our parish. I'm sorry only that we haven't gotten a chance to know each other better.

Would you be our guest for dinner on Saturday night? I'll be making my grandmother's fried chicken, and Herb has promised to whip up one of his famous tortes for dessert. You needn't bring a thing except maybe a hat, as we'll be eating on the lawn if the weather's nice.

Our house is at 34 Deep Hollow Road, about two and a half miles past the refinery. Dinner will be at six. You can reach me at 444-4444.

Sincerely,

• INVITING CLERGY TO BE A GUEST SPEAKER •

Dear Reverend Donaldson,

I am a member of a wonderful support group for the adult children of terminally ill parents. Once a week we meet on the Wakefield University campus to share coping ideas, encouragement, and inspiration. Whenever possible, we like to hear speakers as well. They can be particularly helpful on the days when we just can't seem to inspire ourselves.

Reverend Donaldson, I think you'd be the perfect speaker for such an event. Would you consider attending one of our upcoming meetings (Wednesday, June 15, would be terrific) to speak to this group, which so desperately needs your guidance? You are free to choose any topic. The meeting participants practice a wide range of religions; so if at all possible, I recommend that your comments be ecumenical.

We meet every Wednesday at 7 P.M. in the Kasha Room in the Everett Library. I've enclosed a map to help you find your way around the Wakefield campus. If you decide that you can find the time to speak to our group, I need a couple of days' notice so we can plan accordingly. And if you'd like to attend a meeting beforehand to get a feel for the group, please feel free to drop in.

I realize that you have many demands on your time and will understand if you cannot speak to our group. If your answer is positive, I'll appreciate a call at 478-9985. On behalf of the whole group, thank you for considering our need for an encouraging message.

Sincerely,

(Continued)

P.S. As you may have guessed, we have no budget at all. We don't accept dues or donations (except for time), so we cannot afford to pay our speakers. Even under those circumstances, we hope to hear from you.

COLLEGE

Consider almost any communication to or about colleges as a business letter rather than the typical personal letter. Even though you may be requesting references from friends, your request will generally get a higher priority and you will write a more authoritative, formal reference if you model a business tone in your request.

Summarize your message or request immediately in the opening sentence or two.

"I'm writing to ask that you furnish a reference for…"

"Would you be willing to write a letter of reference to help me…"

"I'd like to ask you for a reference letter, if you would feel comfortable providing one for me on the basis of our past association…"

Then provide all details relative to the situation: full name with initials, dates of past or future attendance, deadlines, fees, identification such as social security number or student number, field of study, future plans, and so forth. Here are some lead-ins that you might find helpful in jogging your reader's mind:

"Let me refresh your memory a bit about my work."

"As I'm sure you may recall, we both…"

"Let me summarize some of the details of our past association that would be of particular interest to a potential employer."

Such prompts will ensure that your reader provides the kind of information that will be useful for landing the job, scholarship, or award.

Enclosing a self-addressed, stamped envelope if you are asking for a written action on your behalf is also a thoughtful gesture that helps ensure a prompt response forwarded to the appropriate person without misrouting.

REFERENCES AND INTRODUCTIONS

• Requesting References •

Dear Dr. Gaines:

I am applying for the Presidential Scholarship, a $5000 annuity to be awarded to a single student. Given that my attendance at Southwestern University is dependent on my receiving financial aid, this is a wonderful opportunity for me.

Would you do me the honor of submitting one of the two reference letters that are required for application? The recipient of the Presidential Scholarship must demonstrate both ability and direction in his or her field of study. In order to assess such qualities, the Scholarship Committee requires that applicants submit reference letters from two professors in their major department.

I took your International Law class in the fall semester of 1996 and your International Organization class in the spring of 1997. I received an A in both classes.

All scholarship materials must be submitted by March 1, and I have enclosed an addressed, stamped envelope for your convenience. I will be stopping by your office during your conference hours this week to confirm. In the meantime, if you need to speak with me for any reason, please call me at (512) 555-5555. Thank you for your time in providing this reference.

Appreciatively,

• Letter of Recommendation — Graduate School •

To Whom It May Concern,

I first got to know Scott Baxter in August 2003 at the Rocky Mountain Writers' Workshop, where I've served as a faculty member since 1999. We met for a one-on-one conference to discuss one of his stories, and since then I've had the pleasure of reading three others.

Though I've seen only a small sample of Scott's work, I consider myself a fan. He is a keen observer and critic of social mores, a writer whose biting sense of humor and gift for irony shine through on every page. More importantly, though, Scott is a writer whose stories demonstrate an understanding that character is at the heart of fiction—but also that a character, no matter how interesting or well drawn, is useless until you've got a great story to tell about him or her.

Scott doesn't need a creative writing program to make him a fine writer—he's already managed to accomplish that on his own. But I have no doubt he would benefit greatly from being able to focus on his writing for two years with the support of a group of like-minded individuals—the kind of opportunity only an MFA program affords. I hope you will see fit to admit Scott. I recommend him without reservation and believe he would be a credit to your institution.

Sincerely,

• SUPPLYING REFERENCES •

Dear Dr. Anderson,

One of my students, Arthur Snell, is making application to the Presidential Scholarship Committee for that award. It is my opinion that Mr. Snell is an excellent candidate for the award in question; he has proven himself well qualified in every facet of the scholarship requirements, both in my classes and elsewhere.

Having served as a college professor in the St. Luke's system for several years, I have had the opportunity to notice a few students who really stand out from the rest. Arthur Snell is one of these rare students. He has demonstrated dedication and serious attention to academic achievement. He has an excellent attitude and work ethic, which will no doubt form the foundation for his success in college.

In my classes with Mr. Snell—namely, macroeconomics and international finance—he has exhibited both creativity and deep insight, far beyond his years, into the world of finance. We at St. Luke's have recognized him a number of times for academic excellence and achievement in various extracurricular activities.

In addition, Mr. Snell is involved in a number of school and community activities that further demonstrate his wide range of interests and his ceaseless energy. He is currently the president of Sigma Iota Rho, the international studies organization; he is an instructional assistant for the Spanish department; and he volunteers for the Feed Birmingham program in his "spare" time.

I might add that I am aware of other professors' opinions regarding Mr. Snell, and to my knowledge, they are in accordance with mine. That is, Arthur Snell is the superior choice for recipient of the Presidential Scholarship.

Sincerely,

• INTRODUCING CHILD OR FRIEND APPLYING TO COLLEGE •

Dear Dr. Dully:

As I know you are aware, it is that time of year when students begin competing with one another to gain acceptance into the university of their choice. My daughter, herself soon to graduate from Bowie High School in Plano, plans to apply to Texas Christian University next month. Her name is Maddy Miller, and as I understand it, she is well qualified by TCU's admissions standards.

Having worked as an administrative professional in a Dallas-based consulting firm for more than ten years, I believe it within my capacity to recognize ability in people. And in Maddy I see someone who possesses certain qualities that, if cultivated under the proper instruction, will lead to a fulfilling and successful career in medicine.

Maddy has exhibited both scholarship and direction as a high school student. Her marks are above average; she holds a grade point average of 11 on a scale of 14. And this May she will graduate in the top 15 percent of Bowie High School's senior class. In addition, she is involved in a number of extracurricular activities, such as the French Club, the Drama Club, Circle K (the volunteer organization), and dance classes and performances.

May we count on you to give her guidance as she seeks to add her name to the freshman roster at TCU? She'll be phoning your office next week to check the status of her application. In the meantime, you can reach her at (214) 489-0986. Her complete admissions package is enclosed.

Sincerely,

• INTRODUCING STUDENT APPLYING TO COLLEGE •

Dear Dr. Suzùki:

I want to take this opportunity to introduce you to one of my best students, Maynard Paul. As I am sure you will agree after you meet him, he would make a valuable addition to Green Bay's student body.

As an English teacher in the Madison school system for more than 10 years, I pride myself on recognizing and encouraging exceptional scholarship in my pupils. And in Maynard, I see unlimited potential. He is bright, energetic, and a serious student.

In my classes with Maynard, he has exhibited both maturity and commitment to excellence in his assignments. As a student in general, his marks are above the norm. He holds a GPA of 3.5 on a 4.0 scale, and this May will graduate in the top 10 percent of his class.

In addition, he is involved in a number of extracurricular activities. This year alone he has performed leading roles in both Bowie's fall and spring plays. Also active on the student council, Michael often brings fresh ideas for new activities to the meetings. And in his precious free time, he plays soccer for a city league.

In conclusion, I would like to add that although Maynard has received very little emotional support and encouragement from his family, he is a responsible young man who is well liked by his teachers and friends. He plans to major in political science. I know he will be an outstanding student at Green Bay.

Sincerely,

• LETTER IN SUPPORT OF TENURE •

Dear Members of the Tenure Committee,

I'm writing in support of Dr. Jason Martin's bid for tenure in the political science department. I understand that research and publication are key factors in any tenure decision, but what is most important to me as an undergraduate is a faculty member's ability to teach. I have met no better teacher than Dr. Martin.

I've been fortunate enough to take three of his classes: POL 101 (Intro to American Government and Politics), POL 212 (Elections in America), and POL 314 (Diversity in American Politics). Before I took his survey class, I thought political science was boring; by the end of the semester, I'd switched my major from sociology to political science and am now looking forward to working with Dr. Martin on my senior project.

In addition to his considerable knowledge of and insight into the American political system, Dr. Martin has a knack for engaging students in the classroom. His effective (and humorous) use of the Socratic method encourages students to think for themselves. This distinguishes him from some of my other professors, who are content merely to disseminate information.

Dr. Martin is also very generous with his time. He offers more office hours than any other faculty member in the department, and on one occasion he even stayed an extra hour to help me with a particularly difficult paper.

In short, Dr. Martin is an exemplary teacher, and his departure would be a great loss to the department. I hope that you will do whatever it takes to ensure that he remains at this university.

Respectfully,

• INVITATION TO FACULTY RECEPTION •

Dear Professor Jones,

Each spring, Sigma Delta Nu hosts a faculty reception to honor the University's best teachers. Each member is encouraged to invite his favorite professor. Would you be my guest?

The reception will be held on March 6 from 5 to 7 P.M. at the Sigma Delta Nu house (1736 College Drive). Cocktails and hors d'oeuvres will be provided. Dress is business casual.

I really enjoyed your Shakespeare class last semester and would welcome the chance to further discuss the plays we studied. Please respond (555-5555) by March 1 if you'll be able to attend.

All the best,

• DECLINING TO SUPPLY REFERENCE •

Dear Jackie,

Thank you for considering me as a source for references as you apply for admission and a scholarship to the University of Alabama.

Of course, I've known your parents for years through various projects in the community, but I'm afraid my knowledge of your own academic abilities, character, and goals is extremely limited. Although I'd be happy to comment about the fine relationship I have with your parents, I hesitate to pass judgment on someone I've had very little association with at all. Therefore, I suggest that you find someone who could give you a much stronger reference than I.

As you know, the University of Alabama is also my alma mater, and I'm still very active in the alumni association. I think you've made a fine choice of universities, and I wish you the best there in your academic pursuits.

Sincerely,

REQUESTS FOR INFORMATION

• REQUESTING INFORMATION FOR APPLICATION •

Dear Mr. Carver,

I am a senior at Stanton High School and plan to graduate in May of this year. It is my intent to attend Northwestern University the following autumn. My major is as yet undecided, though I do have an interest in Spanish and in history.

Please send me an application for admission to NWU and the current spring catalog, as well as the spring schedule of classes as soon as it becomes available. I would also appreciate any additional information you might offer history and Spanish majors.

Can you also provide financial-aid information? (Or possibly route my letter to the correct department for that information?) I am not sure about my eligibility for grants, loans, and/or scholarships. So if you could please send me any relevant information about those requirements too, I would be grateful.

Thank you,

• REVIEW OF FINANCIAL AID PACKAGE •

Dear Director of Financial Aid,

I recently received my financial aid package for the 2006–2007 academic year and was alarmed to see that my aid has been reduced by more than $4500 compared to last year.

Could you review my package to determine if there has been some error and, if not, could you provide me with an explanation? Without a sufficient level of aid, I will be forced to take an off-campus job (in addition to my work-study job) in order to pay my tuition. I worry that a second job will jeopardize my academic performance and thus further threaten my scholarship eligibility.

Enclosed are copies of my financial aid applications for the past two years. Please note that I am enrolled as a full-time student in good financial and academic standing with the university.

Sincerely,

• REQUESTING INFORMATION ABOUT SON'S OR DAUGHTER'S PERFORMANCE •

RE: Student Ashton P. Morrow
     Social Security Number 123-45-6789

Dear Dr. Trevor:

I'm trying to evaluate more thoroughly the performance of my son (Ashton P. Morrow) at your university this year. Although I do receive reports on his final grades, I prefer to be informed on a more regular basis about his general adjustment. As both a freshman and a wheelchair-bound student, he has experienced some difficulty on campus that I'd like to verify.

I would be extremely grateful if you could compile whatever details with regard to his performance that you deem pertinent. I am mostly concerned with his attendance, his professors' opinions about his general attitude, and of course his grades. Is he enthusiastic? Does he appear to be enjoying his classes specifically? Is the work too difficult for him, or does he not exert enough effort?

Ashton entered GMU in the fall of last year as a finance major. Since receiving his grades for the fall semester, I have become very concerned with Ashton's future at the university. You and I are both aware of the pitfalls into which a first-year university student may tumble if he's not careful. Additionally, as you may surmise, his physical condition sometimes limits his potential for social interactions. As a parent, I want to make sure he practices good study habits and that he feels fully welcome among the student body.

Please send all available information and your collective observations to me at the above address. Thank you for your help in this endeavor.

Sincerely,

• WORK-STUDY POSITION •

Dear Mr. Azocar,

I'm writing to request information about the work-study job (student manager of the campus pool hall) you advertised on the bulletin board in the financial-aid office.

Could you tell me what the job entails and how much it pays? Also, is the position for one semester or the entire academic year? Finally, what are the hours? Under my current financial-aid package, I qualify for up to ten hours of work-study per week.

As you can see from the attached resume, I worked in a pool hall in my hometown for two years during high school, handling everything from concessions and table rentals to cue sales. I enjoyed the job very much and would welcome the opportunity to work in the campus pool hall.

I can be reached at 555-5555. Thanks for your time, and I look forward to hearing from you soon.

Thank you,

• REQUESTING TRANSCRIPT •

To the Director of Transcripts:

I am applying to graduate school and so would like to request an official transcript to be sent to the School of Graduate Studies at the University of Nevada, Las Vegas. The address is as follows:

University of Nevada, Las Vegas
School of Graduate Studies Admissions
P.O. Box 4483
Las Vegas, NV 38543-4483

My name as it appears on the transcript is Ana L. Tiant (social security/student identification number: 555-55-5555). I graduated in May 20—with a BA in psychology.

Please charge the cost of sending the transcript to my Visa card (9876-5432-2345-6789; expiration date: 10/08).

Thank you,

RESOLVING CONFLICTS WITH ADMINISTRATION

• FUNDS FOR STUDENT GROUP •

Dear Dr. Ames,

Last week, the Undergraduate Student Government declined the College Democrats' request for $500 to stage a pro-choice rally on the commons on Friday, November 1. However, one week earlier, the USG approved the College Republicans' request for $500 to stage a pro-life rally at the same location and time.

As faculty advisor to the USG, could you look into this matter? I am requesting that the USG approve our request immediately or revoke funding for the College Republicans' rally.

I think we can all agree that college is about the free exchange of ideas—dialogues, not monologues. Students will lose out if only one side of the abortion debate is represented on November 1.

Respectfully,

DECLINING ATTENDANCE AND WITHDRAWING

• DECLINING ATTENDANCE •

Dear Dr. SerVaas:

I would like to thank you for your decision to accept me as a transfer student from Mountainview Junior College. However, I have decided to attend another university because of the generous financial-aid package offered to me there.

I appreciate your taking the time to review my application, and I have the highest regard for your university. Best wishes for your continued success.

Sincerely,

• REQUESTING EXCUSED ABSENCE •

Dear Professor Gaedel,

As stipulated on your syllabus, I'm providing this written request for an excused absence.

On October 11, members of the Medieval Society will be traveling to a conference in Pittsburgh. A flyer from the conference is attached.

As secretary of the Medieval Society, I would very much like to make the trip. However, an unexcused absence would hurt the class participation portion of my grade, so if you aren't able to grant an excused absence, I'll skip the trip and attend class instead.

I can be reached at 555-5555, or we can talk after class on Friday.

Thanks,

• CHANGING MAJOR OR WITHDRAWING FROM PROGRAM •

RE: Fred Galloway
    Student ID 555-55-5555

Dear Dr. Montanez,

I intend to withdraw from the International Relations program for international studies majors at the end of the spring semester of this year. I have decided to pursue an alternative course of study; therefore, I will no longer be studying within your department.

Please make the necessary modifications to my record. I must be officially released by you from the International Relations program before I can register for the next semester under a different major.

I will be changing my major to modern languages. Although I have enjoyed studying the theory connected with international studies, I believe that fluency in a foreign language will be of more practical use to me in the career field that I have chosen to pursue.

Good luck to you and your department. Thank you for the education you've provided me in these last two semesters.

Sincerely,

• Requesting Grade of Incomplete •

Dear Professor Jones,

I'm writing to request a grade of I (incomplete) rather than an F for the fall semester in your English 112 course.

As you know, my mother's illness has caused me to miss several classes, and with only one week left in the term, I don't anticipate being able to complete my final paper. An incomplete would allow me to keep my GPA above 3.5 and retain my scholarship eligibility.

If this arrangement is acceptable, let's meet to set a timetable for me to turn in my final paper in the spring. I would also be happy to complete additional assignments to make up for the classes I missed.

I appreciate your consideration in this matter, especially since it means more paperwork for you at the busiest time of the semester.

Sincerely,

RESOLVING CONFLICTS WITH TEACHERS AND ADMINISTRATION

• REQUESTING REINSTATEMENT AFTER DISCIPLINARY ACTION •

Dear Dr. Heimlich:

I would like to be reinstated at the university, both as graduate teaching assistant and as coordinator of the Instructional Assistantship program. It has been nearly nine months since I relinquished my teaching role and withdrew from my graduate studies. Perhaps your decision and mine were made too hastily.

I urge you to reconsider the situation. If you'll recall, my grades were not the problem; my attendance was sporadic. Unusual family circumstances at that time prevented me from fulfilling my teaching duties and devoting full time to my graduate studies to the best of my ability. These family difficulties have been resolved, and I feel certain that I can now give my full attention to the job and to my graduate studies.

I would like to make an appointment with you to discuss reinstatement and will phone you within the next week. I will be happy to make myself available to you at any time so that we may discuss the matter in greater detail. For now, suffice it to say that my personal life will not interfere with my career again.

For your convenience in reexamining my credentials or conversing with my present employer, I have enclosed a current résumé, along with a copy of my transcript at the time of withdrawal. Thank you for the courtesy of your reconsideration.

Sincerely,

• COMPLAINT ABOUT TEACHER CONDUCT •

Dear Dean Parker,

I would like to register a complaint regarding the conduct of Professor Adam Rupp and request a meeting with you to resolve the matter.

In last Friday's issue of *The Observer*, I published an editorial criticizing the political science department's decision not to offer tenure to Professor Jason Martin. That afternoon, in my POL 267 class, Professor Rupp (who, as you know, is chair of the department) held up a copy of the newspaper and proceeded to characterize my editorial as a "biased, uninformed" attack on the department. He also referred to me as "irresponsible" and guilty of a carrying out a "witch hunt."

I do not think Professor Rupp's remarks were appropriate. He has every right to disagree with my editorial, and had he submitted a letter to the editor, the newspaper would have been happy to publish it. However, in choosing instead to publicly berate me in front of my classmates, I believe he acted in a highly unprofessional manner.

Needless to say, I am now concerned about my grade in Professor Rupp's course. If he's willing to publicly condemn me in the classroom, what's to stop him from giving me a lower grade simply because he disagrees with my views regarding Dr. Martin?

Therefore, I'd like to meet with you and Professor Rupp so that we can clear the air. As dean of student affairs, you are in the best position to help us work through this unfortunate situation.

Sincerely,

• REQUESTING DORM TRANSFER •

RE: Latasha Marie Nye
     Social Security Number 578-54-5555

Dear Mr. Meacham:

With this letter, I am requesting a dormitory transfer. I am aware that midterm transfers are unusual, but undue circumstances make this transfer a necessity. Life at Laurel Hall is not conducive to good study habits, and if I am to do well in my classes this semester, I must relocate immediately.

Both my resident assistant and the hall director are aware of my decision and have given me their approval. Please make whatever arrangements that you can to grant the transfer and then notify them or me. My resident assistant's name is Tatiana Shreve, the hall director's name is Sally Kern. Both can be reached after 4 P.M. at 456-9934.

As a sophomore who has completed 45 hours of credit classes, I prefer to move into Butler Hall or the Women's Resident Tower. Butler Hall is preferable, because I would like to remain in the same price range as Laurel Hall.

Most of the women in Laurel Hall are freshmen, whereas I have begun to take upper-level classes. They still have the time and the energy to stay up until all hours talking and listening to music. I, on the other hand, have to put in more time on my schoolwork, so I find their late-night chatter disruptive. They are not excessively noisy; they are just bothersome to anyone trying to study.

I will appreciate whatever you can do to help make my living quarters more conducive to study.

Respectfully yours,

• DISPUTING UNFAIR GRADE •

Dear Dr. Taguchi:

I'm sure that the most tiresome words a professor can hear at the end of a term are, "I think my grade is wrong." Unfortunately, I really do think mine has been miscalculated.

I had been making Bs all semester in your class, yet my final grade report shows a C. Would you please check your records to verify accuracy? I will call you next week for the results.

I was in your class in Economics 4353, Money and Banking, Section 001, which met MWF at 10 A.M. My student ID number is 555-55-5555. My full name is Walter R. Person.

Enclosed are copies of the front pages of all tests and papers from the class (with the grade recorded in your own writing), as well as my official final grade report. If you wish to speak with me about this before I phone you, you can reach me at 555-5555.

Thanks for your investigation of what I hope turns out to be an honest mistake.

Respectfully,

• DISPUTING UNFAIR DISCIPLINARY ACTION •

Dear Chairwoman Rehagen,

Two weeks ago several of my friends and I were reported for drinking in our dorm room; the subsequent hearing with the disciplinary board is scheduled for March 12. I want to make sure that the board is aware of the special circumstances before that date. Perhaps the board will decide that this case isn't worth hearing. Or perhaps having this information in advance will make the hearing proceed more quickly.

It would be futile to deny that we were drinking. But please consider the circumstances: we were sharing a bottle of champagne given to one of the girls by her parents. The girl, who was also written up, is Carla Goyez. While at home over the weekend, she and her boyfriend had become engaged to be married and her parents had given her the champagne to celebrate with her friends. When Carla returned to the dorm Sunday night, she shared her bottle of champagne with seven of us to celebrate her engagement.

We are all aware of the regulations with regard to drinking on campus. Needless to say, we have all learned our lesson. As you are aware, if the case is not thrown out by the disciplinary board, it will become a mark on our permanent records, and none of us seven has any previous disciplinary infraction. We hope that, upon closer reexamination, you will decide that this one act of poor judgment on our part doesn't merit marring our otherwise excellent records.

Respectfully,

CONGRATULATIONS

Look for opportunities to congratulate others on their accomplishments or happy occasions. Congratulatory notes can nurture a casual acquaintance into a full-blooming friendship. And for those who are already friends, special events take on added significance when shared and recognized by those we care about and love.

With that in mind, offer your immediate congratulations on the event, award, honor, or occasion. Be as informal or "gushy" as your friendship allows. If you're pleased, say so; if you're surprised, say so; if you're thrilled, let your emotions show.

Be specific with your comments. Why exactly does the person deserve the recognition or reward? Your specific praising comments give the reader time to "enjoy" the event or honor once again.

> *"I heard you completed the entire marathon in the top 10!"*
>
> *"Betsy tells me that you were selected for the honor among competition that included more than 400 peers. That's phenomenal."*
>
> *"I understand that you had to give over 250 presentations to win this distinction. What a feat!"*

The other person wants to know for sure that you understand the difficulties in any achievement, the honor in any award, or the pleasure in any event.

Be personal and genuine. Avoid a tone that sounds global, vague, and boilerplate with clichéd statements and sentiments. If a particular phrase seems to "roll off your tongue," that's a good sign that it is a clichéd expression. Try to reword the sentiment with less familiar phrasing.

Your personal note demonstrates that you're the kind of friend or associate who feels excitement and pride rather than jealousy when someone else receives recognition or experiences happy occasions.

• Anniversary •

Marsha and Kennedy,

Rumor has it that you two have spent 20 wonderful years together. Congratulations on having chosen your life's partner so well, for growing more in love through the years, and for being a role model for the rest of the world. In this day and age, marriages like yours should never be taken for granted, and I wanted to take this opportunity to wish you both continued love and happiness together. Have a special celebration.

Cordially,

• BAR MITZVAH •

Dear Preston,

I am so proud of you. You have grown into a terrific young man, and you truly deserve this day and all the recognition it involves.

The way I hear it, you've been studying very hard (*every night!*) to make your Bar Mitzvah readings and recitations perfect. You'll do wonderfully well in school and in life because that is how you do things—with attention to the details and with full enthusiasm.

Congratulations, kiddo. (I have to call you "kiddo" this one last time because after this weekend you'll be too grown-up.) Soon you'll be a man. And nothing could make me prouder or happier for you. This weekend marks a significant event in your life and in the life of our family.

Best wishes,

• BIRTH •

Mindy and Howard,

The long nights walking the floor, the cross-country vacations with stops every half hour, the babysitters who set *your* curfews—your lives will soon be changing. But, of course, there will also be sticky hugs and kisses, starring roles in school performances that will make you proud, and late-night chat sessions about boyfriends. Life will change for the better and for the best. Congratulations on your precious baby daughter! Please continue to keep us up to date on the happenings in your lives.

Our best wishes,

• Birthday •

Reba,

It's your day! Take a long walk in the sunlight. Eat a banana split. Hug somebody special. Birthdays should excite, thrill, and inspire you. You've made a good start, because all those people in my corner of the world are wishing you a terrific celebration. You are special to us. Keep counting.

Love,

• Engagement or Wedding •

Shawanda,

I've just heard the wonderful news—that you've found the love of your life. Turner must be a brilliant man, a gentle and caring man, an ambitious man—and a very wise man. He would have to be all those things to attract someone like you. We're so happy for you. Enjoy each other's love every day for the rest of your lives.

Sincerely,

• GRADUATION •

Hannah,

Graduation marks a significant milestone in life. But the best of everything is yet to come. We know you've worked hard, made excellent grades, and enjoyed many extracurricular activities to develop the skills and attitudes that will continue to make you successful in life. You have our best wishes as you take on the world ahead of you. We are very proud of you.

Cordially,

• COMPLETION OF MILITARY SERVICE •

Dear Greg,

Congratulations on completing your first tour of duty! I can think of few jobs harder—or more important—than serving your country during troubled times like these. Despite the difficulty of being a Marine, it must feel wonderful to know that you are on the front line in the worldwide fight for freedom and democracy. I can't wait to shake your hand and buy you dinner when you get home. You sure have made all of us here in Oakville proud.

All the best,

• Opening Own Business •

Dear Yolanda:

Congratulations on opening your own import-export business! You've accomplished what most people only spend their time talking about—real control over your life and your future.

Back in April when the government threw all that red tape at you, I know how tempted you were just to give up. But true to form, you stuck with it (even when the airlines lost your first shipment of jewelry!), and I know that you now feel all that difficulty has been worth the price of a promising future.

I have every confidence in your success and am so happy for you. Please keep me updated on your progress. I'll be looking forward to sending customers your way.

Regards,

• PERSONAL ACCOMPLISHMENT •

Example 1

Dear Mark,

Well look at *you!* Here you are at age "40-something" and going after your master's degree. It takes courage to do what you've done in switching careers (not to mention endless energy). I want you to know that I admire your risk-taking mindset.

I'm also proud of you for standing up to the criticisms that I know you've received from your family. I guess for some people, education is something to finish and put behind them. I know that for you, getting your MA has more significance than the diploma itself. It represents research into complex new theories, intelligent searching for self-fulfillment, and solid determination to prepare yourself for a new career in service to others.

Good luck to you in this and all the future goals you set for yourself. You're an excellent role model for all of us.

Sincerely,

• PERSONAL ACCOMPLISHMENT •

Example 2

Dear Mrs. Nicholson,

Imagine my surprise when I opened the newspaper this morning and saw that you'd won a Cultural Vision Award from the city council. It's not that you haven't earned it—nobody in this city has done more to feed the homeless than you—it's just that I was beginning to think you'd never get your due. After all, food recycling isn't the most glamorous-sounding endeavor. It is terribly important, though, and I truly admire your innovative approaches to tackling such a tough problem. Congratulations!

Sincerely,

• ATHLETIC ACCOMPLISHMENT •

Dear Steve,

Running a marathon is one of those things that a lot of us dream of doing, but few of us have the determination to make happen. I just wanted to salute you for being among the few. That you finished in the top twenty percent in your division is quite impressive, especially for a first-timer.

Watching you train for the past several months has been a real inspiration. In fact, because of you, I've started training for the upcoming 5K. Thanks for getting me off the couch, and congratulations on your accomplishment.

Sincerely,

• QUITTING SMOKING •

Dear Nicky,

What am I going to do now that I can't nag you about your smoking?

Seriously: I quit almost ten years ago, and I still remember how hard it was. It's great that you've been smoke-free for more than a month now. Hang in there. Soon enough, those stairs at the office won't seem quite so steep. And if you ever need to talk to somebody who's been there, I'm only a phone call away.

Warmest regards,

• FIRST HOUSE •

Dear Liz,

Thanks for the invitation to your open house. I can't wait to see what you've done with the place. Mainly, though, I'm looking forward to congratulating you in person on becoming a home-owner. I know how much discipline and sacrifice it takes to save up for a down payment, and I know how scary it is to sign that first 30-year mortgage. That you were willing and able to take on so much responsibility at such a young age is a testament to your maturity and ambition. Here's hoping your furnace holds up and your roof never leaks.

Love,

• New Job •

Jeff,

I was so excited to hear you landed the executive chef position at Bistro Gigi. I imagine the competition was stiff, but there's no chef in town who deserves the job more than you. After so many years as sous chef at the Hyatt, you must be ecstatic to finally be running your own show. Mandy and I have already booked a reservation for next Friday, and we can't wait to see what you and your staff are cooking up. Bon appetit!

Regards,

• PROMOTION •

Example 1

Dear Barry:

I understand that you've just been appointed vice president in charge of production for the Commercial Film Institute. And the way I hear it, you were more than a little surprised. But I'm sure that no one deserves the honor more than you do.

Your past awards and commercial film successes testify to your extraordinary talent. It must be wonderful to be recognized by your colleagues as well, for the very same qualities.

Congratulations on your appointment. It's a fabulous opportunity and I have no doubt you'll create all kinds of new opportunities for all of us in the industry as you fulfill your new leadership role.

My best regards,

• PROMOTION •

Example 2

Dear Chamique,

I've heard a rumor that turned out to be true for a change—you've been promoted! Congratulations. Am I correct to assume you didn't know about it back when we met for dinner in Sacramento?

In any case, the higher-ups couldn't have made a better choice. We all watched as you almost single-handedly pulled in the Sampson account. Dedication like that deserves to be recognized. I'm glad to see that people get what they deserve in this company. Creativity, good ideas, and hard work really do pay off in your case.

Good luck in your new capacity as director of new accounts.

Sincerely,

• RETIREMENT •

Dear Mrs. Finchel,

The North Point Library won't be the same without you. But after two decades as head librarian, you've certainly earned the right to let somebody else shelve *your* books for a change.

I just wanted to congratulate you on your upcoming retirement and thank you for all your good work. You were the one who first recommended several of my favorite authors—Judy Blume and S. E. Hinton when I was young, Alice Munro and Toni Morrison when I got older. It's been wonderful having a friend who could always point me toward a great book—and toward the right shelf.

I remember you telling me once that as much as you loved your job, you wished you could get outside more, spend time in your garden. I'm so happy you'll finally be able to do so. And I'll look forward, of course, to hearing which gardening books you recommend.

Sincerely,

• PUBLIC RECOGNITION •

Dear Mrs. Weiser,

It is a wonderful moment when a teacher and administrator as dedicated as you are receives the recognition she deserves. I saw the Channel 8 coverage on you and your career in the Fairview public school system several weeks ago and have been meaning to get in touch with you ever since.

You were my sixth-grade homeroom teacher in 1990. I recall that, even back then, you were the kind of person who knows how to motivate. Children can tell when an adult really cares about them, and you demonstrated that concern to us years ago, as you obviously do now.

If anyone deserves recognition for framing young minds, it's you. Thank you for caring. Thank you for teaching. I'm glad Channel 8 took the initiative in spotlighting your career and contribution to the community. Congratulations.

Warmest regards,

• WINNING ELECTION •

Dear Mr. Nytes,

They said it couldn't be done, but you proved that an independent *can* get elected to the Hoover Valley city council. Congratulations on your recent victory.

Your campaign strategy was smart, your speeches were refreshingly candid, and your performance during the debates blew away the other candidates.

As a Republican, of course, I'd love to have you in our camp, but mostly I'm just happy you won and am looking forward to your shaking up what has become an all-too-complacent city council. More power to you as you take on the whole gang!

Regards,

• PUBLICATION IN NEWSPAPER OR JOURNAL •

Dear Kristen:

Someone mentioned to me that you are actually going to have a paper published in *ABD Journal*. Congratulations! You had mentioned to me that you are involved in a research program that's centered around the connection between cancer and nutrition. But I had no idea your concepts and theories were so innovative.

I am anxious to read the article. During our brief group discussion at the party, I was titillated. You really have a mesmerizing delivery, even when you are just *talking* about your research. No doubt that quality comes through bright and clear in your writing. No wonder the publishers selected your work for publication.

The subject of the cancer-nutrition link is well timed too. I am thrilled that someone with your qualifications has spent the kind of time that such an important subject merits. Good luck with your future research.

Regards,

• ON GETTING WELL •

Jack,

I'm so glad to hear you're up and about. Congratulations on a speedy recovery. I have to admit that I believed the doctors when they said you'd be in the wheelchair for four months—they're the pros, right? But I underestimated your grit during what must have been a painful and exhausting course of physical therapy. I hope you'll give me a call as soon as you're ready to hit the links again.

Sincerely,

CONSUMER ISSUES AND CONCERNS

As a consumer, you experience both excellent and poor service. And both should be occasions for writing letters to make organizations aware of exceptional employees—and terrible situations and service.

For the excellent dinner service, for the superb flight in which an attendant took extra care of your traveling loved one, for the special furniture delivery during the rainstorm, you want to express your appreciation immediately. Comment specifically on what the service personnel did to make you feel special or to make your purchase exceptional. Were they quick, efficient, thoughtful, thorough, sensitive? And remember to include names of individuals, not just departments or groups. With a name, the organization that receives your letter can relay your praise to the exact person who deserves it. Often such letters mean raises or recognition.

As for the poor meal, for the flight in which all rights were ignored and needs minimized, and for the furniture damaged during delivery, you need to complain so that your letter gets action.

First, summarize the situation or problem briefly up front. Include enough of the details so that readers can quickly grasp what has happened. Don't assume that they will "fill in the details" about the severity or difficulty of a situation. Often those who receive the complaint letters are far removed from the day-to-day scene.

Then be specific about the action or adjustment you expect on a problem situation. Use a confident, not angry, tone. Avoid sarcasm if your ultimate objective is to have a problem corrected as you want it to be handled. Sarcasm and threats tend to lessen others' motivation for resolving a problem expeditiously.

"We are confident that you see the situation from our point of view."

"We're looking forward to improved service the next trip."

"I'm assuming the new shipment will arrive promptly."

"Thank you for giving this situation your immediate and full attention. We hope you can restore our confidence in your organization."

Don't forget to enclose all necessary paperwork (receipts, past orders or letters, canceled checks, catalog numbers, merchandise labels, warranties, service agreements, and so forth).

APPRECIATION

• TECHNICAL SUPPORT •

Dear Victoria,

I cannot thank you enough for the flawless technical support that you've given me over the last couple of months.

The slides that you created for the Glazton presentation were a big hit; and the multimedia extravaganza unfolded on cue with perfect precision. My colleagues were as impressed with *me* as I am with *you*. You also did a marvelous job researching the report (and I know that I didn't always give you much to go on) and recommending exactly the appropriate graphics software for their preferences.

Without your help, I don't think I could have met the short but urgent deadline. I feel much better knowing that I have such a valuable and capable resource a phone call away.

Regards,

• Helpful Salesperson •

Dear Mr. Ford:

I would like to commend you on the excellence of your sales staff. I was in your store Saturday afternoon, December 26; and given the number of customers who were shopping there that day, I expected less than your best service. To my surprise and pleasure, Kelvin McRae, one of your salespeople, provided exactly the help I needed with an exchange.

Having received a Sony portable compact disc player for Christmas that I didn't need, I set out to your store to return it the following day. Expecting the worst because of the after-Christmas sales, I fought my way through the crowds of holiday shoppers to look for the correct counter to return the purchase. Apparently, I looked as frustrated as I felt, because Kelvin greeted me and then guided me to the correct counter to get a refund on the player. But that was not the end of his effort. The replacement model that I wanted was out of stock. Again, Kelvin spent more than half an hour calling your other stores to locate the appropriate model. During our discussion, I was also delighted by his in-depth product knowledge, something of a rarity in this self-serve era.

Obviously, you know how to train and motivate people, so I expect that Kelvin will receive the attention that he deserves as a result of my writing today.

I will definitely be shopping at your store again, primarily because of the high-quality service and attention I received there on a very busy day.

Cordially,

• Of Safety Personnel •

Dear Richard Burleson,

I would like to commend you on the exemplary service of Juan Alomar, one of your ushers.

On June 2, I attended a Beavers game with my ten-year-old son, Darren. We were seated near the visitor's bullpen in Section 4, Row 2, Seats 11 and 12. During the second inning, Darren was struck in the arm by a foul ball.

Though Darren appeared to be fine, Mr. Alomar convinced him (and me) that Darren needed to be examined by a medic. As it turns out, Darren's arm was fractured.

When Darren realized we'd have to go to the hospital, he was in tears—not because of his arm, but because we'd miss the end of the game.

So imagine our surprise, out in the parking lot, when Mr. Alomar caught up to us as we were leaving. He had managed to track down the ball that struck Darren and had gotten it autographed by the batter, Dickie Nokes. ("To Darren—tough break, kid.") On top of that, he gave us two tickets to the following evening's game.

Mr. Alomar made my son's day; but not only that, his cautious approach to Darren's injury ensured that Darren received the prompt medical attention he needed. I hope you'll see fit to commend him for his level-headedness, his thoughtfulness, and his willingness to go the extra mile for your fans.

Sincerely,

• FOR COMPLIMENTARY SERVICES OR GOODS •

Dear Mr. Seward,

Last night, my husband and I enjoyed a wonderful dinner at Le Chateau compliments of your maître d', Jackson Favreau. I wanted to express my appreciation for his graciousness and for your restaurant's overall devotion to customer satisfaction.

Two weeks ago, during our anniversary dinner, we received the wrong order and then had to wait an additional half hour for our entrées. We didn't complain (as longtime patrons, we're willing to forgive an occasional off night), but Mr. Favreau nevertheless refused to let us pay and furthermore insisted we come back again, his treat, to enjoy, as he put it, "the kind of anniversary celebration you deserve."

It is not uncommon, of course, for a restaurant to offer a free entrée or appetizer when there is a problem with the meal. That wasn't enough for Mr. Favreau, though, and we were truly impressed and touched by his determination that we enjoy an exemplary dining experience.

I commend you for having the city's best maître d', and my husband and I look forward to many more memorable evenings at Le Chateau.

Sincerely,

• HONEST MECHANIC •

Dear Lars:

I would like to commend you for hiring such honest employees. I was at the dealer's service department last Saturday to have my shocks tested, and I was thrilled with the terrific service there. Although I had no appointment and had to wait for an hour for a mechanic to examine my car, his efforts to treat me with courtesy and fairness more than made up for the inconvenience.

Todd, the mechanic, was extremely helpful and honest about the work necessary on my car. He carefully explained the testing he planned to do, the results of his tests, and corrective action he planned to take. I had gone to Saturn expecting to be charged a great deal of money for the work. But Todd discovered the problem and the solution to be far less drastic than we both had originally anticipated. Because of his honesty, I saved several hundred dollars and a great deal of frustration.

I hope that you will extend my thanks to him. And please pass this information on to your supervisor. I want her to know that Todd is the reason that I will be coming back to the Saturn dealership for future repairs as they are needed.

I have owned my Saturn SL1 for several years now. I rarely have problems with it, but when I do, I dread taking it to mechanics. It seems as though they are all so untrustworthy. But my interaction with Todd has definitely changed that previously unhappy perception.

Warmest regards,

COMPLAINTS

• ABOUT DELIVERY OF NEWSPAPER •

Dear Mr. Averill,

Two months ago I bought a subscription to the *Dallas Morning News* when I was solicited by phone. Although I have received an invoice for my order, I have yet to see a single newspaper. The salesperson had promised that I would begin receiving my papers immediately.

Would you please do one of the following: either ensure that delivery begins immediately or cancel my subscription and notify me of that cancellation?

I ordered the Sunday-only subscription for the special rate of $50 on January 7 when I spoke with Sandra. Enclosed is a copy of the invoice received on February 2. Naturally, I will not pay it until I begin receiving a paper.

Thank you for your attention to this matter.

Sincerely,

• ABOUT HIDDEN CHARGES/SURCHARGES •

Dear Customer Service Agent,

Last Friday, I purchased two tickets from Ticket Connection to the Jones Brothers' October 11 concert at the Music Mill in Edinburgh, South Carolina. The tickets cost $20 each plus a $5 service charge per ticket and a $2 service charge per order for a total of $52.

Imagine my dismay, then, when I arrived at the Music Mill and learned that tickets could be purchased at the box office with no service charge (for a savings of $12 on two tickets).

I understand that Ticket Connection offers convenience to ticket buyers, and I would expect to pay a premium for such a convenience. However, I think your service charges (in this case, 30 percent!) are exorbitant. Furthermore, I think you owe it to your customers to notify them in cases where tickets can be purchased without service charges.

I attend between ten and twenty concerts a year. Until you reduce your service charges, I'll be making all of my ticket purchases at box offices that don't charge a Ticket Connection service fee, and I'll be skipping shows where such tickets aren't available.

Sincerely,

P.S. Please see that this letter reaches the appropriate person. I was unable to reach a Ticket Connection executive via your endless automated phone menu.

• ABOUT UNFINISHED WORK •

Dear Mr. Conangelo,

Thanks for the fine job you've done so far in our yard. The landscaping around the garage looks great, and the grading along the foundation has reduced the amount of moisture in the basement.

However, I need to know if and when you plan to finish the rest of the work we agreed upon, including weeding and mulching the flower beds around the pool. You originally estimated the job would take two weeks, but it has been a month since I last saw you.

It's important to me that the work be completed by May 13, when I'll be hosting a graduation party for my daughter. Given the short timeframe, I'm asking that you provide me with a contract stating when you'll complete the work. If you're unable to do so by May 1, I'll have to make arrangements with another landscaper to finish the yard.

Thanks for your prompt attention to this matter.

Sincerely,

• ABOUT RETURN POLICY •

Dear Ms. McNiven,

Last week, I attempted to return a pair of shoes to The Shoe Box, but the sales clerk told me I couldn't because more than two weeks had elapsed since I made the purchase. I'm writing to ask that you waive your return policy and credit my Visa card for the purchase. A copy of my receipt is enclosed.

All of the other shoe stores in town offer at least a 30-day return window, and had I known that The Shoe Box's policy was more restrictive, I wouldn't have shopped there. Also, I noticed that you still have the same shoes on display, so it's not as if I'm asking you to take back a pair of shoes that is already out of season.

Not only do I hope you'll accept my return, but I also hope you'll consider revising your policy to bring it in line with your competitors. That's all it would take to make me a regular—and happy—customer.

Respectfully,

• ABOUT RESTAURANT OR FOOD SERVICE •

Dear Patricia:

Two evenings ago, I was in the MiShack's restaurant on Lovers Lane in Bedrock, and I received exceptionally poor service. It was obvious that the waitress and several others we observed working that night were incapable of keeping up with their customers' requests. The kitchen too was apparently overburdened. What other explanation could there be for the inadequacies that we experienced that evening?

I inform you of this because I suspect that it is not the first complaint you've received from your customers lately; so perhaps you will see your way to do something to rectify the problem. The waitress did inform us that the restaurant was understaffed that night. If this indeed was the case, then the problem and the solution belong to the management team.

Upon arrival, we had to wait 20 minutes to be seated. Such a wait is not so unusual for a busy restaurant on the weekend. I mention it only to establish that I do not expect miracles when a restaurant is so busy. However, I do expect that, once I am seated, the drinks arrive promptly. They did not. I expect the food order to be taken in a timely manner. It was not. And I expect the food, especially after having waited for so long for it to arrive, to be acceptable. It was not. It was cold, and the portions were much smaller than we are accustomed to receiving at MiShack's.

No matter how good employees are at their jobs, if they have too much to handle, they will perform poorly. I have been a MiShack's patron for a number of years, but if this sort of problem is going to persist, I will be forced to dine elsewhere.

Sincerely,

• ABOUT E-COMMERCE POLICY •

Dear PayFriend Customer Service Representative,

This morning, you froze funds in my PayFriend account (under the e-mail address johnsmith@aol.com) after receiving a claim from Bob Richards (eBid user ID dixieboy) regarding item #5171723432. I'm requesting that you immediately release the funds in my account and close Mr. Richards' dispute.

Mr. Richards paid for the lot via PayFriend on March 12, and I shipped the lot to him the following day. He claims he didn't receive the package and is now seeking reimbursement through the PayFriend Buyer Protection Program.

However, I shipped the lot via USPS First Class mail with Delivery Confirmation, and the package was delivered on March 15. The Delivery Confirmation number is 0304-1070-0000-8237-4846. Shipment can be confirmed on the USPS website.

I encourage PayFriend to develop a fairer Buyer Protection Program. Under the current policies, any buyer can, without proof, cause funds to be frozen in a seller's account. I think you owe your sellers a program in which they aren't guilty until proven innocent.

Thank you,

ORDERS AND CANCELLATIONS

• PLACING ORDER •

Dear Vita-Rite:

I saw your ad in *Healthy Times* and would like to order a 6-month supply of Vita-Rite's Detoxification Teas. The ad lists the discounted price at $24.99 (shipping charges included).

I am enclosing a check for the full amount. As I understand it, North Carolina residents don't need to add any sales tax. If that information is incorrect, perhaps I could be billed for the remaining few dollars after delivery. Please send my order to the address above.

Do you offer additional nutritional products? If you have a catalog, please send that along also.

Thank you,

• CHECKING STATUS OF ORDER •

Dear Ms. Rowan,

Last March I was at the Cultural Expo, where I bought a book from your booth. I also ordered a companion workbook two and a half months ago and have never received it. I have enjoyed the book so far, but I think it would be even more helpful, as is mentioned at the end of each chapter, if I could do the workbook exercises that accompany each section.

Would you please check on that order for me?

The title of the book is *Teach Yourself Spanish* by Oscar and Loretta Chavez. The name of the workbook is *Teach Yourself Spanish: Student Handbook of Exercises and Sample Tests.*

Enclosed is a copy of my receipt for both books. The shipping address in my letterhead is still current.

Thank you,

• RECEIVING DUPLICATE BILLING •

RE: Account 5555-5555-5555-5555

Dear Customer Service Representative:

I have just received a bill from Ranger Credit Card Company; it is the same bill that I received and paid last month.

The original bill was received on April 27, and the payment was mailed by regular mail on April 30. Please credit my account with that payment and deduct the interest and late-payment fee incorrectly charged this month.

A copy of my canceled check and also copies of both bills are enclosed.

Thank you,

• CANCELING ORDER •

RE: Order 5895858

Dear Customer Service Representative:

Please cancel my order for the two suits and a pair of shoes (dated September 18). You recently notified me that the clothes were on back order and that you could not guarantee shipment until November. Because I need the clothes for a trip in October, neither outfit will be of use to me.

Please credit my account for the total amount ($413.56) immediately.

Thank you for the prompt notification that the suits are out of stock. That notice will give me enough time to order something else.

Sincerely,

• CANCELING UNSATISFACTORY SERVICE •

RE: Account 95455

Dear Mr. Tulane:

Please cancel my weekly housecleaning service, effective immediately. I have phoned several times in the past year about the poor service that I've received from Metro-Maid, but I've not seen any improvement in the services. My previous calls have focused on the following recurring problems with your workers:

- Failure to bring their own cleaning supplies with them on occasion
- Carpets left unvacuumed behind doors and under movable furniture
- Glass surfaces left streaked and smeared
- Failure to stay the agreed-upon three hours to finish cleaning tasks

Please be sure to notify the team that usually cleans my house. In the past, they have shown up at the regular time—even though I had canceled the service for that week. This time, I am giving a full week's written notice so I will not be liable for any charges should the cleaning team fail to receive this message.

Sincerely,

• RETURNING DAMAGED PRODUCT •

RE: Invoice 4344436

Dear Customer Service Representative:

I ordered the matching Crystal Seaview paperweights on May 24 and received them damaged on June 26. Both are visibly cracked.

I am returning them to you via UPS. Please reimburse me for the full amount of postage, and send me replacement paper-weights immediately.

These paperweights are a birthday gift for my business partner. Although I ordered them in plenty of time, the delay in having to wait for undamaged ones will certainly create a short dead-line. Do you pay for shipping them overnight in such cases where the error is yours? I must have them by July 10.

Enclosed is the return order form and a copy of the UPS receipt.

Thank you,

• REQUESTING REFUND FOR DEFECTIVE PRODUCT OR POOR SERVICE •

RE: Invoice 49494

Dear Customer Service Agent:

I am returning my Compton Color Printer to you for an immediate refund. It has not worked properly since the day we purchased it, and we no longer have the inclination to wait for you to send other technicians to "adjust" it.

Please refund me in the full amount ($432.13), plus the shipping charges ($25.95) incurred when sending it back to you (shipping bill and original receipt enclosed).

The printer smears and smudges almost any document that it prints out, even those done only in black and white. The repairman that you sent out to examine it told us that he could find nothing wrong with the machine; he stated that the quality of the printed documents was simply the best we could expect from such a printer. Assuming that his diagnosis of the situation is true, we will be looking for a higher-quality printer that better meets our printing needs.

Sincerely,

• Requesting Replacement under Warranty •

RE: Invoice 00012

Dear Mrs. Flaherty:

I bought a vegetable steamer/rice cooker about 6 months ago at Mincefield's Department Store (Model 120-V, with a 1-year warranty). When I tried to use it last week, however, the power button would not work. I returned the item to the store, but Mincefield's would not honor the guarantee, because it is going out of business. The manager suggested that I contact you, the manufacturer.

I need to have the steamer either repaired or replaced. Also, I assume that I will be reimbursed for shipping charges, so I'm enclosing the post office receipt with this letter. Please return the new or repaired steamer to my work address: 2003 Mountainview, Suite 320, Houston, TX 79050.

I use the steamer/cooker quite frequently so I would appreciate your promptness. Except for the fact that it suddenly broke last week, I find it extremely convenient, a product well worth buying.

Thank you for honoring the manufacturer's warranty. I'll look forward to purchasing other of your products.

Thank you,

REQUESTS

• REMOVE NAME FROM MAILING LIST •

RE: Account 686869566

Dear Customer Service Agent:

I recently became a new MasterWorld credit card member. From the time that I received my first statement, I have been inundated with a never-ending stream of advertisements and mail-order offers through, I suppose, this credit card mailing list. I do not like to shop by mail and simply discard my "junk mail."

I would be much more satisfied with my credit card services if you would please remove my name from your mailing list. The only mail that I wish to receive from your organization is my monthly billing statement.

Thank you for removing my name from your direct-mail marketing lists and refusing to sell it to other companies.

Sincerely,

• REMOVE NAME FROM CALLING LIST •

Dear Jenkins Mortgage,

On September 9, I received a telephone solicitation from your company. I asked to be removed from your calling list, but a week later, I received a second call, once again interrupting my dinner.

I'm asking that you remove me from your calling list immediately. I am currently on the state's no-call list, and if I receive another call from your company, I will report Jenkins Mortgage to the attorney general via the website the state has established for just that purpose.

Thank you for your prompt attention to this matter.

Sincerely,

• REMOVE NAME FROM E-MAIL LIST OR GROUP •

RE: Frequent Flier #3477789

Dear Northern Airlines,

Please remove me from your e-mail advertising list. I appreciate the convenience of receiving my frequent flier statement online, but I don't appreciate the weekly barrage of advertisements and special fares. When I signed up for online statements, I did not knowingly give my consent to receive such e-mails. Be assured that if I'm planning a trip, I will take it upon myself to check your website for special fares and offers.

Sincerely,

• REQUESTING RETURN OF DEPOSIT •

Dear Apartment Manager,

Last month I placed a deposit on an apartment in your complex. The representative with whom I spoke promised me at that time that I would be able to move into my new apartment within two weeks. It has now been four weeks and the apartment still isn't ready for me.

The lease on my old apartment expired a week ago, so I was forced to find other accommodations in another apartment complex. Since I am now leasing from them, I am requesting that you send me a full refund of the deposit I made to you a month ago.

Please send the check to my new address at 22 Bluebonnet Lane, #221, Dalworthington MD 39473. Or you may contact me by phone (555-5555) and I will pick the check up personally.

Thank you,

• STATUS OF ONLINE AUCTION PURCHASE •

Dear Jerry Alexander,

I'm writing to check on the shipping status of a Chinese vase I won in one of your eBid auctions (item #5171723432). My user ID is vase_collector_#1, and my address appears at the end of this e-mail.

The auction ended on July 12, and I made payment of $52 ($46 + $4 shipping + $2 insurance) via PayFriend instant transfer on July 13.

As of today, August 15, I still haven't received the vase. Can you tell me when it will be shipped or, if it already has been shipped, provide me with the tracking number?

I will be happy to leave positive feedback should the vase arrive within the next week, by August 22. If not, I will have little choice but to open an "item not received" dispute via eBid in an effort to recoup my money.

Sincerely,

• To Expand Service Area •

Dear Mr. Parker,

I'm writing in hopes that you'll consider expanding your delivery area north of 23rd Street to include the Aiken Heights neighborhood.

I understand that Aiken Heights was once viewed as dangerous, but the neighborhood has undergone a renaissance in the past few years. Police records show that the crime rate is now lower than in most surrounding neighborhoods.

Furthermore, Aiken Heights comprises only 24 city blocks (four blocks east to west, six blocks north to south), meaning your drivers would not have to travel more than a half mile or so beyond your existing delivery area.

At present, only Pizza House and Sinatra's deliver here. I much prefer Amici's, as do many of my neighbors. I sincerely hope you'll give us the opportunity to give *you* our business.

Sincerely,

• NOTIFYING COMPANY OF HAZARDOUS PRODUCT •

Dear Mr. Luckman,

A few weeks ago I bought a decorative bowl manufactured by your company. Although it makes a beautiful centerpiece, I noticed on the enclosed information leaflet that the bowl contains lead.

Knowing how dangerous lead poisoning is and how easy it is to get lead poisoning from food served in a lead dish, I think it's important that you warn customers. I suggest that you use bold print on the outside of the box. Clarify that the notice of lead content is a warning, not just a characteristic of the clay.

The bowl I now own is the size C serving bowl from the Printemps collection. I have enclosed my proof of purchase here as well as a copy of the leaflet that came with the dish.

I think that many customers are unaware of the danger of lead poisoning. Please do everything that you can to see that unnecessary poisoning does not occur.

Sincerely,

CREDIT, BANKING, AND FINANCIAL CONCERNS

Nothing captures the attention of readers so much as the issue of money—their money or yours. Whether depositing, withdrawing, lending, or borrowing, you want to make sure you provide all the facts.

When you have borrowed money, assure the reader that you intend to repay the money owed, even if that becomes necessary under altered terms with lesser amounts or over a longer period. Although many people consider their financial situation confidential, you will do well to explain your current difficulties to those who are lending you money. They consider explanations a show of good faith. Another way to motivate creditors to work with you during difficult times is to remind them about past business you've given them and state your intention to do business with them again under better conditions.

When requesting a loan, give a full explanation of how you intend to use the money and state your plans for repayment. Be specific as to your calculations for where the money will come from to repay the loan. Even when addressing friends or family, use a businesslike (not flippant or pleading) tone to convey your sincere need for the money and your firm intention to repay the loan.

When refusing a loan to friend, remember that you are not obligated to give a reason—although doing so makes your refusal sound less arbitrary and more thoughtful. Statements such as these may seem firm, yet less harsh.

"I feel uncomfortable making personal loans for any reason to anyone."

"I'm not financially in a position to make loans to anyone."

"My spouse and I have made a personal commitment to each other never to lend money to a friend or a relative because of the hard feelings that inevitably develop around such circumstances."

"My own job is rather unstable."

When refusing a loan, however, do express your understanding of the need for the money. Often, when the requester hears a "no," he or she thinks that you are saying no simply because you don't earnestly see the need as critical or urgent. Consider these comments:

"I understand how much you need the money."

"I can understand the difficulty of the situation."

"You have cause for concern. I see your predicament."

"A couple of thousand dollars, I know, would make a big difference in your situation. I understand that."

Try to use positive phrasing with your turndown:

"I'm afraid I simply can't make such a loan. I need all my available resources to handle my own commitments."

"I wish I could help in this instance, but I can't."

"I wish I had the extra money for situations like this, but I just don't. We live on a limited income ourselves."

Instead of focusing on what you're not going to provide, focus on your own needs or plans for the money or your own positive philosophies about personal loans.

"I myself have similar commitments that will require all my available cash. We plan to spend any excess cash above our expenses this year on X."

End with a goodwill statement about the outcome of the situation or resolution of any problem.

"I do hope you can resolve the issue."

"I'll hope to hear that you've been able to handle the situation on your own."

"I hope you'll understand. I do value our relationship and want what is best for both of us."

In delicate matters such as lending, borrowing, and collecting, tone becomes very important in reaffirming commitments and in keeping any personal relationship intact.

On other miscellaneous matters of banking, finance, and taxes, summarize your message succinctly without irrelevant detail: What do you want your reader to know or do? Include all necessary dates, account numbers, amounts, full names, and form or receipt numbers so the reader can investigate your history and situation with ease. The image that you create in your writing style and with your thoroughness often makes an impression that spills over into the business transaction and decision itself.

If you decide to grant a loan, state your positive response immediately.

"I'm enclosing the money asked for."

"Yes, we will agree to lend you the money under the terms you mentioned."

"We are glad to be able to help you out in this instance."

Outline the conditions under which you will make the loan, including all repayment terms and any collateral you expect.

"We understand that you intend to begin repaying the money in June."

"I can agree to the 10 percent interest over the term of the loan."

"The details you outlined for repayment dates and amounts sound fine."

Provide a written agreement of the loan and repayment schedule for the friend or family member to sign. This formality underscores your own firm intention that the borrower will repay the loan by the agreed-upon date. This agreement also offers protection in case the borrower dies; you'll need proof of the money owed to you from the deceased's estate.

"I've drafted a letter, including the details of the loan."

"I've put together a confirmation of the loan and terms."

"Just so we both understand the terms of the loan, I've outlined here something for you to sign so that both of us are clear about the situation."

"In case something happens to me or you before this loan is repaid, I've jotted down the particulars..."

CREDIT AND COLLECTIONS

• ADDING PERSON TO ACCOUNT •

RE: Checking Account 099090933

Dear Mr. Dotel:

I have recently married and would like to add my husband to my checking account.

An account manager at Corporate Bank told me last week that my husband and his bank (Service Corp. United) must complete a few forms for an electronic transfer of his account balance to your bank. Please send me those forms immediately so that we can take care of this transfer before we leave town on April 30.

Thank you. We're looking forward to continued excellent service at your bank.

Sincerely,

• REMOVING PERSON FROM ACCOUNT •

RE: Checking Account 3434898755534

Dear Customer Service Representative:

My mother and I have been cosignatories on the same checking account since 1995. She is now moving to Florida, so she plans to open a separate account there in her name only.

Please take the necessary steps to remove her name from our joint account. Any paperwork to be completed may be sent to me at the address on the letterhead.

My mother plans to move within the next three weeks, so we'll appreciate your making this change promptly.

Thank you,

(Signatures of both parties)

• CHANGE OF NAME •

RE: Account #3232 1770 4444 9809

Dear Watkins Bank,

Please change the name on my Watkins Bank Visa account from Martha Posey to Martha Posey O'Neal effective May 1 and send me a new card reflecting the change.

I'm getting married on April 30 and will thereafter be using my married name. A copy of the marriage license is enclosed. Please contact me if you require additional documentation.

Sincerely,

Martha Posey

• NOTIFYING OF PAYMENT NOT CREDITED TO ACCOUNT •

RE: Service Card Account 7878-9033-9933

Dear Ms. Riggs:

Three weeks ago, on November 20, I sent a payment of $200 to the Service Card. However, when I received my last billing statement, dated November 30, that payment had still not been credited. What is more, I was charged a $15 late fee for failure to pay.

Would you please verify your receipt of that payment and see that I am credited in the full amount? Once the first discrepancy is remedied, please subtract the $15 late fee erroneously added to my balance.

I mailed the payment ten days before the due date (as I usually do), so the Service Card should have received my check in plenty of time to apply the payment before the closing date for November's statement.

Enclosed is a copy of my check carbon, on which is imprinted the check that I wrote to the Service Card three weeks ago.

Sincerely,

• REQUESTING RECONSIDERATION FOR DENIED CHARGE ACCOUNT •

Dear New Accounts:

I received your notice that I was denied a personal charge account with your department store. I cannot understand this refusal of credit, because my credit history is exemplary.

The income from my salary and my husband's business totals $52,000. Perhaps you considered us a credit risk because his income is from self-employment and I've just begun my new job this month. Yes, I have recently changed jobs, but you'll notice that I was with my previous employer for more than seven years. As to my husband's income from his small business, I'm enclosing his corporate tax returns for the past two years to substantiate his average income at $31,000.

We respectfully ask that you reconsider your decision regarding our credit status. I'd be happy to resubmit the application to ensure that no discrepancies exist. Or, if you must adhere to your decision, please notify me (my address and phone number are on the letterhead) of the reasons that led to your decision.

I submitted my application to you on March 19, and your response (enclosed) is dated March 31. We hope to hear from you promptly with a more positive answer so that we can begin to do business with your fine department store.

Sincerely,

• REQUESTING A LOWER INTEREST RATE •

RE: Account #3232 1770 4444 9809

Dear Watkins Bank,

I'm writing to request a lower interest rate on my Watkins Bank Visa card.

I've recently received preapproved offers from several credit card issuers for Visa cards with a lower rate than what I'm currently paying (not to mention even lower, limited-time introductory rates).

As a longtime customer, I'd prefer that the Watkins Bank Visa remain my primary credit card, but without a reduction in the interest rate, I simply can't afford not to switch to a card with a lower rate.

Thanks for your time and consideration.

Sincerely,

• REQUESTING INCREASE IN CREDIT LIMIT •

RE: Account #3232 1770 4444 9809

Dear AmeriBank,

I'm writing to request an increase in my Visa credit limit from $5000 to $10,000. Please note that I've made all of my monthly payments on time during the three years I've had an AmeriBank Visa. My annual income has also increased by more than $4000.

Lately I have begun receiving offers from other credit card issuers for cards with limits greater than $5000 (as well as interest rates comparable to what I'm now paying). I'd prefer to continue using the AmeriBank Visa as my primary card, but in order to do so, I will need the flexibility of a higher credit limit.

Thanks for your time and consideration.

Sincerely,

• CLAIMING BANKRUPTCY PROTECTION •

Dear Capital Bank:

Please discontinue immediately your calls and letters demanding payment. You were notified that I filed bankruptcy in Atlanta, Georgia, on February 1, 20—, under Docket number 499993433872983459595. (Enclosed is another such copy of that action.)

As you may be aware, all creditors, once they have been notified of such action, are subject to stiff penalties and fines should they persist in collecting their debts directly or through a second party.

If you have further questions about the bankruptcy proceedings, you may contact my lawyer: Ms. Carol Humphrey, 4885 Westlake, Ste. 344, Atlanta, GA.

Yours truly,

• DOCUMENTING LOST OR STOLEN CREDIT CARD •

RE: Stolen card 456-999-30303

Dear Credit Services:

One week ago (September 16) I noticed that my credit card had been lost, and I immediately called to report it. Now I'm following up that report with a letter for your records.

If you have not already done so, please take the necessary actions to change my account numbers and discontinue the old card. Also, please send my new card as soon as possible.

According to your credit card contract, I will not be responsible for any authorized charges above $50 resulting from this lost card and my subsequent report.

For your convenience, I am enclosing a copy of the last statement from Capital Credit. The only missing information is my full name as printed on the card (Domingo J. Balint) and my current address: 2102 Rue-de-Calais, Pendleton, MO 87726.

Thank you,

• REQUESTING CREDIT REPORT •

Dear Credit Bureau:

I would like to request a personal credit report. Please send the report to the current address listed below.

The necessary personal information is as follows:

- Social security number: 555-55-5555
- Date of birth: February 24, 1968
- Current address: 14300 Oak Tree Lane, #21A, Mobile, AL 39957. (I have lived at this address since December 1996.)
- Prior address: 1520 Maple Avenue, #917, Mobile, AL 39902. (I lived at that address for four years, from January 1992 to December 1996.)
- Name change: Maiden name (Conroy) legally changed to Chacon in April 1995.

I understand that you need address information going back only five years. If this requirement has changed, please notify me immediately so I can include more information.

Also, enclosed is a copy of my driver's license to verify my current address. Because it still shows my maiden name, I have enclosed a copy of my marriage certificate as well.

Sincerely,

• DISPUTING CREDIT REPORT •

RE: Social Security Number 455-90-9000

Dear Mr. Liebowitz:

The mortgage loan that I applied for on October 12 was denied on the basis of information supplied by your credit bureau. The erroneous information contained in your credit bureau's report involved "late payments" on my car for 36 months. I assure you that I made those payments on time.

Please contact Ford Motor Company to verify that this is fact, and correct my credit report with your bureau. Then please send me a new, corrected credit report at the above address.

I have already been in touch with Ford Motor Company and received an explanation of the mix-up on the car payments. When I bought my car, I made the first two months' payments immediately. For some reason, however, the first payment was credited as two January payments instead of one January and one February payment. So when I made no payment the next month (for February), my record was marked as "late." From that point on, all my payments were logged as a month behind, even though I was paying them on time.

I am enclosing a copy of the credit bureau report you supplied to the mortgage company, containing the erroneous information. Also included is a printout of my Ford Motor Company record of payments, and a business card from Jayne Ripton (the Ford customer service agent who supplied me with the printout). She will be happy to speak with you regarding this issue.

Sincerely,

• REQUESTING SWITCH TO ELECTRONIC STATEMENTS •

RE: Account #3232 1770 4444 9809

Dear Watkins Bank,

I'm writing to authorize a switch to electronic monthly statements for my Watkins Bank Visa card. Please send confirmation of this switch and all future electronic correspondence to the following e-mail address: gladys@meachams.com.

Thanks for your help.

Sincerely,

• REQUESTING REFUND OF LATE FEE •

RE: Account #3232 1770 4444 9809

Dear Heartland Bank,

I just received my Heartland Bank MasterCard monthly statement, which includes a late fee of $20 for my June payment. I did, in fact, mail the June payment two days after the due date. I had the envelope stamped and ready, sitting on the kitchen counter, and simply forgot to take it to the post office. I apologize for this oversight.

However, in light of the fact that this is my first late payment in more than two years as a Heartland Bank MasterCard customer, I'm writing in hopes that you will waive the fee.

I would greatly appreciate your understanding and can assure you I will be more conscientious about mailing future payments on time.

Sincerely,

BANKING

• OPENING ACCOUNT •

Dear Mr. Sanguillen:

I would like to open a personal checking account. Because it is difficult for me to find the time to come in during business hours, I would like to handle the transaction entirely by mail.

Please send me the proper signature forms to be filled out, as well as any pertinent information you may have for me with regard to bank policies and regulations.

I need a checking account with unlimited checking privileges and would like to avoid monthly service charges by maintaining your minimum balance requirements. As to my choice of checks, please select a style comparable to the sample I'm enclosing from my current account with another bank. As you open the account, please order the minimum number of checks (that is usually 200 checks, I think) and debit my account for that cost.

My current address is 2410 Lakebetter Court, Oklahoma City, OK 83432. If you need any additional information in order to send the signature forms and open the account, please call me at my daytime work number (555-5555). Your bank has an excellent reputation in the community, and I'm looking forward to a solid banking relationship.

Sincerely,

• CLOSING ACCOUNT •

Because of Better Rates

RE: Joint Checking Account 89983334555

Dear Mr. Face:

I am closing my account with First United Bank and moving my account to my credit union because of the convenience involved.

Would you please send a final statement and a cashier's check for the closing balance of $1249, according to my records, to the address above?

The service at First United has always been fine, but a credit union better serves my needs at the present time. In fact, its savings accounts offer much better interest rates than your bank does.

Please note both my wife's and my notarized signatures below.

Sincerely,

• CLOSING ACCOUNT •

Because of Moving

RE: Checking Account 9883440003

Dear Mr. Ramirez:

I have a regular checking account with Eagle Bend Bank, and I am moving to New York City next week. Because Eagle Bend doesn't have a branch there, I must close my account here and build a new banking relationship in New York.

Please send me the latest statement and any other information that I may need to close the account. I don't plan to write any more checks on the account, and I want a chance to review your records before I close the account and accept the final balance as accurate.

I leave Eagle Bend on Thursday, March 31. That is only nine days away, so I'd be grateful for your expediency in sending the paperwork.

Thank you,

• CLOSING ACCOUNT •

Because of Poor Service

Dear Account Manager,

I have had both checking and savings accounts with Bank of Trust since 1993, but I'm closing both of my accounts today. Why? I can no longer tolerate the poor service that I've been receiving the past year.

When I phoned the bank on Monday, account manager Stephanie Maxwell informed me that a letter of intent is all that is required to close my accounts. Please make the necessary arrangements to properly close my accounts with Bank of Trust.

Over the last year, I have been subject to a number of accounting errors on the part of Bank of Trust. On more than one occasion, for example, I was charged for overdrafts that occurred because of a teller's error. (Notice my August, October, and November statements for those improper charges.) Mistakes happen, but my attempts to have the problems redressed were most often met with more bureaucracy, incompetence, and even rudeness.

I am enclosing copies of my last bank statement and my last savings account summary for your convenience in closing the accounts.

Yours truly,

• DISPUTING ACCOUNT STATEMENT •

Service Charge

RE: Checking Account 987654321

Dear Ms. Irabu:

On my last checking account statement, I noticed that I was charged for calling the Certified Bank automated teller information number. I have been using that number (toll-free) to verify deposits and withdrawals for years (ever since I opened my account in 1992) and was unaware of any new policy about charges for using that number.

If indeed some new policy imposes a charge for its use, I will no longer call that number. In any case, I think it only fair that you credit my account for the $7 charge for the seven times that I called the number during my last banking cycle.

If there was a policy change imposing that new usage fee, notification prior to the start of the new policy was in order. I never received such notice and, therefore, do not expect to be charged for a service that I have been receiving free for so long.

Enclosed is a copy of my last statement with the extra service charges highlighted in yellow. I will appreciate your removing these charges.

Sincerely,

• DISPUTING ACCOUNT STATEMENT •

Failure to Credit Deposit

RE: Checking Account 34889893483

Dear Mrs. Sizemore,

One week ago, on November 22, I deposited $637.12 in my regular checking account through your automated teller. However, the deposit has not yet been credited to my account.

Please verify that deposit and call me immediately (456-0004) if there is some problem.

It is my understanding that a deposit is always credited the day it is made (or the following business day if it is made after 3 P.M.). If this policy has changed, please notify me at once. Otherwise, I will assume that it remains the same and will continue to do my banking accordingly.

I am enclosing a copy of the deposit slip to help you track the deposit.

Sincerely,

• DISPUTING ACCOUNT STATEMENT •

Insufficient Funds

RE: Checking Account 00939399087675

Dear Ms. Boyd:

I just received a notice of insufficient funds from Interstate Bank. The notice states that a standard $20 service charge has been assessed to my account to cover administration fees involving a returned check. I have double-checked my records and verified that I made a deposit on August 6 that was not credited to my account until August 8. Therefore, check 2223 to Doyen's Department Store was returned through no fault of my own.

Please double-check your records, and correct the date of the deposit in question. Then please credit back to my account the $20 service charge for the overdraft. Finally, as you are aware, there is embarrassment in having a check returned marked "insufficient funds." I'd appreciate it if you would notify the department store that the error was the bank's, not mine.

As you will see on the deposit slip enclosed with this letter, I made the deposit before 3 P.M. on the same day that the check was cashed (June 22). There should have been more than enough money in my account to cover the check.

Thank you for your attention in correcting this error promptly.

Sincerely,

Enc. Your notification of insufficient funds
     Deposit slip

• REQUESTING LOAN •

Dear Mrs. D'Amico:

I am in the process of paying off a number of small debts. In an effort to simplify my finances, reduce the aggregate interest that I am charged every month, and reduce the total of my overall monthly payments, I would like to acquire a consolidation loan.

Please review the enclosed loan proposal. I am seeking approval by the end of this week, if at all possible, before I incur additional interest charges on my various debts.

The loans that I would like to consolidate include four credit cards (two majors and two department stores), my remaining six car payments, a furniture store credit plan, and a few small payments for dental work last year. Other details and numbers are, of course, included in the loan proposal. As collateral for the loan, I'm suggesting my 1997 Jeep Cherokee and my wife's 1997 Buick.

My total annual income amounts to $43,550. That income should certainly be sufficient to pay off the loan. My past financial problems have been the result of a six-month period of unemployment. Now that I've found a new job, I find that I'm still "playing catch-up" with the bills. Until this past difficulty, my credit rating was fine and with this consolidation loan, I'm hoping to regain my footing and establish consistent payment patterns.

My net worth calculations (assets and liabilities) are contained on the completed form supplied by your customer service representative. Thank you for your consideration.

Sincerely,

• REQUESTING EXPLANATION OF LOAN DENIAL •

Dear Loan Officer:

Your bank recently denied my request for a $4000 personal improvement loan. I am puzzled by your decision and respectfully request an explanation for refusing the loan.

I have been steadily employed with the same company for the past three years, earning $32,000 annually. I have always paid my bills on time and have an excellent credit rating.

What other possible risk factor could your loan committee be considering? If its decision was based on some erroneous report by a credit agency, I'd like to be made aware of that so I can correct any discrepancies immediately.

Was there some other error or reason? What will be necessary for you to reconsider my loan application? I'll look forward to either an explanation or a positive decision upon a second analysis.

Sincerely,

• REQUESTING LOAN PAYMENT ADJUSTMENT •

RE: Loan 585857

Dear Loan Officer:

My spouse was recently laid off from his job, and we are having difficulty meeting our financial obligations during this interim period while he seeks other employment.

We are asking that you defer or reduce our $425 monthly loan payments until he finds other employment. If you cannot defer payments completely for a few months, we believe that we can continue to make payments of about $100 each month until our employment situation improves.

My job is steady, and we intend to pay the loan in full as soon as possible. I'm enclosing a $100 payment in good faith, hoping you will agree to this reduced-payment arrangement, if not a complete deferral.

When conditions improve for us, we will look forward to continuing our banking relationship with your organization in future years. Thank you for your understanding and patience in this difficult time.

Sincerely,

• REQUESTING DEFERRED PAYMENT ON LOAN •

RE: Loan 88844

Dear Loan Officer:

My car loan payment falls due on the seventh of the month, and I'm requesting that you change the payment due date to the first of the month. I travel frequently on my job and therefore try to write all my checks twice a month. The current due date creates either the inconvenience of having to mail the payment from the road or the necessity of making the payment early.

I'll appreciate your changing the monthly due date and am willing to make any partial payment necessary to cover the interest on the interim days during the changeover.

Sincerely,

• CASHING CERTIFICATE OF DEPOSIT •

RE: Certificate of Deposit 3239995

Dear Customer Service Representative:

The above certificate of deposit for $10,000 will mature on November 1, and I intend to cash the CD on that date. Would you please deposit the full value at maturity in my personal checking account 4949477002, also at your institution?

Sincerely,

• CHECKING STATUS OF INVESTMENT ACCOUNT •

RE: Heritage Mutual Fund Account 4958882

Dear Fund Agent:

Would you please forward a current statement of my investment account to the above address? I'd also like a summary explanation of the performance of my investments with your fund since my initial deposit of $4560 on January 10, 1997.

As a means to analyzing my overall return, would you please provide any further information, analysis, ratings, or comparisons with other funds sharing the same investment objectives?

Also, it would be helpful to know if investment philosophies will change now that you have a new fund manager.

Sincerely,

• REQUESTING BETTER CHECKING ACCOUNT •

RE: Account #643790

Dear Community Bank,

I'm writing to request an upgrade in my checking account. Specifically, I'd like an account that requires no minimum balance, provides free checking, and offers checking reserve with a credit line of $500.

Now that I've been banking at Community for three years, I think that I should no longer be penalized when my balance dips below $100 nor be charged for writing checks above a monthly allotment of twenty. Furthermore, with checking reserve, I'd no longer have to worry about bouncing checks when my balance is low.

I know these features are available at no additional charge at other area institutions. I'd like to continue banking at Community Bank, though, and I hope you'll be able to accommodate me.

Sincerely,

• DOCUMENTING LOSS OF SAFETY DEPOSIT BOX KEY •

RE: Safety Deposit Box 59995

Dear Customer Service Representative:

I have either misplaced or lost the key to my safety deposit box. This letter is being sent to follow up my telephone report of the lost key on May 2.

Please make your staff aware of any possible attempts at unauthorized use in case someone has stolen or found the key. The last time I entered the box was almost five months ago, in early January. Could you please check your records and let me know if there has been any unauthorized activity on the box in this intervening time? If so, I'll appreciate your sending me a copy of the transaction/entry dates, names, and signatures.

Finally, would you please assign me a new box? If you will phone me when it's ready, I'll stop by to complete the necessary signature form. I appreciate your effort on my behalf to ensure safekeeping of my valuables.

Sincerely,

• AUTHORIZING AUTOMATIC BILL PAYMENT •

RE: Loan #643790

Dear Calvin College,

Please enroll me in your E-Z Pay Student Loan Repayment program. It is my understanding that instead of sending a bill for my student loan, you will simply deduct the payment from my checking account electronically on the fifth day of each month.

Enclosed is the completed authorization form as well as a canceled check, as you've instructed. Please contact me at the address below if there are any problems.

Sincerely,

TAXES

• REQUESTING EXTENSION FOR FILING RETURN •

RE: Social Security Number 123-45-6789
  Tax Year 20—

Dear IRS Representative:

With this letter, I am requesting a second extension on filing my income tax return for this past year. I filed Form 4868 for the first extension on April 1, along with my payment of $450 for additional taxes.

This second extension has become necessary because my job has required that I unexpectedly be out of the country for an extended period (November 2005 to the present). When I left the United States in November, I had no idea that my stay here in the Philippines would be extended on a month-by-month basis. Because of the delay in forwarding information overseas, I am having difficulty collecting all my 1099s and other financial reports from various investment accounts.

Also, my CPA tax preparer from past years has retired, and I'm trying to select a new one to prepare this year's return. The process of interviewing CPAs by letter and checking references with their long-time customers has become complicated and time-consuming because of my overseas work.

For both of these reasons, I'm requesting an additional extension of the filing deadline. Would you please confirm this extension by writing to me at the above address?

Sincerely,

• DISPUTING REFUND RECEIVED •

RE: Social Security Number 123-45-6789

To Whom It May Concern:

I have just received my refund check for $3488 on my 20—return, $1500 less than the amount due me according to my records and the submitted return.

Your attached letter explained that you had discovered unreported earnings from royalties of $6000 on a 1099 submitted by my publisher. However, those royalty earnings *have been reported.*

That royalty amount was reported on my business return rather than my personal return for this past year. All personal royalties go into my business account. If you'll cross-reference my corporate tax return for Trudeau and Associates, you'll notice that these earnings have been reported in that income total.

Therefore, please correct your records and forward to me the remainder of my refund, $1500, along with the accrued interest to date. Thank you.

Yours truly,

• REQUESTING FEE ESTIMATE FROM A TAX PREPARER •

Dear Mr. Niven,

I'm interested in hiring a professional tax preparer to handle my taxes this year. Could you provide me with a written estimate of your fees for this service?

To give you an idea of the work involved, I am enclosing copies of both my state and federal returns for the past two years. My financial situation is basically unchanged except for the fact that I recently purchased a new home in Morgan County and am still trying to sell my old home in Jackson County.

I look forward to hearing from you at your earliest convenience.

Sincerely,

• RESPONDING TO AUDIT OR CLARIFICATION OF RETURN •

RE: Social Security Number 123-45-6789
   Audit Number 34999333399393
   Tax Year 20—

Dear IRS Representative:

In response to your notification that my 20— federal tax return is being audited, I am enclosing the following items you requested to support my charitable contributions deduction:

• My contribution record to my church
• Receipts for items donated to Goodwill Industries
• Transactions receipts for stock sold and contributed to Star Hope Mission

These receipts and contribution records should answer your questions about the return. If not, please phone me at (344) 444-4444 (daytime) or (555) 555-5555 (evening).

Yours truly,

• REQUESTING REVIEW •

RE: Social Security Number 123-45-6789
      Audit Number 94949491223
      Tax Year 20—

Dear IRS Representative:

The auditors have completed their review of my 20— income tax return. They have assessed my tax liabilities at $13,478 rather than the claimed $8232, calculated by my own CPA tax preparer.

I disagree with your auditors' conclusions and the additional proposed tax liability. The auditors have questioned my charitable contribution of an unimproved lot to the First United Methodist Church. Although churches do not assess a value to the property they receive but rather simply acknowledge receipt, I secured and submitted two appraisals from independent appraisal companies attesting to the value of the land. The appraisal estimates were within $1000 of each other. Although the IRS auditors consider the value to be excessive for an unimproved lot, its prime location as a parking lot for surrounding businesses is the basis for those appraised values.

Granted, the appraisal value shown by the Barrington Independent School District is $15,000 less than that assessed by the appraisers, but all properties in the district have been undervalued. A recent newspaper article states that property owners can expect all tax assessments to rise by 30 to 50 percent in the next two years. (Copies of that article and the two appraisals from the independent appraisal companies are enclosed.)

Therefore, with this letter, I'm requesting an independent review of my tax return and the examination findings by the Appeals Office.

(Continued)

My daytime phone number is (477) 555-7878. Thank you for your prompt review.

Yours truly,

Enc. Auditing findings and IRS letter
       Two appraisals on land
       Newspaper article about appraisals

• DISPUTING PROPERTY TAX ASSESSMENT •

County Tax Assessor

RE: Lot 789879
    Block 37B
    Index Number 8999833

Dear Tax Assessor:

The recent tax assessment on my lot on Hughes Road seems excessive. The current assessment of $4888 represents a 48 percent increase over the amount assessed last year on the property.

I realize that almost all property taxes were increased this past year, but the assessment is far greater than that for the lots surrounding the property. The lot to the left was assessed at $3600; the lot to the right was assessed at $3598; the lot across the street was assessed at $3489. These are all comparable investment lots, with no improvements on them. None is a corner lot, and none has utilities.

I can imagine only that someone made a clerical error in computing the assessment. Would you please review this situation and respond to me at my home address (124 Zimmer Avenue) immediately about this assessment? If I do not hear from you within two weeks, I will plan to appeal the assessment to the State Board of Review.

Sincerely,

INSURANCE

• REQUESTING INFORMATION ON INSURANCE COMPANY •

Dear Insurance Commissioner:

I would like information on the Universal Insurance Company before I make a decision about applying for coverage.

Specifically, I would appreciate answers to the following questions:

- Is the company licensed to operate in our state?
- How is the company rated by the industry?
- Is the company financially stable? Are there any bankruptcy proceedings in the past or in progress?
- Have you received any complaints about the company or its representatives with regard to the way they have represented themselves, paid claims to policyholders, misrepresented their services, or failed to provide adequate customer service?

One of Universal's direct-mail pieces came to my home recently, advertising an annual premium for health coverage that seems quite low and that triggered both my interest and my doubt. Any information you can provide will be most helpful to me in making my decision about talking with the company representative further about coverage. Thank you for your assistance.

Sincerely,

• REQUESTING REVIEW OF POLICY •

RE: Policy #46547 and Policy #22114

Dear Insurance Agent,

At present, I have two policies with your agency, a State Mutual homeowner's policy (#46547) and a Keico auto policy (#22114). I'm writing to request a review of both policies to see if there are others that provide comparable coverage with lower premiums.

I am particularly interested in consolidating my homeowner's and auto policies with a single insurer—for the sake of simplicity and for the discount that many companies offer in such circumstances.

Thanks for your help in finding me the best, most affordable coverage available.

Sincerely,

• CONVERTING COMPANY POLICY TO INDIVIDUAL POLICY •

Dear Insurance Representative:

I currently have life and medical insurance coverage with your company through my employer, McDonnelly-Dudley, Inc., policy number WTYl345. Effective May 1, I will be leaving this company and am considering my option to convert my group coverage to an individual policy.

Would you please provide me with an overview of the procedure to make this conversion within the next 30 days? I also need information about coverage and costs: the monthly premiums for various amounts of coverage, any deductibles involved, and any health maintenance services or discounts.

I am married, with one child. For the purpose of computing our premiums, our birthdays follow:

Dennis L. Joss: 1/30/62
Charlotte Bay Joss: 2/26/64
Dennis L. Joss, Jr.: 7/1/92

Although I have not accepted a new position with another employer, I do not anticipate my occupational duties to change significantly, and, therefore should pose no additional insurance risks.

I'll appreciate your fast response with this information because I must convert to an individual policy by May 31.

Sincerely,

• CHANGING LIFE INSURANCE BENEFICIARY •

RE: Term Life Insurance Policy 4449099

Dear Insurance Agent:

I want to change the beneficiary on my term life insurance policy, effective immediately. The current beneficiary is Louis J. Mencken (husband). I'd like the new beneficiaries to be my parents: Chad and Holly Berley. All other provisions and clauses of the policy will remain the same.

I am enclosing my notarized signature below. Should there be other forms required, please send those immediately to my work address: 3499 Beltway Drive, Suite 395, Dallas, TX 75252. Thank you.

Sincerely,

• REQUESTING NEW AGENT—POOR SERVICE •

RE: Homeowner's Policy RT3889

Dear Manager:

My current insurance agent (Abner Keane of Ardmore, Oklahoma) has not been as attentive as necessary to my insurance coverage in the past, and I am requesting that a new agent service my account. Would you please have a new agent (preferably one a little closer to my current location) contact me immediately?

I've been a policyholder for more than ten years and think that some additional coverage is warranted because of various jewelry and computer purchases through the years. My current agent has never mentioned updating my coverage. Additionally, I recently had a small claim (broken picture window) and found it difficult to get Mr. Keane to return my calls.

Please let me know if any further action is required on my part, and I'll look forward to having a new agent from your organization contact me about taking over the account.

Sincerely,

• REQUESTING REDUCTION OF HEALTH
INSURANCE PREMIUM •

RE: Medical Insurance Policy 5899985

Dear Insurance Agent:

I am requesting a reassessment of the risk associated with the premiums on my current insurance policy, issued eight years ago.

A recent physical exam shows that I am now within the standard weight guidelines; also, I am no longer a smoker. With these improvements to my lifestyle, my doctor agrees that my health risks have decreased. (His letter is attached.)

Would you please let me know if I now qualify for lower rates, and send me any necessary forms and verification of the change in premium payments?

Sincerely,

• INQUIRING ABOUT MEDICAL COVERAGE ABROAD •

RE: Policy 4444-4444

Dear Insurance Agent,

This spring, my daughter and I will be traveling to Japan for three weeks. Could you review my health insurance policy, explain any travel-related coverage, and advise me as to whether or not I should consider purchasing additional health insurance for the trip? I can be reached at 555-5555. Thanks for your help, and I look forward to hearing from you so that we can travel with complete peace of mind.

Sincerely,

• REQUESTING REDUCTION OF AUTO INSURANCE RATE •

RE: Auto Policy 58838

Dear Insurance Agent:

I've just received my new premium notice reflecting the addition of my son, Troy Ott, age 16, to my auto policy, effective August 6. That increase in premium seems to be excessive for his limited use of my car.

Would you please reevaluate the risk factors associated with his driving and let us know what discounts you can offer in his case?

Troy completed the state-approved safe-driving course this past spring at Lamar High School. As an honor student there, he has shown considerable maturity for his age and has never been involved in acts of delinquency or irresponsibility. His driving will be limited to trips to school and to church youth functions, all within a ten-mile radius of our home.

We'll look forward to a positive decision about reduced rates for responsible, limited driving by my son.

Sincerely,

• CLAIMING LIFE INSURANCE BENEFITS •

RE: Life Insurance Policy 44922

Dear Insurance Agent:

Richard Q. Hunt, your policyholder, died on August 1 in Houston, Texas. His latest legal residence was 4788 Elmhurst in Houston. As beneficiary of his life insurance policy, I am requesting immediate settlement of the lump-sum distribution.

I would prefer to have electronic transfer of the funds direct to my bank account 0039884993 at BankFirst, Houston, TX 77013 (routing number 0009999). If for some reason you are not set up to make an electronic transfer, you may mail the distribution check directly to me at the above address.

Enclosed is the required, signed certificate of death.

Sincerely,

• DISPUTING AMOUNT OF SETTLEMENT •

RE: Homeowner's Policy 5500003

Dear Claims Adjuster:

Today I received your letter and settlement check for replacement of my television sets, security system, and stereo equipment, which were damaged when lightning struck our home on March 6. That settlement amount is unacceptable.

Please review the attached documentation (original receipts for purchase of each item), which shows the total cost to be $9456. It seems that your settlement check is for $7092, representing a payment of 25 percent lower than actual value. I suppose this discounted replacement payment is based on a typical deduction for normal wear and tear.

From the dates on the receipts, you'll notice that all the equipment was new. In fact, we purchased our newly constructed home only six weeks ago. Although we closed on the home January 27, we took possession from the builder only three days before the lightning incident. (Our receipt for the move with Bekins, showing the move-in date as March 3, is enclosed.) Therefore, the damaged items were virtually unused. We believe that we are entitled to full replacement values under these circumstances.

We ask that you reevaluate our situation and send us another check for $2364 to bring the total settlement to the appropriate replacement amount of $9456.

Sincerely,

• CANCELING POLICY •

RE: Homeowner's Policy 778890
    Auto Policy 5588839
    Term Life Insurance Policy 488779

Dear Mr. Quinn:

I would like to cancel all three of the above policies, effective May 31. Please return any portion of the premium payments due me under the six-month payment plan for each.

Since applying for the life policy, I have discovered another policy that will meet my needs for coverage at better rates, and I plan to convert to whole life insurance with that new company.

Additionally, I have been disappointed with the way my homeowner's account has been serviced for the past 18 months. When I recently reported a claim for carpet damage due to a broken plumbing line, I had great difficulty in getting a quick estimate for repairs and replacement carpet installed through your designated vendor (M. C. McElrath Flooring).

And because of dissatisfaction with these two policies, I've simply decided to move all three of my insurance accounts to another company.

Thank you for your prompt processing of this cancellation notice and premium refund.

Sincerely,

• APPEALING POLICY TERMINATION TO COMPANY PRESIDENT •

RE: Homeowner's Policy 998822

Dear Mr. Walker:

I have been a policyholder with your company for the past eight years and to date I've paid premiums totaling $9350. Yet, unexpectedly, I've received a notice from your company stating that you plan to cancel my homeowner's coverage, effective February 1. Certainly, there has been some mistake.

Would you please investigate the matter and let me know why this action is planned?

During the past eight years, I've filed one claim for $4200 for roof damage after a hailstorm on May 18 of this year. Your claims adjuster investigated the roof damage, and I selected your recommended roofer for the repairs. There are no other extenuating circumstances of which I'm aware.

If after reviewing the situation, you decide not to reverse the decision and reinstate my coverage, I plan to cancel my other policies with your organization:

Policy 009898   Auto insurance, in effect for ten years
Policy 899998   Auto insurance, in effect for six years
Policy 777888   Auto insurance (son, Don Lee), in effect for two years

Additionally, I plan to contact the State Department of Insurance and ask for a review of this decision, fearing that other homeowners who were victims of hail damage in the same storm have received or will receive similar cancellation notices.

(Continued)

I'll look forward to your explanation about the homeowner's cancellation notice and hope that you can reverse that decision so that I can continue my coverage with your organization.

Sincerely,

• APPEALING POLICY TERMINATION TO REGULATORY AGENCY •

RE: Policy T388872
Wobbly Insurance Company
4889 Wimbledon Drive
Albany, NY 12207

Dear Mr. Mitchum:

On October 15, my Jeep Cherokee was stolen from the airport parking lot. I filed a claim with the Wobbly Insurance Company according to the standard procedure. The settlement has been unacceptable, and I'm appealing to you to arbitrate the decision and review Wobbly's license to sell insurance in our state.

The company sent me a settlement check for $9400, nearly $2000 below the blue-book value of Jeeps of the same year and comparable mileage and condition as mine. I wrote the company to protest its arbitrary decision, enclosing a copy of the blue-book page and a copy of an appraisal from a local dealership. Wobbly refused to increase the amount offered in its settlement.

Therefore, I'm appealing to you for your arbitration and will abide by your decision in this case. Additionally, I suggest that you review the company's standard procedures for paying other auto claims; in my dealing with Wobbly representatives, their cavalier attitude seems to indicate that such treatment is rather commonplace. I strongly urge you to revoke the company's license for selling insurance in New York.

Sincerely,

• INQUIRING ABOUT PET INSURANCE •

RE: Policy 4444-4444

Dear Insurance Agent,

We were recently hit with a huge vet bill when our golden retriever, Jake, got into a nasty tangle with a raccoon. I'd like to avoid similar surprises in the future. Do you offer pet insurance? If so, please review the available policies and make a recommendation. If not, I'd be grateful if you could refer me to an agency that handles such policies.

Sincerely,

• NOTIFICATION OF SURGERY •

RE: Policy 3333-3333

Dear Insurance Agent,

On April 1, I'll be undergoing surgery for a kidney transplant at Baptist Memorial Hospital. Please let me know what steps I should take in order to ensure that everything goes smoothly with the insurance paperwork. Thanks for your prompt attention to this matter.

Sincerely,

DECLINING INVITATIONS OR REQUESTS

Most people hate to say no—but not nearly as much as other people hate to hear it. Your challenge in declining invitations and solicitations, therefore, is to extricate yourself from the situation or obligation while maintaining the relationship or good standing.

To do so, state your empathetic understanding of the need, request, or situation. Often people assume that your "no" means that you do not thoroughly understand the real situation or need. You have to take care to demonstrate to readers that you do have an appreciation of the situation and their need for your services or money.

As a first step then, agree, if you can do so honestly, that the need is real or the cause is worthwhile.

"I understand that this need is real."

"I identify with your goals."

"I concur with the action you plan to take."

"The cause is certainly deserving of support and attention."

Add your reason for a negative response, if you wish. Giving a reason makes your decision sound less arbitrary and more thoughtful.

"I've simply overcommitted myself at this point."

"My schedule has just become too unpredictable."

"I've made previous commitments for the funds this year."

"I simply couldn't feel comfortable making that commitment, because other commitments for my time would have to go lacking."

237

Be firm about your decision not to contribute, participate, or attend. On occasion, you may find it easier to phrase a negative message positively by focusing on what you *do* intend to do with your time, money, or possessions rather than on what you can't do. Example:

"This year I plan to spend my time exclusively in helping the X Committee to..."

And by all means, end with a goodwill statement about the positive outcome for the event, occasion, situation, or cause.

"I wish you every success with the project."

"Thank you for thinking of me."

"I appreciate your letting me know of the efforts and goals of your group."

"I know you'll be outrageously successful with such an event."

"The party sounds like a wonderful idea. I'm sorry I'll have to miss it."

Saying "no" does not have to mean the end of the relationship.

• ATTEND EVENT •

Dear Mabel,

I appreciate your invitation to join your group for lunch at the Kenmore Foundation and a tour of the new facilities. It must be very satisfying to see all your months of construction finally come to a successful completion.

I'll not be able to attend the lunch, but want to thank you for thinking of me. I wish the foundation much success in all its philanthropic efforts on behalf of our community.

Sincerely,

• ATTEND EVENT—PRIOR COMMITMENT •

Example 1

Dear Stan:

Thank you for the invitation to join the group of friends at your table at the annual Professionals' Prayer Breakfast at the Hyatt on March 28. The speaker lineup sounds impressive. Unfortunately, I'll be in Atlanta that week attending to a key customer account. Otherwise, I'd love the opportunity to meet your colleagues at the table and hear an inspiring message.

Thanks so much for thinking of me. I'll take a rain check for next year.

Regards,

• ATTEND EVENT—PRIOR COMMITMENT •

Example 2

Dear Tamika,

Unexpectedly, my company is sending me to Los Angeles the week of March 9 and requiring me to stay over the weekend for a training session. I'm so disappointed that I'm going to have to miss Charlie's wedding. I had already returned my reply card to the bride's family, saying that all four of us would attend. Would you please pass on this development and our regrets?

Give our love and best wishes to Charlie and his bride as they start their lives together.

Cordially,

• HEAD PROJECT COMMITTEE—TIME CONFLICT •

Dear Esther,

Your list of potential members for the Economic Development Committee reads like a "Who's Who" of Tyler. I feel flattered that you have invited me to join that illustrious group.

Flattered and disappointed. Disappointed that I can't commit the kind of time this committee work deserves. The projects you outlined as part of the objectives sound truly worthwhile and certainly should attract new corporations to the neighborhood— a prospect that would benefit all of us.

However, this year I've decided to devote all my available time to my continuing work with the symphony. There are still several ongoing projects there that I'd like to complete.

My best wishes as you continue to put together such an all-star lineup.

Regards,

• SPEAKING ENGAGEMENT •

Dear Professor Tovar,

Thanks so much for the invitation to speak to your journalism class on Thursday, May 4. I know the course is a valuable one because we've been fortunate enough to hire some of your former students here at the *Gazette*. They still rave about your class.

I'm sorry I won't be able to come, though, because I'll be out of town that day. Could I get a raincheck?

Sincerely,

• CHAPERONE FIELD TRIP •

Deanna,

I'm glad you asked me to be a chaperone for the fifth-grade field trip to Washington, D.C. I know how important this trip is to the kids—and how important it is to have enough parents to make sure things go smoothly.

Unfortunately, I'll have to pass. As you know, I've been very involved in the production of the spring theater performance, and with opening night fast approaching, I wouldn't feel right leaving for five days.

I'm sure you'll find another willing chaperone among our school's many wonderful, involved parents, and I'm sure you and the kids will have a great time in D.C.

All the best,

• ORGANIZATION POSITION •

Dear Mr. Denning,

It brings me great satisfaction to serve as a board member of the Clarksburg Music Center, and I'm honored that the governance committee has seen fit to nominate me for vice president.

However, because my work schedule has become so unpredictable, I must decline the nomination. I simply don't feel I can give the time and energy that the Music Center deserves from its vice president.

For the time being, then, I look forward to carrying on as a regular board member. Please pass along my regrets to the rest of the governance committee.

Sincerely,

• BE A GODPARENT •

Susie,

I'm so touched you've asked me to be Michael's godfather. My own godfather, William Percy, was an important figure in my life, always quick to offer support and guidance (spiritual and otherwise). One thing I loved about him is that he was always there for me, and because of my experience with Godfather Bill, I feel it's important that a godparent be a steady presence in a child's life.

Unfortunately, in my line of work, transfers and relocations are the norm. As you might already know, I've lived in three states in the past eight years. I would hate to see Michael end up with an absentee godfather. I'm truly sorry to disappoint you. But it's even more important that my absence doesn't disappoint Michael as he grows into the fine young man I'm sure he'll be. All my best wishes for both of you.

Cordially,

• PET SITTING •

Mike,

Sounds like you and Michelle have a great trip lined up. I could use a couple of weeks on the beach myself. With the way things are going at work, though, I won't be taking a vacation anytime soon. In fact, most nights I'll probably be working past eight. That's why I can't look after Patches while you're gone. I won't be home in time to let him out, much less take him for a good, long walk in the park. I'd be happy to check in on him from time to time, but—as much as I love your pooch—I better leave the day-to-day responsibilities to someone else.

Yours,

• HOST PARTY—EXPENSE •

Dear Latoya:

The dinner party to honor Luke and Ursula as they move away sounds like a nice idea. I'm sure everyone will want a last opportunity to wish them well on their new venture in Oregon.

Thank you for asking me to join you as host, but I'm afraid I'm going to have to say no because of the expense involved in such an elaborate setting. Melvin and I plan to spend some time with Luke and Ursula individually before they go.

I do know you'll understand, and I hope the event turns out to be a huge success. Luke and Ursula will appreciate your efforts so much.

Cordially,

• NEIGHBORHOOD FUNCTION •

Jill,

I think a neighborhood progressive dinner is a great way to kick off the holidays, and I'm glad you thought of me to host one of the courses. I'm guessing attendance will be strong, though, and with one of the smaller houses on the block, I doubt I'd have room for everybody. Is there some other way I might contribute?

Thanks for all the work you've put into organizing this event. It's neighbors like you who make Collinswood such a wonderful place to live.

Sincerely,

• SELL PERSONAL ITEM •

Jake,

I just got your message about the Mustang, and I'm sorry to say it's not for sale. My father and I spent three years restoring that car—the engine, the body, you name it. I doubt I'll ever be able to part with it at any price. Even so, I appreciate your more than generous offer, and I'd be happy to put you in touch with some other muscle-car enthusiasts who might have a Mustang for sale. Meanwhile, what do you say we take a spin this weekend?

Yours,

• LOAN OF PERSONAL ITEM — PERSONAL POLICY •

Dear Hester,

When I returned to town yesterday, I received your message about borrowing some of my crystal bowls and silver serving pieces for the upcoming graduation party.

On occasion, I have let a family member or friend borrow these serving pieces. But the last time a tray was returned chipped, I promised myself I'd not lend them again. Because each piece is a memento from a special trip, I have an emotional attachment to all of them. They really are irreplaceable.

I do hope you understand, and I don't want this to ruin our friendship.

Sincerely,

• JOIN LEGAL DISPUTE •

Dear Brad,

I can certainly appreciate the troubles you've been having with Mr. MacGregor. On several occasions my family has been disturbed by late-night parties in his building, and the tenants loitering out front are a detriment to the neighborhood.

That said, I'll have to decline your request to join the suit against him regarding use of the alley. I agree there is a problem, but I'd much prefer to work it out as neighbors, without involving the courts.

Perhaps we should start by having a survey done to establish the property lines. I'd be happy to chip in for such a survey if Mr. MacGregor and the other involved property owners are willing to share the cost.

Sincerely,

• PARTICIPATE IN FUND-RAISER—DISAGREE WITH ORGANIZATION •

Dear Mr. Garrett:

I received your personal letter asking for financial contributions to keep the doors of Star Mission open for this coming year. Generally, I look forward to such charitable opportunities, but I must decline on this one.

Frankly, some of the comments from my acquaintances have raised serious doubts about flagrant misuse of funds at the mission. I don't mean illegal use, but simply a misrepresentation about how the money has been used in the past. Also, I have difficulty understanding the mission's philosophy about not imposing a limit on the time that the homeless can stay in the center without seeking training or employment.

For these reasons, I'm reluctant to commit funds. I do wish you success in collecting contributions from those who've had a more positive experience with that organization.

Sincerely,

• BIBLE STUDY GROUP •

Dear Mrs. Murphy,

Thanks for your recent invitation to join the Bible study group at First Fellowship. Since I moved to town, you and other members of the congregation have made me feel so welcome. But until I decide where I'll be buying a house and living permanently, I'm reluctant to get too involved in church or civic activities. I look forward to seeing you at Sunday's worship service.

Sincerely,

• SUPPORT POLITICAL CANDIDATE OR ISSUE •

Dear Nikki,

Thank you for making me aware of your support for Brandy Stallone in her bid for the newly vacated city council seat.

I've been keenly interested in several of the candidates because of the ongoing problems in the district and have analyzed their positions on several key issues important to the community. Unfortunately, we have differing views on several points. Therefore, I'm going to have to say no to the request that I work in the election campaign and hope that you'll understand my position.

By the way, Ms. Stallone certainly has a cast of admirable backers with the experience you bring to the table on her behalf!

Sincerely,

FRIENDS AND RELATIVES

Some "touchy" situations become even more sensitive when friends or relatives are involved. Those awkward situations include having to remind friends that they promised to write a letter of reference on your behalf, pay for their share of a family gift, or reimburse you for damage done to your belongings. While you want to keep the relationship intact, you still need to remind and motivate people to take some promised or appropriate action. Tone becomes paramount.

State the gist of your message in the opening paragraph: Why are you writing? Don't let this letter ramble into unrelated issues, leaving the relative or friend actually wondering about your overall intention for the letter.

In a negative situation, offer encouragement rather than blame. Don't make the other person feel guilty that things aren't as you hope, expect, or wish. Instead, stick with the situation "as is" and ask for what you need or state your decision about what you can or cannot do to accommodate the other's needs.

When offering encouragement or praise, remember that specific statements sound more genuine than global sentiments. Instead of "I miss you," try "I miss hearing your laugh when we watch TV."

Finally, express your commitment, love, or appreciation despite any problems or negatives in the current situation. A "no" message or a "please do it" message does not have to mean the end of a relationship.

FRIENDLY REMINDERS

• OPEN INVITATION •

Todd,

Last month, you mentioned you might be coming up for a convention this summer. I just wanted to remind you that you're welcome to stay with us—then or any other time you find yourself in Portland. We've got plenty of room now that the third floor is finished, and Mary and the kids would love to see you. Don't be a stranger!

Yours,

• FAMILY REUNION (INVITATION ALREADY SENT) •

Josephine,

As you (hopefully) already know from the invitation, our annual family reunion is going to be held out at the farm again this year, Saturday, September 5, starting at ten in the morning and going until who knows when.

I sent the invitation last month, and when I didn't hear from you, I began to worry that it got lost in the mail—so this reminder. (I know, of course, that you try to make it to all of these get-togethers.) Everybody is looking forward to seeing you, especially me.

Love,

• RELATIVE'S BIRTHDAY •

Dear Son,

Just a little reminder that your grandmother's birthday is coming up. When I talked to her last week, she was so excited about seeing you. At the same time, she knows how hectic your schedule has become and doesn't want to be, as she put it, "a burden."

Will you still come visit your dear old grandma on May 4 and let her know she's no burden? I'll be at the nursing home most of the day and can help you with the wheelchair if you decide to take her out to lunch. If you're pressed for time, you might also consider eating at the home. The dining room is open from 11:30 A.M. to 1 P.M., and the food's not as bad as you might expect.

And don't worry about shopping for a gift. I have it on good authority that there's nothing she'd like more than a nice picture of you and the girls.

Love,

• To Contact Mutual Friend •

June,

Just got a piece of news yesterday—Terri will be going to New England for the summer to stay with her parents for a long visit. As we agreed, she really needs to hear from you so we can mend fences over the political divisions that developed this winter.

I thought I'd let you know of her plans so you can make contact before she leaves; time only seems to aggravate rather than improve these situations. We've all three had such a positive relationship in the past that I know you're looking forward to getting this present difficulty behind us.

In case you've misplaced it, her address is 232 Lemmons Avenue and her phone number is 333-4242. Thanks for agreeing to get in touch with her.

All best,

• TO FULFILL PROMISE •

Example 1

Thelma,

My niece, Karina Zolot, and I were having lunch last week and she again mentioned how much she was looking forward to meeting your colleagues at Harris Foundation. Her heart is set on finding a job with a nonprofit organization. And, of course, Harris is the ideal match because of her college major in psychology.

I'm hoping that you're not having difficulty in making suitable arrangements for an informal get-together. If so, may I help in some way? I'd be pleased to schedule a conference room here if you think your colleagues wouldn't mind walking across the street for cocktails and hors d'oeuvres after work some afternoon.

Thanks for your offer to introduce Karina to your colleagues at the foundation. With the respect this group has for you, you will be doing her a very big favor. We'll both be very appreciative.

Regards,

• TO FULFILL PROMISE •

Example 2

Dear Jermaine,

It was so kind of you to offer to mow our lawn until Charlie's leg heals. He's such a perfectionist about the yard, but he has seen how nice yours looks, and he knows his grass is in good hands.

Let me know when you think you'll come, and I'll make sure the garage is unlocked. There are lawn bags, gas, and oil on the shelf above the mower. And if you get thirsty, or hungry, please help yourself—the refrigerator beside the work bench is stocked.

Sincerely,

• TRAVEL PLANS •

Todd,

It was great talking to you last month. I just wanted to let you know I'm still coming to Raleigh. I'll be arriving on Tuesday, late afternoon, and departing Sunday morning. The conference runs from Tuesday through Friday, but I'm free after that and would love to get together. Saturday brunch, perhaps? You can reach me on my cell or leave a message at the hotel. I'll be staying at the Ambassador Hotel (555-5555) downtown.

Best,

• TO PAY FOR DAMAGE •

Dear Patsy,

I finally have been able to get the last estimate on re-covering the chair. The bid from Hilton's Upholstery was $545; Graham's Designs quoted $350; and Motley's Designs gave me a figure of $650. (The bids are enclosed.) As you can see, there's quite a difference in price. That difference is probably due to their varying charges for labor and delivery, the fabric price being the same in all cases from the manufacturer.

I was pleased to learn that the manufacturer still had the same fabric in stock, because the chair was purchased so recently. That was the only stroke of luck in this whole unfortunate incident.

I've seen the quality of Graham's work and am, frankly, quite afraid of the final product. I'd feel much more comfortable having Hilton's Upholstery do the work, but I'll do whatever you think is fair. Just make your check payable to me, and I'll pay the company upon completion of the work.

I know you regret as much as I do Kimberly's accident while here, and I appreciate your offer to take care of the damage.

Sincerely,

• TO PAY FOR SHARE OF GIFT •

Michael,

Brenda and Ted seemed thrilled with the pottery that our group sent for their Open House. I think they were totally shocked—and so pleased that we thought of them on that occasion, especially since they had dropped their membership a few months ago.

The total tally came to $457, including the shipping charges. That amounts to $50 per couple. You could give me the cash at our next event, but since that won't be until August, I'd really prefer a check (if you don't mind) so we can get this all taken care of. I'd like to report back to the members that all's over and done with it on this end. Just make it payable to either me or Johnny Tuttle.

Thanks for chipping in for the pottery. I really appreciate being able to count on a group as solid as ours.

Regards,

• TO RETURN BORROWED ITEM •

Dear Agnes,

Carrie has finally landed a part in the upcoming school theater production, and we're going to be the proud parents mingling with the cast, taking all the irritating photos during the curtain bows and following festivities.

Have you had a chance to pack up all my camera gear yet? I'd appreciate it if you could give me a call and let me know when you can drop it by before "the big week" of April 6.

I hope it served you well on your vacation; we've always liked the way our photos have turned out. But then, of course, it's hard to have operator trouble when all you have to do is push a button.

If this weekend will be convenient for you, we plan to be home.

Regards,

• TO PAY CLUB DUES •

Dear Tiffany:

Oops—did you forget? We sent out an earlier notice about annual dues ($45) for our writers' group and had hoped to have all the funds collected by February 1. Our records show that we still have not received your check. Did we miss it somehow?

If so, please let us know the check number and date. If you discover that you have not yet sent your check, please mail it to me directly at 4589 Hanover, Arlington, TX 76015.

As you probably know, we try to keep our dues collection informal and quick because all of us are so busy trying to get that next chapter written. Looking forward to seeing you at the next meeting. We have some great programs lined up for this coming year.

Sincerely,

• APPROACHING DEADLINE •

Dear Rick,

So far 18 Delta Sigma alums have signed up for the canoe trip on July 26, and I'm really hoping you'll make it 19. The registration deadline is July 20, and the fee is $30 per person.

You seemed pretty enthusiastic about the trip last time we talked, so I just wanted to make sure it hadn't slipped your mind. If you're coming, the check should be made out to White Water Adventures, and you can drop it off at my office any time before Wednesday.

Here's hoping you can make it—and that you bring your harmonica along.

Regards,

PERSONAL LOANS

• REQUESTING LOAN FROM FRIEND OR RELATIVE •
Example 1

Dear Uncle Floyd,

I'm writing under difficult circumstances. I've had a recent car accident and the insurance company totaled my car. Thank goodness, no one was hurt. But my primary concern now is finding transportation to and from work. I've located a used car for $2000 from a colleague at work, but I haven't yet worked long enough to be able to save that kind of money.

Would you consider lending me the $2000 to buy the car? I can repay the loan at $150 a month until it is paid in full. I'd be more than willing to pay interest on the loan also.

As you may be aware, there's no metro bus or subway service in this part of the country, and I'm in danger of losing my job if I can't find dependable transportation. I've tried to get a loan at my local bank, but all my credit reports still show the evidences of my college escapades 4 years ago. Although I learned my lesson about handling easy credit long ago, the bank has nothing but my word to prove it. If you will consider the loan, please let me know and I'll telephone my colleague before she sells the car to someone else. If not, I'll understand.

Sincerely,

P.S. I'm writing rather than phoning to give you ample time to consider my request before giving me an answer.

• REQUESTING LOAN FROM FRIEND OR RELATIVE •

Example 2

Jeff,

You've always said I could come to you if I needed cash, and I've always said I wouldn't do that. But now I'm asking.

Megan and I have spent the last six months looking for a house. We finally found the perfect place, but we're $5000 short on the down payment. We could put down less than 20 percent, but then we'd have to pay private mortgage insurance, which would make the monthly payments unmanageable.

Would you consider lending us the money? I'd pay you back (with interest) before the end of the year, and, if you like, we could work out a monthly repayment schedule.

If you can help, we'd need a cashier's check by Wednesday. If not, I understand completely and appreciate all the generosity you've shown us over the years.

Your friend,

• PROMISING REPAYMENT TO FRIEND OR RELATIVE •

Dear Liz,

Whatever you do, don't assume that I've forgotten about the $300 I borrowed from you for car repairs.

I am sorry that I haven't yet repaid you, but I *will* do so. By the end of the month, you should have received at least half the money. And within a few weeks after that, you'll have the other half too.

Meanwhile, rest assured that I am watching every penny until my debt is settled. Thanks for your patience with me.

Sincerely,

• FORGIVING LOAN •

Shack,

Last year, you borrowed $500 and promised to pay me back by Christmas. I haven't heard from you since, and I assume it's because you're having trouble coming up with the money.

I know you would have paid me back if you could. I also know you and Theresa are going through some tough times. That's why I want you to forget about repaying the loan. Consider it an early Christmas present, and know that there are no hard feelings on my end. I'm glad I was able to help and only wish I were in a position to do more.

Sincerely,

• GRANTING LOAN TO FRIEND OR RELATIVE •

Dear Marty,

As we discussed on the phone last night, I'm enclosing a check for $2000 for your car purchase. Also, I've computed the interest rate we discussed and have drafted a note to confirm your repayment arrangements on the last day of each month. Please keep a copy for yourself and sign and return a copy.

Through the years, I've found that having a written confirmation of what everyone has agreed to makes things clear for all concerned. All my best with the car. Keep in touch.

Your Uncle Floyd

• REQUESTING REPAYMENT •

Rich,

Have you "settled into" your new job by now, and do you still feel as enthusiastic about it as you did at the beginning? Of course, any job has its drudgery tasks, but all in all, from what you told us, it sounds like a good match for you.

We're writing to ask when we can expect repayment of the $1500 loan for your car. We were glad to help you with the purchase of your Toyota so that you'd have transportation back and forth to your new job. You agreed to pay all, or at least half, of the loan by June. If you have decided that you cannot repay the total $1500 at once, we understand. But we do need to receive at least half that amount within the next two or three weeks.

We hope the car you selected has not disappointed you. We, too, thought it was a good buy. Please let us know how things are going.

Sincerely,

• DECLINING REQUEST FOR LOAN FROM FRIEND OR RELATIVE •

Example 1

Dear Candace,

I appreciate your sharing your current financial difficulties with me. I understand how disappointed you must feel about the unexpected expenses in your first few months in operation.

Now that I've had time to think over the situation, I've decided that I must say no on the loan. Personal loans have always been "off limits" with me, because so many good relationships have been broken over this issue.

Starting your own business is always risky, I guess. I've never had the courage to venture out on my own as you have. I hope you will accept my answer as nothing personal—just a reflection of my own philosophy about friendship and finances.

Sincerely,

• DECLINING REQUEST FOR LOAN FROM FRIEND OR RELATIVE •

Example 2

Shack,

I'm glad we're close enough that you felt comfortable asking me for a loan. And believe me—I wish I could help. I know what a tough time you and Theresa are having right now.

Megan and I are working hard to save up for a down payment, though, and we simply don't have any cash to spare. If there's anything we can do for you short of a loan, please call on us for that help.

Regards,

GOVERNMENT PROGRAMS

From time to time, you will have to contact government agencies about Medicare, social security, or veterans' issues for yourself or on behalf of your loved ones. And dealing with government agencies can be exasperating because of the sheer volume of letters these agencies receive. That is, their volume of correspondence means that you will likely receive a form response—and often an inaccurate or inappropriate one—unless you take special care to provide all necessary information and ask questions specifically about your situation.

To lessen the likelihood of incomplete information or repeat requests, use a reference line to identify yourself before you begin the body of your letter: social security number, case number, account number, member number, or any other identifying information for quick reference to a previous file and related data. Such a reference will help supply the government employee with all the available information in interpreting regulations pertinent to your situation.

Try to summarize your message or request in a sentence or two at the beginning of your letter:

"I'm writing to ask for the status on…"

"I need information about…"

"Would you please provide information about X and any necessary forms and guidelines to take this action?"

Provide supporting detail of your position or request. Answer the questions: who, what, when, where, why, how, how much. Let your reader know that you will not settle for a general response in a form letter. Make it clear that you expect a direct answer/interpretation/

decision for your specific situation rather than a general citing of a written policy or law. For example:

"Would you please answer these two specific questions as they apply to my situation? First…"

"Am I or am I not eligible for these benefits?"

"The earlier form letter I received did not provide a full explanation of how this policy applies to my situation. Specifically, I need to know…"

Finally, include written documentation of past action, claims, notifications, or requests.

Persistence pays.

MEDICARE

• REQUESTING INFORMATION ABOUT AVAILABLE HEALTH AND HUMAN SERVICES •

To U.S. Department of Health and Human Services:

Would you please send information about government services or resources available to me because of (*physical condition, death of family member, immigration, and so forth*)?

Also, I'd like to have the name, address, and phone number of any regional offices nearby that I may decide to visit or contact about this issue.

Sincerely,

• REQUESTING STATEMENT OF EARNINGS •

U.S. Department of Health and Human Services

Dear Sir or Madam:

I will be 65 on my next birthday, and need to have information about my eligibility for social security and Medicare benefits, along with the procedure and forms to apply for these benefits.

To verify my eligibility and compute my likely earnings, I'd like to receive a copy of earnings that have been attributed to me during my employment years.

The pertinent identification details follow:

    Full current legal name: Pearl Atkins Greenwood
    Maiden name: Pearl Atkins Baylor
    Former married name: Pearl Atkins Baylor Cotto
    Social security number: 123-45-6789

Thank you for your prompt response in sending the appropriate forms and procedures to begin these benefits.

Sincerely,

• REQUESTING LIST OF PHYSICIANS •

Dear Medicare Representative:

As a recently retired widower, I am now enrolled in Medicare. Would you please send me a list of physicians and facilities in my local area that accept Medicare assignment for the health services they provide?

Sincerely,

• REPORTING INCORRECT BILLING •

RE: Invoice Number 234890

Dear Dr. Montefusco:

Your office sent me an incorrect statement for my recent treatment of gastrointestinal tests done the week of May 5. Would you please send a corrected statement for the service?

Your office submitted the claim directly to Medicare for me, and Medicare has paid its limits on these services. Your bill still shows an outstanding balance of $92 due from the patient. It was my understanding that you accepted the Medicare limits as total payment for these services, rather than charging your typical fee for these tests. I appreciate the seniors' discount for this service, and evidently this recent billing to me for the "difference" between the insurance payment and the full fee is an inadvertent error on the part of your staff.

Thank you for your competent medical services. I'll appreciate a correct invoice showing no balance due.

Sincerely,

• DISPUTING DENIAL OF BENEFITS •

RE: Case Number 78333

Dear Mr. Sakata:

I'm asking for a reversal of your earlier decision to deny benefits to my mother, Pauline Righetti, for hospitalization for her gastrointestinal testing procedures.

We understand that this normally is an outpatient procedure. However, because of my mother's medical history of internal bleeding and complications with heart ailments, she clearly needs to be hospitalized for this testing. Enclosed is a copy of her medical history, including ailments and treatment dates, along with a letter from her attending physician about the advisability of hospitalization for this current testing.

Please reassess this situation and respond to me about allowing coverage for the hospitalization that her current condition warrants during this testing procedure. We would appreciate your immediate response, because my mother's condition grows worse by the day.

Sincerely,

SOCIAL SECURITY

• APPLYING FOR SOCIAL SECURITY CARD •

Social Security Administration

Dear Sir or Madam:

I want to apply for a social security card for my minor child. Please send the necessary information and forms to me at the above address.

Sincerely,

• APPLYING FOR BENEFITS •

Social Security Administration

RE: Social Security Number 333-33-3333

Dear Sir or Madam:

My husband, Philip T. Lynn, is terminally ill, and I am writing to determine what benefits my two minor children and I will be eligible for under social security at his death. My husband's social security number is listed above.

Sincerely,

• CHANGING NAME AFTER MARRIAGE •

Social Security Administration

RE: Social Security Number 456-98-9889
     Darlene Sue Henderson (maiden) Cowley

Dear Sir or Madam:

I recently married and need to have my social security records changed to my married name: Darlene Sue Cowley. Enclosed is a copy of my marriage certificate. Please send me the appropriate forms to complete this change and let me know of any other supporting documentation required.

Sincerely,

• CHANGING NAME AFTER DIVORCE •

Social Security Administration

RE: Social Security Number 444-44-4444
    Libby Connor Fisher

Dear Sir or Madam:

I have recently divorced and need to have my name changed on your social security records. Would you please send me a replacement card also? (A copy of the old card and the divorce decree is enclosed.) Please issue the new card in the name of Libby Fisher at the above address.

Sincerely,

• REQUESTING DIRECT DEPOSIT OF CHECKS •

Social Security Administration

RE: Social Security Number 777-77-7777

Dear Social Security Administration Representative:

My social security checks are now coming to my home at 457 Lassiter Road, Colleyville, TX 76034, and I would like to change this arrangement and have them deposited directly into my bank account:

Account Number 490093331
Routing Number 00046010
BankNow
38894 Arbor Road
Arlington, TX 76031

Please either make this change immediately or send me the appropriate forms to do so.

Sincerely,

• CANCELING DIRECT DEPOSIT OF CHECKS •

Social Security Administration

RE: Social Security Number 777-77-7777

Dear Representative:

My social security checks are currently deposited directly into my bank account: Account Number 490093331, BankNow, 38894 Arbor Road, Arlington, TX 76031.

I'd like to change that arrangement and have the checks come directly to my new home at 457 Lassiter Road, Colleyville, TX 76034, effective with the *June check*.

Please either make this change immediately or send me the appropriate forms to do so.

Sincerely,

• REPORTING CHANGE OF ADDRESS •

Social Security Administration

RE: Social Security Number 777-77-7777

Dear Social Security Administration Representative:

I need to change the mailing address for my social security checks, effective immediately.

Current Address: 457 Lassiter Road
                 Colleyville, TX 76034

New Address: 9355 Trail Lakes
                 Fort Worth, TX 76180

Please either make this change immediately or send me the appropriate forms to do so.

Sincerely,

• NOTIFYING ADMINISTRATION OF DEATH OF SPOUSE •

Social Security Administration

RE: Social Security Numbers
    Crystal Hudler: 555-55-5555
    Scott Hudler: 666-66-6666

Dear Sir or Madam:

My wife, Crystal Hudler, died on October 5. Her monthly social security benefit was $689 at the time of her death. I am writing to determine my eligibility for survivor's benefits. Her death certificate is enclosed.

Please send me the necessary forms and information for applying for these benefits. My address remains the same as on the letterhead above.

Sincerely,

• REPORTING LOST OR STOLEN SOCIAL SECURITY CARD •

Social Security Administration

RE: Social Security Number 888-88-8888

Dear Sir or Madam:

My social security card has been lost. Would you please send me the appropriate forms and guidelines to receive a replacement card? My current address is 3888 Billings Street, Tallahassee, FL 32399.

Sincerely,

• REQUESTING STATEMENT OF EARNINGS OR BENEFITS •

To Social Security Administration:

Please send the form *Request for Earnings and Benefit Estimate Statement* to me at the above address.

Sincerely,

• DISPUTING AMOUNT OF ENTITLEMENT •

Social Security Administration

RE: Social Security Number 222-22-2222

Dear Representative:

There seems to be some mistake in your computation of my social security benefits. I received my first check (a copy enclosed) for $758, almost $120 less than the amount that your earlier letter (copy enclosed) reported that I would receive.

Please review your records, clarify the correct amount, and send me a copy of your computations and figures used in the formula.

Sincerely,

• DISPUTING DENIAL OF BENEFITS •

Social Security Administration

RE: Social Security Number 123-45-6789

Dear Sir or Madam:

I recently received notice that my social security benefits have been terminated because my wages from part-time employment exceed the specified limits.

Before I accepted the new job, I inquired with your office and was assured that my $6-per-hour job (total monthly income $180) was well under the limits. Obviously, someone gave me incorrect information or your recent termination action was inappropriate.

Please review the situation, and forward the outstanding checks immediately. Copies of your termination notice and my last check stubs are enclosed.

Sincerely,

VETERANS' AFFAIRS

• REQUESTING MILITARY RECORDS •

Personnel Records Center

RE: Service Number/Social Security Number 123-45-6789

Dear Military Official:

I have been unable to locate the original copy of my discharge papers from the Navy. Would you please send a duplicate copy to the above address?

My full name is Marla Curtis Ray. I served in the National Guard from May 2000 to March 2004.

Thank you for an immediate response. This verification is necessary for a scholarship application for the upcoming fall semester.

Sincerely,

• REQUESTING CIVIL SERVICE PREFERENCE CERTIFICATE •

RE: Service Number 123-45-6789

Ladies or Gentlemen:

I understand that I may be entitled to special employment considerations because I am a veteran of the Desert Storm era and recently completed my active duty assignment (service dates: April 1989 to April 2005).

Would you please provide a Civil Service Preference Certificate to be included with my job application at the oil company with which I'm seeking employment?

If there are any forms I must complete, please send them, along with any published information or testing requirements that may help me should I decide to seek civil service employment opportunities.

Sincerely,

• REQUESTING VA-GUARANTEED LOAN •

RE: Service Number 09983
   Social Security Number 389-55-9999

Dear Representative:

I plan to purchase a new home in the next few months and would like verification of my eligibility for a VA-guaranteed loan and general information about the loan (guidelines, restrictions, current mortgage rates, and so forth).

I served in the Army from March 1982 to April 1984. I received an honorable discharge and left the Army with the rank of captain.

Please forward information and forms to the above address. I'll appreciate a quick response, because a house-purchase decision is pending.

Sincerely,

• REQUESTING EXCHANGE AND COMMISSARY PRIVILEGES •

RE: Spouse's Service Number 333-55-5555

Dear Administrator:

I understand that as a widow of a veteran who suffered a disability in connection to his service in the U.S. Army during the Bosnia operations I may be entitled to privileges through the local exchange and commissary.

Would you please send me the appropriate form to apply for these privileges and receive an identification card? Thank you.

Sincerely,

• REQUESTING REIMBURSEMENT FOR BURIAL MONUMENT •

Dear Administrator:

My husband, Henry R. Winfield, died on April 29 and was buried at Heartland Memorial Gardens here in Omaha, Nebraska. We purchased a gravesite marker for $855. I understand that the family is entitled to reimbursement for an "average" cost for a government marker.

Would you please either process this reimbursement or send the necessary forms to complete so that we may receive this reimbursement?

The pertinent details regarding my husband's service follow:

Branch: Marines
Dates of Service: October 1, 1984, to December 1, 1988
Discharge: Honorable

I've enclosed a copy of his death certificate and a copy of the receipt for our purchase of the gravestone from C. C. Rosenburg Funeral Home.

Sincerely,

• CLAIMING INSURANCE BENEFITS •

RE: Service Number/Social Security Number 666-45-4444
   Life Insurance Policy 44494949494

To Whom It May Concern:

My husband, Lee K. Randolph, passed away on March 15 of this year. Would you please let me know what benefits or disbursements I'm entitled to as surviving spouse and beneficiary to his life insurance policy:

Date of Birth: 2/12/46

Branch of Service: Army

Service Dates: 2/27/64 to 2/26/94

Rank: Lieutenant Colonel

Discharge: Honorable

Enclosed is a certified copy of his death certificate. Thank you for your prompt response about disbursement of the life insurance benefits.

Sincerely,

• DISPUTING DENIAL OF BENEFITS •

RE: Service Number 394-55-8888

Dear Veterans' Office Representative:

I received a letter from your office, saying that my recent claim for additional compensation had been denied. It appears that the letter is a form letter and does not disclose the reason that I was denied the additional bonus pay for having completed the 14-month language training program with a passing grade.

Therefore, I am requesting a review of this claim and a full, specific explanation about the reasons for the denial. If I do not receive a reversal of this decision, I plan to file an appeal within the required time frame to follow up on my rightful claim to this bonus.

All appropriate documentation is enclosed (service letter explaining the language bonus, grades, my original letter to you, your form letter to me).

I expect to hear from you immediately about this review and to receive the full compensation due me under this recruitment arrangement.

Sincerely,

HOME CONCERNS

Unfortunately, you can't leave all your problems at the office. As a homeowner or renter, you will undoubtedly be faced with neighborhood or environmental concerns. You'll be negotiating to buy, sell, lease, or evict. You'll need repairs completed. You'll have to move and handle associated details, from address changes to utility refunds. And as a landlord of rental property, you'll have to handle two sets of books and correspondence on all the above.

Keep in mind these general guidelines: Summarize your message or request in the opening sentence or two. Then provide specific details on effective dates, fees and payments, names, and addresses.

Ask specifically for what you want and add a deadline for response, if appropriate. If you become embroiled in a conflict, show your willingness to compromise, if appropriate, to meet all parties' needs:

> *"I can arrange to alter my school schedule to be there to let the repairperson into the house if you can give me a specific time."*
>
> *"I would be willing to forfeit $100 of my deposit if you could release me from the contract and find a suitable tenant by that date."*
>
> *"I understand your needing to keep the apartments leased and am trying to work out some compromise that will meet my needs as well."*

Remember to enclose copies of related documents to make the reader's verification or action quick and easy.

Neighborhood and environmental issues will be of special concern and deserve special handling. Summarize the issue or the situation. State why it is dangerous to you or the community. Finally, be clear about what action (or inaction) you want the reader to take. Convey the attitude that you assume the reader will make attempts to correct the problem or improve the situation once he or she becomes aware of the hazard.

Generally, you should refrain from making specific threats unless you are prepared to carry them out. In a negative and recurring situation, simply state what other options you will be forced to consider:

"If I don't hear from you, I will be forced to contact the proper authorities."

"Frankly, if I have to contact a lawyer, it may cost me more than the repairs, but I'm determined to do that if that's what it takes to get this matter resolved."

"I'm hoping you can meet your commitment so that we can avoid any legal action in this situation."

"I'm hopeful that you can install the new heater before I have to escalate the problem further."

"I will wait to hear of your decision before I notify the owner about the situation."

"I hope no further action will be necessary."

"Any further correspondence should be directed to my lawyer at…"

Home is where the heart is, so you'll want to make sure you keep the hearth burning brightly by taking care of all the persistent and pesky concerns that plague renters and homeowners.

NEIGHBORHOOD AND ENVIRONMENTAL CONCERNS

• REQUESTING ROAD REPAIR •

Dear Mr. Frisch:

I want to warn you of a problem about which you may be unaware. The potholes in the service road near my office are as dangerous as they are maddening. I cannot tell you how many times I have seen a near-accident on this road as cars and trucks swerve to avoid the holes. In the interest of safety, I beg you to please do what you can to address this potentially disastrous problem.

The stretch of service road to which I refer is on the westbound side of Highway 183 between Shallot Avenue and Geller Lane. I work in the Enterprise Building at 503 Geller Lane, on the northwest corner of Geller and 183.

A number of my coworkers and I have discussed this predicament of the potholes repeatedly. I have also overheard disgruntled grumbles about it in the lobby, on the elevator, and in the café that is located inside the Enterprise Building. We are all anxious to see this problem remedied.

To signify to you the magnitude of our discontent, I have enclosed a petition signed by the staff of the entire Enterprise Building. Mr. Frisch, we would all be deeply grateful if you could give this issue the much-needed attention it deserves.

Respectfully yours,

• REQUESTING TREE REMOVAL •

Dear Asheville Power & Light,

On Monday, April 11, one of your tree-trimming crews was in my neighborhood cutting limbs away from power lines. A worker told me that Asheville Power & Light will remove, on request, any dead or dying tree that interferes with a power line.

I'm writing to request the removal of the hard maple in the northwest corner of my yard at 345 Landhaven Street. A major power line runs right through its branches. I'm attaching a tree inspection report from Arbor Tree Company indicating that the tree is dying.

If I need to complete any additional paperwork, please send it to the address above.

Sincerely,

• COMPLAINT ABOUT GARBAGE COLLECTION •

Dear Head of City Sanitation Department,

For the past two weeks (July 11 and July 18), city sanitation workers have failed to empty trash receptacles in the alley behind our house at 56 McMillan Street. As a result, the alley smells awful and has been attracting raccoons and possums, which have eaten through several bags and strewn garbage across the alley. Please send a crew to collect the garbage and clean up the mess as soon as possible.

Sincerely,

• REQUESTING CARCASS REMOVAL •

Dear Mr. Connor,

For almost a week now, the carcass of a large dog has been lying in the street in front of my house at 29 Park Avenue. Could you send out one of your crews to haul it away?

Normally the city is quick to remove dead animals from the roadway, so I'm guessing this one simply escaped your notice. Thanks for keeping our streets clean, and thanks for your prompt attention in this particular case.

Regards,

• PROTESTING POLLUTION •

Dear Mrs. Fong:

I have just had my tap water tested for various contamination levels and am aghast at the increase in the amount of heavy metals in our local water source. Such contaminants can lead to any one of a number of long-term illnesses, to decreased mental capacity over a long period of time, and even to birth defects. We must do something about the quality of our drinking water.

I implore you, for the sake of our families, our friends, the environment, and the generations yet to be, to tackle this problem now! We need your help, Mrs. Fong. We need action. Cite those responsible for the environmental violations. Provide guidelines for cleanup. Insist that people meet them lest they incur additional fines. Stand up to their economic power.

I have done some research on the origin of the pollution of our water source. Not surprisingly, the decline in our water quality coincides with the inception of the new Ashlake facility in our area in 1989. Here is a company that has received countless citations, including several multimillion-dollar fines for environmental degradation. The EPA and the state of Virginia have both repeatedly demanded that the company clean up its act. Yet it is cheaper for Ashlake to pay the fines as just another business expense. If this reckless treatment of the environment is to be curbed, the fines must be large enough to hurt Ashlake's profit margin.

I have circulated an informative memo on this exigency to residents in the area. I will include it here so that you too may increase your awareness of our dire circumstances. Please take this seriously. If we don't do something immediately, the consequences could be devastating for all of us.

Very respectfully yours,

• PROTESTING WORK OF CITY CONTRACTOR •

Dear Mayor Brown,

I appreciate the city's replacing the sidewalks in the 2100 block of Glendale Street earlier this year. Unfortunately, the city used a poor quality seed mix for portions of the yards that were dug up in order to install the new sidewalks. As a result, all of the lawns in our block now look like overgrown weed patches.

I'm writing to request that the city remedy this situation by either 1. reseeding the area with a higher quality seed mix or by 2. enlisting a professional lawn care company to restore the lawns to their original condition using fertilizer and weed-control agents.

Like most of my neighbors, I've worked hard to establish a good lawn, and I hope the city will ensure that work wasn't wasted. For your reference, I'm enclosing before and after photographs of our yard at 2113 Glendale Street.

Sincerely,

• COMPLAINT ABOUT SNOW REMOVAL •

Dear Mayor Brown,

During last month's snow emergency, I was unable to get my car out of the garage thanks to three-foot snow drifts that accumulated along the curbs in the 1600 block of Wichita Street. I also observed two cars that got stuck in the snow and had to be abandoned in the street overnight.

I understand that the city uses a priority system whereby roads are cleared based on the amount of traffic they serve. Though Wichita Street is by no means a main artery, it sees more traffic than you might expect as a popular shortcut among commuters headed to and from the Interstate 65 interchange at Clarence Boulevard.

In future snow emergencies, I hope you will see fit to have Wichita Street plowed as soon as possible. I'd also like to know whom I should contact if the plows don't arrive and the street becomes impassable. Please have someone at your office contact me at the number below.

Sincerely,

• PROTESTING CITY PLANNING •

Dear Mr. Ferrell:

I find Dallas–Fort Worth's plans to expand the airport for five square miles southward absolutely disturbing. I live in northeast Tarrant County, where already an occasionally low-flying plane rattles my windows as it thunders toward the nearby runway. Should the airport planners have their way at the zoning hearing and be allowed to construct more landing strips five miles even closer to my house, I'm afraid that what remains of our suburban tranquility here will disappear.

Mr. Ferrell, as the chairperson of the Zoning Commission, you should be informed of all pertinent opinions with regard to this issue. Speaking for myself and an entire community's worth of potentially irate families, I strongly encourage you to decline DFW's request for southward expansion.

I live in the 2400 block of Trinity Boulevard in Arlington. It is a relatively peaceful neighborhood, which was a key factor in my husband's and my decision to buy our house back in 1990. At that time, we were told that zoning ordinances prevented the airport from expanding in our direction.

I have enclosed a copy of the zoning ordinance that was designed to preclude any such construction; it is still current. Please don't amend it in order to accommodate DFW's airport. It was this piece of legislation that convinced us to move into the neighborhood six years ago. I don't want it to be the reason we take a loss on our house and leave our neighbors this year.

Sincerely,

• REQUESTING ZONING VARIANCE •

Dear Board Members:

We recently purchased property in the Trail Lakes Estate of the city. In talking with the architect preparing our house plans, I was told that the city has specified no side-entrance garages. I'd like to request a variance on this ruling to permit such a structure.

The original decision was made to ensure that homes left adequate space for city sidewalks that might possibly surround the complete large-acre lots. The esthetics of the situation demanded that pedestrians on the sidewalks not see into others' garages. However, the situation has changed. All homes in the subdivision are now complete, and no such "surrounding" sidewalks have been constructed.

My neighbors, the only people that this issue affects, have no objection to the side-entrance garage, and their signed statements to that effect are attached.

If you will approve this variance, please send me the written documentation immediately in the enclosed self-addressed, stamped envelope. If I need to complete any forms, please include those as well. Thank you for your prompt attention to this matter; my wife and I are eager to move ahead with our housing plans.

Sincerely,

• REQUESTING POLICE PATROLS •

Dear Chief Barker,

I'm writing to request additional late-night and early-morning patrols in Wiggins Terrace, particularly between the 200 and 400 blocks of McCabe Street.

As you know from reports filed by several of my neighbors, we've experienced a rash of petty crime since the start of summer, including several car and garage break-ins. (A comprehensive list is attached.)

Officer Peter Thompson has told me that extra patrols are allocated based on the number of reports filed in a particular area, but I haven't noticed a stepped-up police presence in the neighborhood.

Please let me know if such patrols are available and, if so, when they'll begin. As captain of the McCabe Street Crime Watch block club, I'd like to share with our membership the specific steps being taken by the Bayville Police Department to address this problem.

Thank you,

• REQUESTING SPEED TRAP •

Dear Chief Barker,

I'm writing to request a speed trap in Wiggins Terrace.

Since the weather got warm, the neighborhood has seen a sharp increase in the number of vehicles speeding northbound on McCabe Street, particularly between the 200 and 800 blocks. Rush hour is bad, but weekends are the worst, when packs of motorcycles race up the street after nightfall. An officer who lives on my block estimated that some of the motorcycles are traveling in excess of 80 miles per hour—in a 35-mile-per-hour zone!

Please let me know if you're able to arrange a speed trap. As captain of the McCabe Street Crime Watch block club, I'd like to share with our membership news of the Bayville Police Department's aggressive efforts to address this problem.

Sincerely,

BUYING AND SELLING

• REQUESTING AMORTIZATION SCHEDULE OF PAYMENTS •

RE: Loan Number 388355

Dear Miss Wheat:

My husband and I have a mortgage with your company for our home at 4689 Windy Way Circle. Would you please send me a new amortization schedule of payments from the start of the loan? We want to verify the calculations since we made our lump-sum payment of $35,000 last month against the principal.

Sincerely,

• REQUESTING PAYOFF BALANCE OF MORTGAGE •

RE: Home Mortgage Loan 8889300

Dear Loan Officer:

We intend to pay off the mortgage on our home at 4998 Bristol Avenue on March 9. Please provide us with the payoff balance on this loan as of that date. Our contract shows no penalty for an early payoff. Would you please verify that issue also in your response to us?

Finally, would you let us know if any amount of escrow money for taxes and insurance will be refunded at the time of payoff?

Thank you for a prompt response; we have a pending sale.

Sincerely,

• ENLISTING REAL ESTATE AGENT (SELLER) •

Dear Mr. McGinnity:

We are considering putting our home at 8945 Brentway on the market in February and are investigating various real estate agencies with experience in this locale. Previously, we had our home up for sale about two years ago for $198,000, and the listing agent at that time made very little effort, in our opinion, to sell the home, although she suggested that listing price. We had no offers during the entire six-month period, and only one potential buyer came to see the house.

If you would be interested in selling the home, would you please run comparable prices for recent home sales in our neighborhood and send us a copy of your standard three- to six-month listing agreement? After we review this information, if we are still interested in moving ahead with the listing, we'll phone to ask that you meet us here to inspect the property.

Sincerely,

• ENLISTING REAL ESTATE AGENT (BUYER) •

Dear Mr. Daniels,

My wife and I are looking for a real estate agent to help us in our search for a downtown condominium. While we've met several agents who are knowledgeable about the condo market on the city's north side, few seem informed about downtown condos, especially those in the older, renovated buildings along Michigan Avenue and in the warehouse district, the areas that most interest us.

Could you give me a call at your earliest convenience to discuss your expertise in this area? I'm particularly interested to know what percentage of your business comes from downtown and how long you've been handling downtown properties. I'd also like to know if you've served as a buyer's or seller's agent for any properties in these specific areas.

I look forward to speaking with you.

Regards,

• THANKING REAL ESTATE AGENT •

Dear Kate,

Now that the boxes are unpacked and the dust has settled in our new home, we want to thank you for handling both the sale of our Overlake property and the purchase of our new home in Montclair Parc.

In a nutshell, you were thoroughly up-to-date in your knowledge of the market, adept at interviewing us to identify the criteria most important in selling our home as well as in building a new one, creative in identifying potential buyers, aggressive in your follow-up calls to potential buyers who looked at the home, and finally attentive to all the details throughout the nine-month process on both homes. And, of course, we appreciate the little extras—like selling our used refrigerator to another client couple and setting up the appointment to introduce us to potential customers for our consulting business. Finally, after-the-sale service is important to us; you continue to come through in that regard with the last-minute items still needing attention from our builder.

Please feel free to use our name as a reference for any potential home buyers or sellers. We can have nothing but good things to say about the extra effort you made in making sure we were satisfied. Thank you for your efforts on our behalf. Now we know why you're consistently among the top agents in the region!

Sincerely,

• CANCELING REAL ESTATE LISTING WITH AGENT •

Dear Ms. Turchi:

Please consider this letter as notification that when our listing expires on April 1, we do not plan to renew the agreement with your agency. As you know, we have been very disappointed in the efforts you've made to call attention to the property. We do not consider a sign in the yard as appropriate advertising for our out-of-the-way location.

We also think the asking price that you suggested is off target and suspect that you intended to recommend our lowering the price with your renewal for another six months. However, we cannot afford the luxury of a long wait for that ideal buyer. As we first explained, we must sell our home immediately—at a reasonable price.

Sincerely,

• WITHDRAWING OFFER TO PURCHASE •

Dear Mr. Kroecker:

With this letter, we are withdrawing our offer of $258,000 to purchase the property at 811 Bellview Court. Since there has been no response in the past three days either to accept or to reject our offer, we ask that you simply void the contract immediately.

Sincerely,

HOME REPAIR AND IMPROVEMENT

• REQUESTING INFORMATION ABOUT PERMIT FOR IMPROVEMENTS •

Dear City Inspector:

We are planning to construct an eight-foot wooden fence around our investment property at 3499 Glennlake. The area is zoned as residential, although there are no other houses under construction. Do we have the city's permission to proceed with that construction?

We are unaware of any code restrictions. If a special permit is necessary, would you please forward to us the appropriate forms?

Sincerely,

• REQUESTING INFORMATION ABOUT RESTRICTIONS •

Dear Wrightsville Historic Preservation Commission,

I recently purchased a home at 999 Jonesbury Street in the Logan Bluff historic district and am interested in renovating the front porch. As I understand it, all exterior modifications are subject to the commission's approval and must contribute to the architectural character of the area.

I'd like to schedule a consultation with one of your staff members before proceeding with the renovation. My goal is to ensure that all of the necessary steps are taken and that the work is completed in a timely fashion.

Regards,

• REQUESTING PRICE QUOTE •

Dear Mr. Dickens:

Your representative, Red Lyons, dropped by our home last Friday to give us an estimate on recarpeting our floors. At that time, he measured our home, but did not give us a complete estimate for total installation, with padding and labor charges added.

Would you please provide in writing your quote for recarpeting our home in all the same rooms that are now carpeted? Please include in the quote your total fee for our carpet selection at $22 per square foot, including the highest-grade quality for your padding and all labor charges.

Also, would you please mention in your quote any guarantees you offer and provide a list of three or four customers we may call for references?

Thank you for your time in providing this bid. We hope to make a decision by midmonth.

Sincerely,

MOVING

• Complaining about Movers •

RE: Invoice 8900933

Dear Mr. Mize:

We are writing to make you aware of the difficulties we had when your staff handled our move from 1010 West Ryan Road to 2598 Towering Oaks. The movers arrived late and wasted time during the day on several "breaks," several items were damaged, and the move took two days rather than the promised one day.

We expect immediate payment for the damaged items and a refund of $280 for the excessive hours charged for labor.

As you will see from the enclosed estimate from your sales representative, Jill Wallace, your movers (four of them) were to arrive at 8:00 A.M. the day of the move and work until the local move was complete. Ms. Wallace estimated the move would take nine hours at a fee of $160 per hour. The first two movers arrived at 8:15; the last two movers arrived at 9:00. During the day, they took a two-hour lunch break and then several breaks randomly, during which time the rest of the crew slowed their pace "to wait for help." Consequently, they did not finish the move at the estimated time and had to return the second day for three hours to unload the truck completely. This delay was another unplanned inconvenience.

Additionally, four paintings were damaged when the movers packed them in the flat cardboard boxes. They decided that crating the pictures was unnecessary because of the short-distance move. When the movers unboxed them upon arrival, the glass was cracked on each of the four and the frames were scratched.

(Continued)

I've enclosed your completed claims form, along with purchase receipts for the pictures, and a copy of your original estimate, showing the estimated total weight of our household goods.

Please give this matter your immediate attention. We expect full and prompt settlement of this claim.

Sincerely,

• CANCELING ACCOUNT WITH UTILITY •

Refund Deposit

RE: Utilities at 810 Busier Lane

Please cancel our electricity service at 810 Busier Lane, effective May 10. You can refund our deposit to our *new* address at 47 Orton Road.

Sincerely,

• CANCELING ACCOUNT WITH UTILITY •

Transfer Deposit

RE: 810 Busier Lane

We are moving from 810 Busier Lane to 4900 Hogan Avenue on May 1. Please cancel our electricity at Busier Lane on May 1, and begin our service at Hogan Avenue on the same day.

Please transfer our deposit from the old address to the new address. If a deposit is no longer required because of our on-time payment record during the past four years, would you please refund that deposit to me at my new address?

Sincerely,

• CHANGING ADDRESS WITH FAMILY OR FRIENDS •

We've moved!

And we wouldn't want to miss any of those invitations, announcements, or periodic updates of what's going on in your life, so please make a note of our new address. While you're at it, write and let us hear from you!

5206 Orville Avenue
Laurenceville, GA 30244
555-555-1234

RENTER'S CONCERNS

• COMPLAINING ABOUT PROPERTY EMPLOYEE •

Dear Mr. Chesbro:

I want to let you know of my concern about the behavior of one of your maintenance people, Rip Hooper. On two occasions last week, I passed Mr. Hooper as he was repairing the fence near the swimming pool. On both occasions, he made suggestive remarks to me, which I tried to ignore without acknowledgment.

Then last Friday, May 3, Mr. Hooper unexpectedly knocked on my door, saying he was sent to check the thermostat. When I told him that I had not called for repairs, he mumbled something about having the wrong apartment but then stayed to try to engage me in conversation. Again, I told him I was busy and terminated the conversation.

Would you please talk with Mr. Hooper about the suggestive remarks at the pool, and then verify that he indeed did have a call to check a thermostat last Friday? This behavior causes me concern about my safety here. I'd appreciate your phoning me in the evening (555-5555) to let me know the outcome of your conversation.

Sincerely,

• REQUESTING INFORMATION ABOUT TENANTS' ASSOCIATION •

Dear President,

I recently moved into apartment 12C. Please send me information about joining the building's tenants' association. I've already had some trouble getting the superintendent to repair my toilet and am interested to learn how others in the building have dealt with similar problems. I'm looking forward to meeting you at the new neighbor mixer later this month.

Sincerely,

• Requesting Rent Extension •

Dear Ms. Barker,

I'm writing to request an extension of my July rent due date. I'm in the process of switching jobs and, as a result, will be receiving my paycheck a few days later than usual.

Would it be all right if I make payment on the fifth instead of on the first? In August, I will resume my usual payment schedule.

If this arrangement is satisfactory, please provide me with written approval according to the conditions of my lease. Thanks for your understanding in this job-change situation.

Sincerely,

• COMPLAINING ABOUT FELLOW TENANTS •

Dear Mr. Ladendorf,

Three times during the last month, Carla Bombera in apartment 4C has parked her vehicle in my reserved space. On the first two occasions (June 3 and 11), I asked that she not do so, and she assured me it wouldn't happen again. On the third occasion (June 14), she told me she had no choice—no street parking was available, and her reserved space was occupied by her son's vehicle.

I'm writing to ask that you intervene in this situation before it gets any worse. My lease clearly states that I am entitled to one reserved parking space. Though Ms. Bombera has been a good neighbor in other respects, I need my parking space and am prepared to do whatever it takes to see that the terms of my lease are honored.

Regards,

• PROTESTING RENT INCREASE •

Dear Manager:

I received your notice about the rent increase of $80 a month, effective July 1, and I strongly protest this increase on behalf of my fellow tenants.

We understand that your costs for taxes and maintenance have increased, but living costs have escalated for all of us as well. Many of us as tenants were promised new installation of carpet when we signed our leases. My carpet, as yet, has not been replaced, nor has that of those renters to whom I spoke about the issue.

Please give me the specific date of carpet installation. If that installation has not been scheduled, we strongly urge you to reconsider the effective date of the rent increase. Otherwise, many of us will be forced to seek other living arrangements when our leases expire.

Sincerely,

• REQUESTING RENT-TO-OWN ARRANGEMENT •

Dear Mr. Ladendorf,

At the time I signed my first lease, 5625 Jupiter Avenue was being offered as either a rental or a rent-to-own property. I've really fallen in love with the house these past three years and am now in a position to make the higher rent-to-own payments.

Is the property still available on a rent-to-own basis and, if so, what are the terms? If I can handle the terms, would you be willing to let me out of my current rental lease in order to buy the house? I look forward to your reply.

Regards,

• REQUESTING APARTMENT SUBLET •

Dear Mr. Keefe:

My company has unexpectedly notified me that I will be transferred to New York on April 30. As you know, my apartment lease runs until June 1 of next year, and I must find a way to handle that commitment.

Although your contract doesn't provide for a sublease arrangement, I'm requesting that you make an exception in this case, since my lease runs for another 14 months. I plan to announce the apartment availability on my company's bulletin board and run an ad in the newsletter. I feel certain that I can find a suitable tenant immediately.

Because I will be ultimately responsible for on-time payments, I guarantee that I will take utmost care in finding a responsible, creditworthy tenant.

If you will not allow such an arrangement, I have an alternative suggestion: I'd like to pay you an extra month's rent at the end of April in exchange for an early release from my contract. That extra month's rent will allow you time to find a suitable tenant yourself.

I've been very pleased living in your apartment complex this past year and will recommend it highly to my colleagues moving into the area. Would you please let me have your decision about the subleasing or the early-cancellation arrangement as soon as possible?

Thank you for considering these options.

Sincerely,

• REMINDER OF REQUEST TO REPAIR APARTMENT (WITHHOLDING RENT) •

Dear Ms. Walsh:

My cooking range in Apartment 322 is still not working properly. I have phoned you twice (May 2 and May 8) and written once (May 16) to ask that you send a maintenance person to check it (the burners on the left don't heat at all). I mentioned that I would be home in the evenings after 7 and all day Saturday. To my knowledge, no one has been by to make the repair.

If the range is not working by June 1, I will be forced to escrow a portion of my rent until the burners have been repaired or replaced. Should such an arrangement become necessary, I will deposit the escrowed rent with my lawyer and you can contact him when you've completed the repairs.

I hope that you will complete the promised repairs and that this escrow action becomes unnecessary. My cooking range is not an "extra," but rather an essential appliance; I eat most of my meals at home. Please complete the repairs immediately.

Sincerely,

• VACATING PROPERTY •

Dear Manager:

I plan to vacate Apartment 450 in the Villa Capri Complex at 5400 Lawndale on October 15. Please let me know the prorated rent to that date so that I can prepare my final payment accordingly.

After final inspection, you can mail my deposit to me at 3445 Runner's Circle, Apartment 230, Pacifica, CA 94044. I will be leaving the apartment clean and all appliances in good working condition.

Sincerely,

• REQUESTING CREDIT IN EXCHANGE FOR UPKEEP, REPAIRS •

Dear Mr. Ladendorf,

Would you be willing to discount my rent in exchange for repairs and/or upkeep not currently designated as my responsibility under the lease?

In return for such a discount, I'm willing to assume the weekly yard work you currently do yourself, paint the apartment, clean the gutters, or perform any other tasks as you see fit.

If you're interested in such an arrangement, let's meet to work out the terms and revise the lease.

Thank you,

• TERMINATING LEASE •

Dear Manager:

I am terminating my lease on Apartment 14 at Haven Living on Fuller Parkway. This letter provides a full 60-day notice, as required by the lease contract.

After I secure another apartment closer to my new job, I'll let you know where you can mail the deposit refund. There has been no damage to the apartment, and I'm anticipating a full refund.

Thank you for efficient responses to all requests for repairs during my tenure in the apartment.

Sincerely,

• REQUESTING RETURN OF DEPOSIT •

Dear Manager:

When I vacated Apartment 350 in Mellon Manor on Arbor Street, I was denied a refund of my initial $450 deposit because the apartment was not vacuumed and the bathrooms not cleaned. At the time of checkout, Mr. Vasquez, the local manager, provided an inventory showing that all appliances were intact and working properly and noted only the unclean apartment as the reason for refusing the refund.

I cleaned the apartment the next day, requested a reinspection, and was told by Mr. Vasquez that he would mail the deposit check. The check has never arrived, although I've made three follow-up calls to his office.

Please check into this matter immediately and mail the deposit refund to me at the address above. Otherwise, I'll be forced to report this issue to the Better Business Bureau and escalate the matter for appropriate legal action.

Sincerely,

• REQUESTING PERMISSION FOR PET •

Dear Ms. Holmes,

Recently a friend of mine became very ill and is no longer able to care for Butch, his six-year-old cat. Would you be willing to modify my lease so that I can adopt Butch? I would consider paying a pet deposit or meeting any other terms as you see fit.

In addition to being neutered, declawed, and fully house-broken, Butch is very laid-back and quiet. I hope you'll consider waiving the no-pets clause of my lease so that he doesn't end up at a shelter. Thanks so much for your consideration of this request.

Sincerely,

LANDLORD'S CONCERNS

• Notifying Tenants of Rent Increase •

Dear Tenants:

Much to our chagrin, the taxes on our apartment complex have been reassessed and increased by 15 percent this past year. To offset these additional costs, we find it necessary to increase rent as detailed in the attached flyer, which gives current and new rates for each building location, floor, and size.

This new amount will go into effect with your rental payments due on July 1. We regret the increase, but want to be able to continue to provide you with the same amenities you've become accustomed to at Buena Vista.

Thank you for your cooperation, and we look forward to continuing to make your apartment living comfortable and safe.

Sincerely,

• Notifying Tenants of Sale of Property •

Dear Tenants:

I have just completed sale of the condominium building in which you are residing to T. R. Stone and Associates. Effective with your October payment, you should mail your rent checks directly to the new owner at the following address:

T. R. Stone and Associates
P.O. Box 499
Nashville, TN 37234

Thank you for your cooperation and prompt payments while I owned the building.

Sincerely,

• REQUESTING TENANT TO REMOVE PET •

Dear Mr. Mauch:

Last Friday, when my son-in-law was in your apartment to repair the dryer outlet, he noticed evidence of a dog in your premises. This letter is to remind you that your lease prohibits pets in the apartment.

Please remove the dog immediately and permanently from the apartment. We will be checking the premises on or before March 10 to ensure that you have complied with the terms of your lease agreement. We will expect your full cooperation.

Sincerely,

• REQUESTING TENANT TO PAY FOR DAMAGES •

Dear Mr. and Mrs. Ward:

When we drove by your house last week, we noticed that the front lawn and row of hedges around the driveway have been damaged. Thank you for your responsiveness and honesty in our phone conversation about the matter on August 10. We know you regret that your summer houseguests have wreaked such havoc with your yard in your absence.

However, your house lease with us clearly states that you are responsible for any damage to the house as a result of the behavior of your guests. We regret that your houseguests have not been as responsible as you have been during your time with us, and regret to have to tell you again that you are ultimately responsible for the damage.

We can arrange to have the lawn and hedge replaced through our landscaper and have him bill you directly, or you can select the landscaper of your choice—so long as the lawn and hedge are of comparable look and value as the original landscaping. We need to approve any changes to the original design.

Please let us know which way you plan to handle the situation.

Sincerely,

• WARNING NOISY TENANT OF COMPLAINTS •

Dear Ms. Hafey:

Several of your neighbors continue to complain about the noise coming from inside your apartment and from your back patio during weekend parties. We, of course, do not care to dictate what goes on in your apartment. But when your behavior and that of your guests infringes on the rights of other tenants to a quiet environment, then we must insist on a change.

Please consider this warning carefully. If we continue to receive other complaints and our investigations prove them to be valid, we will have no choice but to terminate your lease immediately without further warning.

We hope you'll be able to change the disruptive situation.

Sincerely,

• Warning Tenant about Delinquent Rent •

Dear Mr. and Mrs. Tinker:

For the past several months, your rent payments have been late, arriving even five to ten days past the "grace period" provided in your lease agreement.

This letter will serve as a reminder that your rent in full is due on the first day of each month. If you are having a temporary difficulty, please make us aware of the problem. Otherwise, we'll expect to have your rent on time, as agreed when you assumed occupancy of the duplex.

We appreciate your full cooperation so that no other action will be necessary.

Sincerely,

INVITATIONS

Often, the most pressing part of a party or event revolves around deciding how to word the invitations so that you clarify details and minimize questions.

To make things easy, begin by stating the occasion or event, including date, time, location, and purpose. And don't forget to mention whether spouses, children, or other family members are invited. Either throw open the gates enthusiastically or limit surprises—but do so tactfully.

"Children will have other activities provided."

"Only members of the immediate family are invited for this occasion."

"Our accommodations have limited our guest list to include only those who…"

"If you plan to bring a guest, please let us know by calling…"

"Come and bring your guest."

"If you know of others who may be interested, invite them to attend with you."

Overview scheduling for any planned activities. These details will help guests understand about the appropriateness of arriving early or late or other schedule conflicts during the event.

State the appropriate dress, if that is not obvious from the occasion, activities, and site.

"Business attire is required."

"All our guests will probably be coming straight from work, so your professional attire is appropriate."

"Business casual is the appropriate dress."

"Beachwear is the order of the day."

"Wear something comfortable for working and walking."

"We'll be outdoors, so dress accordingly."

"Dress in your partying clothes."

"Festive attire is appropriate."

Ask for a response by a certain date so that you aren't left with indecision about food and space logistics. Or, if a response isn't necessary, say so.

State tactfully preferences or appropriateness of gifts. No mention of gifts leaves readers to do what they wish, or nothing at all. If you want to leave the giving decision open, avoid any mention of gifts.

"Gag gifts, OK."

"Please send your love in lieu of gifts."

"No gifts, please."

"Mary has asked that no gifts be sent. Please send any donations to..."

"Tara's planning a color scheme of green and plum in the bath and kitchen."

Having this arduous chore of composing the invitations behind you, enjoy the party!

FORMAL

• BABY SHOWER •

It's a girl—or at least that's what the doctors say at this point.

You're invited to a baby shower for Marilyn Ewing.
May 5 from 12 to 2 P.M.

Carter's Tea Room
455 Oak Lawn

RSVP by May 2 (555-5555).
We're planning a light lunch.

• BIRTHDAY PARTY •

You are invited to a party honoring Lauren Lazzeri on her nineti-eth birthday, December 1. Lauren has gone from horses to jets, from no phones to mobile phones, from inkwells to computer chips. What a fantastic day to gather around and hear her varied experiences with life!

The party will be at the Carver Room, in the Hartford Civic Center. Please stop by sometime between the hours of 2 and 5 P.M. to express your best wishes to Lauren. No gifts, please.

• BRIDAL SHOWER •

You are invited to a bridal shower honoring Brenda Hulman, on January 14, from 4 to 6 in the afternoon. Please reply to Mary Cox (555-5555) if you will be able to join us after work for cocktails and hors d'oeuvres.

The bride is registered at the following stores: Dillard's, Foley's, The Kit and Kaboodle, and Bradford's.

Big Tip 1: Since Brenda has experienced apartment living for several years, she has the necessities in the kitchen. But the extras, well, that's where you come in.

Big Tip 2: Colors throughout the apartment are burgundy and forest green.

• CHRISTENING •

Christening of our daughter
Kaya Ann Waddell

Sunday, February 6, at 6 P.M.

St. Thomas Episcopal Church
388 Foster Road
Wyatt, Iowa

RSVP for the dinner following: (123) 333-4894

• WEDDING AT CLUB •

Friends and Family

You are invited to join us in celebrating our love, on Saturday, November 6, at the Grand Kapinski Hotel, in the Love Nest, 39393 Los Alamos Freeway, Los Angeles.

We ask that you, our very closest friends, be with us as we say our wedding vows at 7 P.M., and then join us at the reception following the ceremony. Your being with us on this occasion will complete our special day.

Regrets only: 555-5555

• WEDDING AT HOME •

We are pleased to invite you to the wedding of our daughter, Louise Jean Flick, to Ross Moranville on Friday, May 7, at 8 P.M. in our home at 5782 Miramar Road in the Southlake Vista.

After the couple exchanges vows, we invite you to join us for a buffet dinner honoring our children. Please respond (555-5555) by April 15 if you will be able to attend.

• CANCELLATION OF INVITATION •

Mr. and Mrs. Ludwig Stack
are recalling their invitations to the
marriage of their daughter
Sally Stack
to
Herb McCarthy

The wedding will not take place
because of Herb's
prolonged illness.

Note: If the reason is not meant for common knowledge—if it's something other than military obligations, illness, or death in the family—you may simply wish to end with this generic explanation: "The wedding will not take place."

INFORMAL

• ANNIVERSARY PARTY •

For Friends

Myrna and Casey Tastabul
are celebrating their
Golden Wedding Anniversary
on February 1, at 7 P.M.

Please join us in our home for a buffet dinner
to congratulate the happy couple.

Given by Deanna and Wayne Fisk
973 Blair Lane
(555) 555-5555

RSVP by January 21.

• ANNIVERSARY PARTY •

Your Own Anniversary

We're celebrating our twenty-fifth wedding anniversary
and hope you'll join us.

What? Sit-down dinner, followed by dancing
When? June 22 at 8 P.M.
Where? Harvey Hotel at 848 Lamar Boulevard
Why? We appreciate our friends and family.

Burt and Deb Smith

RSVP by June 1 (card enclosed)

• SUPER BOWL PARTY •

Won't you join us as the
New England Patriots take on the Philadelphia Eagles
(as if it matters who's playing)?

Come for the game, stay for the commercials.
And the snacks. And the chatter.

February 6—6 P.M. till closing
Ted & Lou's Place
789 Tanwell Court, Apartment 6A

Eagles fans are requested to use the back door and
wear gorilla suits.
All others, come as you are.

• Bachelor Party •

It's Andy's last chance to tie one on before he ties the knot.

What: Bachelor party
When: Friday, August 5, from 6 P.M. till?
Where: Moe & Johnny's Restaurant

After dinner, we'll head downtown to the warehouse district.
Limo transportation provided. RSVP to Kevin Nordquist
(573-0986) by August 1.

• RETIREMENT PARTY •

On May 6, Duane Ward will retire after 16 years as branch manager.

On May 7, Duane says he'll be fishing the Cuyatuck River and may never come home.

Please join us in giving him a great send-off—it might be the last time you see the guy.

Duane Ward's (Surprise) Retirement Party
Fifth floor conference room
Friday, May 6, 5 P.M.
Plenty of food and drink provided.

• BIRTHDAY PARTY •

No Gifts

It's the big 50 for Pauly Beane.
He'll never have a good night's sleep again.

Dress casual and be prepared to party
on March 31 at 7 P.M.
Rinehart's Restaurant at Central and Bowen Expressway

RSVP: 555-5555 by March 28

No gifts; just come eat our grub.

• BIRTHDAY PARTY •

Surprise

It's a surprise!

Teddy Skinner turns into superman on his twenty-first
birthday.

Come party with us!
January 14 at 8 P.M.
Backyard Barbecue

Aaron and Greta Owen's Place
292 Westway

No need to call; for those who don't show up, we'll
send out a posse.
Gag gifts only.

• Holiday Season •

Join us for a preholiday party to meet and greet your neighbors!

Dessert and Drinks

November 29 from 8 to 11 P.M.

Henry and Carmen Hobart's Home
4899 Casablanca Boulevard

Dress: Festive

• PARTY FOR VISITING FRIEND OR GUEST •

It's a party for our summer houseguest!
Our niece, Annie Raines

Saturday, June 1, at 7 P.M.

Stop by to meet and charm Annie, and then say hello to friends and neighbors you haven't seen in a while. You might be surprised at what they've been up to lately!

Dress: Casual

• Public Reading •

Please join the Brownville Book Club for an evening of poetry and conversation as we host Josephine Calder. Ms. Calder is the award-winning author of three chapbooks, including *Brood City*. She has also published essays in the *Oxford American, Southern Review*, and other magazines.

Archibald & Diana Knox's home
994 New Jersey Street
Thursday, June 11, 7 P.M.

The reading will be followed by a wine and cheese reception. A $5 donation is requested at the door. All proceeds will benefit the Brownsville Literacy Association.

• SOCIAL CLUB MIXER •

Try us; you'll like us.

Chapter Mixer, sponsored by the Laketon Literary Club
Date: August 7
Time: 7 to 8:30 P.M.

Program: Roundtables with local authors
Chilton Library, Conference Room B
Foster at Central Expressway
Reception following at Ernie's Eatery, across the street.

• Neighborhood Event •

The Landsdowne Neighborhood Association requests your
presence at the fifth annual

Landsdowne Progressive Dinner

Hors d'oeuvres
5:00–5:30 P.M.
56 West Street
Charles & Gail McMillan

Soup
5:30–6:00 P.M.
49 Ironwood Avenue
Nikki Rodriguez

Salad
6:00–6:30 P.M.
59 Ironwood Avenue
Jack & Lisa Tan

Entrée
6:30–7:30 P.M.
29 West Street
Aaron Hamilton

Dessert
7:30–8:00 P.M.
93 Reese Avenue
Chuck and Lola DeRossa

Dress is festive. All neighbors are welcome.
Bring a bottle of wine or appropriate dish to the course of
your choice.

• BLOCK PARTY •

The Emerson Avenue Crime Watch Block Club invites you to
its third annual . . .

Block Party & Barbecue!!

Saturday, April 16, 5 P.M.
5604 Emerson Avenue (Martha Pickerell's house)
Rain or shine

Brautz, burgers, and beverages will be provided.
Everyone encouraged to bring a covered dish . . . and a neighbor!

• ALUMNI OUTING •

The Cubs are out of the pennant race again. So what?

The Chicago chapter of the Dickson College Alumni Association cordially invites you to an afternoon of sunshine (hopefully), baseball (sort of), and suds (guaranteed).

Wrigley Field
Chicago Cubs vs. Washington Nationals
Friday, August 29
1:20 P.M. (Central Time)

Tickets must be reserved in advance by contacting Brian Ridge (555-555-5555). Tickets will be available for pick-up one hour prior to game time at the Goose Island Brew Pub, 3535 North Clark Street, 222-222-2222.

• THEME PARTIES •

1980s

It's a 1980s Rerun

Party Hearty!

Friday, June 5 at 7 P.M.

Jolene and Dirk Rice's Place
5900 Dill Drive, Apartment C

Dress as you did in high school: casual and comfortable.
Bring a snack tray, bowl, or basket with your favorite goodies.

• THEME PARTIES •

Movie Madness

Movie Madness after the Holidays

January 6 at 7 P.M.

We're planning to have videos of all the classics playing in the background.

Come prepared to laugh and cry with the stars!

Dress: Clothes, any flavor will do
Bring a dessert and a beverage

Sponsored by the Mavericks' Club

• THEME PARTIES •

Romeo and Juliet

Romeo and Juliet Party
Come in costume as a famous, romantic twosome

February 14 at 8 P.M.

Wyndham Hotel, Wedgewood Room
3833 Lovers Lane

Pay at the door: $45 per couple for all the
food, music, and fun you can enjoy

RSVP: Call Vivian Hatcher (555-555-5555)
or Julia Herrerra (555-555-1234)
by February 12

• SCHOOL FUNCTION •

She was a good girl. He was a bad boy. How could their
love survive?

The ninth grade class of Maple Academy
invites you to the premier of its spring play, *Grease*.

Maple Academy Auditorium
April 29, 7 P.M.
Limited seating
RSVP: 666-4534 by April 25

• GET WELL PARTY •

Just because Mike's leg is broken doesn't mean the rest of us can't dance.

Surprise Get Well Party
February 3 at 7 P.M.

Mike & Mindy's house
8009 Winding Way

No need to call. Please arrive 15 minutes early and park around the corner on Sherman Oak Drive so Mike won't see your car and get suspicious. Enter the house through the back door. Mindy will bring Mike home at 7:00 sharp.

JOB REFERENCES AND INTRODUCTIONS

On occasion, you will be the go-between for friends, relatives, and associates. They'll need character references, nominations, and introductions. Don't let the task of phrasing a good letter keep you from helping someone in these situations. Writing a reference letter puts your friend or family member in the limelight and banks a favor for your own future.

When you can enthusiastically introduce or refer someone, get to the point immediately; introduce or recommend the person in the first sentence or paragraph. Then overview the person's association or acquaintance with you: In what capacity did or do you know this person? How have you become aware of his or her skills, talent, character traits, or success?

> *"I've known Johnny for years as a fellow swimmer on the neighborhood team."*
>
> *"Johnny's children and mine have grown up together. We've lived in the same neighborhood for almost 16 years."*
>
> *"Over the years I've served with Johnny on several boards in which I've noted his financial savvy about..."*
>
> *"Sara's creative talents often came in handy in PTA fund-raising projects."*
>
> *"Sara has been a faithful attendee of my congregation for almost ten years, and during that time, I've often called upon her to..."*

Be as specific as possible about the person's skills, attitudes, and accomplishments. If possible, relate them to benefits for the group or association to which you're making the referral, recommendation, or introduction.

> *"Cary's flexible attitude in fast-changing environments would certainly come in handy in dealing with your membership."*
>
> *"Because your organization depends on the fund-raising efforts of its members, I know that Ming would be willing to access her network of friends to tap into their resources and energies."*

Express confidence that any future association between the reader and your friend or family member will be mutually rewarding.

> *"We know you'll profit from any conversations; you are both so well versed on the subject."*
>
> *"We think you'll really hit it off together."*
>
> *"Any association between you two can only be mutually rewarding."*
>
> *"I'm very confident that Michael will become an outstanding student at your university."*
>
> *"Dominick, if he should win this award, will bring great distinction to your organization for having recognized his talents."*

When writing reference letters, you have a unique chance to do a favor for two people with only a few strokes on your keyboard.

• Supplying Reference for Student •

To Whom It May Concern:

I highly recommend Sandra Moses for summer employment in your organization. As a freshman and sophomore, Sandra worked for me as assistant in my law practice. She performed various clerical duties, including word processing, copying and collating, filing, courier services, and errands to clients' and vendors' offices.

My staff and I found her to be extremely mature in dealing with clients and flexible in changing priorities almost daily. We were pleased with her word processing speed and accuracy in customizing our tedious technical forms and documents. In addition, she was punctual and had no absences during the two summers with us—quite a record, considering the schedules of today's busy teens.

Regrettably, Sandra will not be continuing employment with us this coming summer, because we have moved our law practice out of the neighborhood where she attends high school. The extra 15 minutes in commuter traffic makes the move for her impractical.

If Sandra accepts a position with your firm, we think you'll be very pleased with her work and attitude.

Yours truly,

• Supplying Reference for Employee •

To Prospective Employers:

Darla Shields has provided cleaning and nanny services for our family for the past four years, and we have been very pleased with her work. We became acquainted with Darla while we were visiting a friend in Germany. Later, when we learned that she wanted to come to the United States, we quickly invited her to work for us and helped her get the necessary legal clearances to do so.

Darla's job responsibilities with us have included the typical household duties, cooking for our family of four, and caring for two preschool children. Darla speaks impeccable English, demonstrates a congenial attitude toward all in our family, and understands the importance of giving loving attention and discipline to the children—not to mention her considerable culinary talents!

We were very disappointed when Darla told us of her plans to enroll as a full-time university student and seek only part-time employment. Had we not needed someone full time to care for our preschoolers, we would still insist on having Darla with us.

Any family who employs Darla in the future will find her personable, efficient, and honest.

Sincerely,

• SUPPLYING CHARACTER REFERENCE FOR FRIEND •

Dear Mr. Hoynes:

Craig Dewey, a good friend of mine, has recently left his job at Atwood Engineering to start his own consulting practice, specializing in computer training for small businesses. His 16 years inside a major corporation that manufactures and installs various telecommunications systems around the country have certainly prepared him for the new venture.

What's lacking is a solid list of prospects needing his services. That's where I come in. I offered to contact a few friends of mine who have their own professional practice or small business and need his services to train themselves or staff in the array of new software packages flooding the market.

Craig's previous employer and satisfied customers can attest to his technical skills. I myself know this man's attitude and character. He is a creative individual with the perseverance to get the job done—whatever that takes. He's patient with those who suffer from computer phobia (personal experience here), and can quickly grasp the business applications of your operation and identify the must-know from the nice-to-know tasks that you or your staff need to perform on the computer. That translates into increased productivity sooner rather than later.

Should you have need of computer training at the moment, I encourage you to give Craig a call at (555) 555-5555. I think you'll find it a mutually rewarding relationship. Best wishes for your own continued success.

Sincerely,

• SUPPLYING REFERENCE FOR FRIEND FOR CLUB MEMBERSHIP •

Dear Committee Members:

With this letter, I am recommending Xander Cottier for membership in the Brighton Club. Xander and his family moved to Bynum three months ago from Chicago, where he served as hospital administrator for the Medicare clinic system. His wife had her own practice there as a pediatrician in Napersville. Currently, both of them are pursuing the same careers here. She has established her pediatric practice with the Methodist Hospital, and Xander has assumed a similar administrative position with the same hospital.

Our family's association with this family began more than ten years ago, when our sons played on the same Little League team in Chicago. We struck up a casual acquaintance and then a closer friendship as we served on several corporate boards together.

I find Xander and his wife to be dedicated professionals in their medical careers, capable leaders in the community, and of high moral character. Our organization could profit immeasurably from their membership, talents, and insight.

Sincerely,

• NOTIFYING REFERENCE OF USE •

Dear Professor Abbott,

Thanks for offering to serve as a personal reference for me. I've recently applied for a position as drug rep with Bailey Pharmaceutical and provided the human resources department with your contact information. The director, Janet Orozco, said she'll likely be calling you some time in the coming week. If you would rather she reach you via e-mail, let me know and I'll be happy to communicate your preference.

I'll drop a line as soon as I know if I got the job.

Sincerely,

• INTRODUCING RELATIVE TO EMPLOYER •

Dear Jessica:

My brother Barney has just returned to Dayton to seek employment so that he can be near our elderly parents. When he told me that he wanted to continue his long sales career with a premium organization—selling a service that he believes has lasting value for people—I immediately thought of you.

Barney has sold both products and services in the past 20 years: telephone systems, copiers, software, training, and public relations services. And, I might add, he has done very well at it, having been recognized by two previous employers for exceeding revenue goals and landing in the Top 10 Percent Club at their respective organizations.

If you need a self-starter with a track record, you may want to set up an interview with Barney. He'll be moving here in July, but he can fly in for an interview at your convenience. Let me know if you think you could benefit from meeting Barney to see if there's a match in temperament and philosophy.

I always love being a matchmaker—especially when the relationship could be so rewarding for both parties involved. If I don't hear from you, I'll assume you have no positions available at the present. In any case, do stay in touch. Hope you're having another great year at FlexMart.

Cordially,

• Nominating Candidate for Award •

Dear Committee:

With this letter, I am nominating Geraldine Magadan as Citizen of the Year at Summersville.

For 15 years, Geraldine has devoted countless hours to community projects. But this year, her efforts have been unsurpassed and invaluable to our citizens. As chair of the United Way campaign for the city, she raised more than $14 million, representing a 22 percent increase over any previous year. That in itself is a gargantuan achievement.

But Geraldine's efforts have also extended to service on the board of directors for Habitat for the Homeless, Snyder's Mission, and the Glasgow Art Museum. Through her countless efforts on these boards, she has indeed created a caring and nurturing environment in our community. We owe much of our heritage to similar efforts of hers in the 20 years since she and her family have made their home here.

The Citizen of the Year award could go to no finer resident than Geraldine Magadan. It's time Summersville offered a sincere thank-you for her many contributions.

Sincerely,

• RECOMMENDING GUEST SPEAKER •

Dear Members:

Kim Witt is the epitome of a professional speaker extraordinaire: expertise established through years of solid research, a dynamic delivery style, and ethical standards so important to today's audiences.

I'd like to recommend Kim to you as a valuable resource for your next annual meeting. I've known Kim for about three years through my employer, Frito-Lay. We engaged her to deliver various concurrent sessions at our national sales meetings, and our attendees found her to be always prepared, on target with the latest research, and focused with practical marketing strategies for immediate use. We had more positive comments on her sessions than on all the others combined.

If you'd like to know more about the results we were able to achieve with the information Kim provided, give me a call to review our audience profiles and evaluations in greater detail.

Although I've left Frito-Lay, Kim is still traveling the country addressing the top corporations in the area of her expertise: marketing in the global economy. If you ever find yourself looking for an expert on that topic, you could not find someone more qualified or more effective in moving audiences into action than Kim Witt.

Sincerely,

• DECLINING TO SUPPLY CHARACTER REFERENCE •

Dear Rodney,

I received your message yesterday about using my name as a reference in your job search.

Through our association at the club, as you probably recall, we did not often agree on our budgeting priorities and membership goals. Therefore, I'm afraid any comments I might pass on to a prospective employer would be biased by those difficulties at the club. So I've concluded that it might be in your best interest for me not to comment on those differing views.

I wish you success in finding a suitable job.

Sincerely,

• DECLINING TO MAKE INTRODUCTION •

Dear Peggy,

Liz and I are so thrilled you're moving back to Williamsport. I only wish that I could be more useful in helping you land a job.

As you know, I was hoping to introduce you to some of my contacts in the school district. It wasn't until I went through my Rolodex that I realized that most of the administrators I once knew have either retired or moved on to other districts.

I'm sorry that I won't be able to provide any useful introductions, but I'd be happy to serve as a character reference or provide a letter of recommendation. Let me know what I can do to help.

All the best,

LETTERS TO YOUNG CHILDREN

On first blush, you might consider writing a note or letter to a child an easy task. But writing that does not sound condescending or silly and that demonstrates to a child that you understand his or her world takes a little thought.

Generally, you are safe to start by complimenting the child specifically for behavior and action. Instead of "You've been a very good student," try:

"Your mother tells me that you've earned all A's this semester. And I imagine that's not easy with the two science courses you're taking."

Make the child feel special by mentioning details (names, occasions, toys or games, comments, feelings) that are special to him or her personally. Empathize with and accept feelings he or she has expressed in the past.

"I know that you must have been afraid to try something like this."

"I know that you have spent hours working on the project."

"Most children feel very disappointed when something like this happens."

Above all, express your love and appreciation, focusing on the child's concerns, not your own.

• ENCOURAGEMENT FOR SCHOOLWORK •

Julio,

That's too bad about your D in math. I'm guessing it was especially tough since you've always gotten As in the past. Hang in there, though. The important thing is to do your best and not be shy about asking for help when you need it.

If you ever want to go over some problems together, I hope you'll call. And for the record, I once got an F in algebra myself. (Let's not tell the other accountants at my office, okay?)

Love,

• CONGRATULATIONS ON SCHOOLWORK •

Dear Francisco,

Thank you for writing to me and sending your grades for this year. I'm always so concerned that you're studying hard. And it certainly looks like you are. Your math grades came up two points from last time. That must mean you understand your fractions now well enough to do those word problems. I still have difficulty with fractions myself from time to time when I'm drawing those house plans.

Thanks for keeping me updated. I'll expect more good news next semester.

Love,

• CONGRATULATIONS ON PERSONAL ACCOMPLISHMENT •

Nicky,

Your mother tells me you passed your swim test with flying colors. Congratulations! I know you've worked hard at your lessons, and I'm so happy all that work finally paid off.

Your Uncle Rick and I are looking forward to swimming in the ocean when you come to visit. But let's still build a sand castle too, okay?

Love,

• CONGRATULATIONS ON GRADUATION •

My dear Samantha,

Graduating from elementary school is quite an accomplishment. I still remember how proud I felt that first day of middle school with all of the "big kids." I just wanted to say congratulations and wish you a great three years at Seabrook Middle School. And please let me know what sports you end up playing. I'd love to come cheer you on.

Lots of love,

• HAPPY BIRTHDAY •

Cory,

Happy birthday on your seventh big event. I understand that you're planning a great camping trip for the weekend to celebrate with your friends. Be sure not to forget to eat an extra hot dog for me—with lots of mustard, just the way you and I like them.

I'm proud of the kind and bright young man you've become.

With love,

• SUMMER CAMP •

Alex,

So how's the swimming up there at Camp Cheerio? And the riflery? And the soccer?

All's well here in the city. We're saving the Sunday comics for you, and I've been taking Mix for a walk every night, just as you asked me to do. He misses you, but the squirrels have been keeping him company until you get home.

I'm sure you're plenty busy, but your mom and I would be so happy to hear from you. Can you spare a few minutes to drop us a postcard and tell us about all the fun things you're doing? We'll get a care package together as soon as we hear from you.

Love,

• PLEASE VISIT •

Dear Jackson and Miranda,

Would you be able to spend a few days with us in Seattle while you're out of school for the holidays? We'd love to send you airline tickets if your mother thinks you can arrange to come. If you can be with us, here are some suggestions for what we might do. (*Fill in details.*)

What do you say? I'll be waiting to have you call me after you and your mom have had time to look at your schedules.

Love,

• PLEASE COME AGAIN •

Felipe,

I can hardly believe you've already come and gone. Your grandaddy is still adding snow patches to Frosty in the backyard. His hat is lopsided, but otherwise, he's still in fairly good shape.

The most fun we had with you was tucking you into bed each night and reading those new stories we bought last weekend. Do you still remember what happened to Donald, the Muckety-Muck?

Please ask your dad to call us on the weekend to let us know if you need a refill on the books.

With love,

• THANK YOU FOR GIFT •

Dear Katrina:

How sweet of you to send the pictures to me. I really like the one you took on top of the mountain. Where was that? How high were you?

You were pretty sharp to remind your folks to get double prints made for me. Let's you and me keep working with those two and we'll have them remembering to do that every time! Thank you for including me in your vacation.

Love,

• LOSS OF PET •

Dear Max,

I was so sorry to hear about Zeke. They say cats have nine lives, and I suppose he finally used his up. He was certainly lucky to have you for a friend, though. I've never seen a boy take such good care of a cat, and I've never seen a cat who loved a boy so much. It always made me happy to look out my window in the afternoon and see you taking Zeke for a walk on his leash. Not many people are patient enough to train a cat so well. I hope that when you think of him now, you think of all the good times you had together. And remember what else they say: All good kitties go to heaven.

Love,

• APOLOGY •

Dear Joel,

I'm sorry I wasn't able to take you to the Lakers game on Saturday. I was really looking forward to the two of us enjoying some hot dogs and rooting for Kobe together, and I know you were too. Something came up at work that just couldn't wait, though.

How about next weekend? The Suns are in town, and I already have tickets. And if they call me from the office with another emergency, I'll tell them to get somebody else to take care of it because I'll be at the arena with my favorite nephew.

Can't wait to see you,

• NEW RESPONSIBILITY •

Katrina,

I enjoyed stopping by your refreshment stand on Saturday. The lemonade was delicious, and, at fifty cents, a bargain. I'm impressed that you've taken on such a big responsibility and made it a success. I'll be sure to send some customers your way. Meanwhile, here's hoping you save up enough by the end of the summer to buy that Schwinn.

Yours,

• REMINDER •

Dear Zachary,

Thanks for raking my leaves on Saturday. I just wanted to remind you that the side yard needs to be raked, too. Knowing how responsible you are, I figured you planned to come back later and finish up. I'm hosting a reception on Friday and would like the leaves gone by then. Are you free sometime before Thursday? Let me know, and I'll have a check waiting for you.

All the best,

• GET WELL SOON •

Dear Keisha,

Your mom told me you just had your tonsils removed. Is it true they're making you drink milkshakes *every day*? Sounds rough, but I guess somebody has to do it.

I heard the operation went well and that you were the bravest girl Dr. Palmer ever saw. I'm not surprised a bit.

Get well soon, okay? I think about you every day and look forward to seeing you back at school. Meanwhile, have a double chocolate malt for me.

Sincerely,

MEDIA: ISSUES, CONCERNS, POSITIONS

You need to deal with the media—to conduct your life and fulfill community obligations—in various frames of minds, from elation for coverage about hazardous situations to anger about offensive programming. Your purpose must determine your tone.

To request services, begin by stating the action you want—that's your message.

> *"Please retract immediately the statement that…"*
>
> *"I'd like to request equal time to present the opposing views about…"*
>
> *"Please place my ad in Sunday's paper in the section called…"*

Answer these questions for public service announcements: what, who, when, why, where, how, how much. Finally, provide contact information for further questions.

On those occasions when you intend to show support, express your appreciation for the media's position on an issue, ad, or controversy or for media sponsorship of decent, beneficial programming.

> *"We wholeheartedly embrace and welcome the new program you've decided to air about…"*
>
> *"I commend you for taking a strong stand against…"*
>
> *"I read with great appreciation your editorial about…"*
>
> *"Thank you for calling attention to the often overlooked issue of…"*

Then add your own reasons for agreeing with the media's position or action.

Commend the media for shedding light on any complex issue and spending time and effort in the investigative process, and thank them for bringing issues or problems to the public's attention.

> *"I'm sure the background facts you printed were not easy to dislodge from such protective agencies."*
>
> *"I appreciate the fact that your reporter made several trips overseas to get to the bottom of this matter."*
>
> *"This situation is complex and your investigation shows that you did more than a cursory review."*
>
> *"You have done us all a big favor."*

When you object to the media's position or action, speak up. That's your right as a citizen. Identify yourself so as to add authority to what you say:

> *"As a well-known citizen frequently speaking to civic groups about…"*
>
> *"As a taxpayer who contributes over $X in property taxes each year…"*
>
> *"As a principal of the high school who intends to advise teachers and students against the policy stated in the media…"*
>
> *"As an active voter and grass-roots supporter during election campaigns…"*

Give your reasons for the disagreement or objection, pointing out any erroneous information and giving your sources of information in support of your position. Take care to point out the ill-will, harm, or other negative ramifications of the media's position and urge them to reverse their position or action or broadcast a retraction.

Finally, don't forget the positives within the power of the media. If you know of an issue that needs coverage or a problem to be resolved, be proactive in contacting the media and suggesting a story. They need more, not fewer, concerned citizens.

• PRESS RELEASE—PUBLIC SERVICE ANNOUNCEMENT •

For Immediate Release

As publicity director of the Bonnham Supplies for Students Fund this summer, I'm making you aware of a drive to collect used school supplies for the needy children in our local districts. We'd appreciate it if you would announce this drive—its purpose, the collection points, and the distribution center—during your after-school driving time.

> Join us in our Bonnham Supplies for Students Drive. Many children find that they outgrow or stop using their old school jackets, sweats and warm-up suits, notebooks, and supplementary reading texts as they complete various courses. We're asking parents and students to donate these used-but-still-good items to our collection for use by other children.
>
> I've listed below the various collection points around the city. We will be sending a truck to pick up these items and bring them to a central location on Monday evenings. Those students and their parents needing such items will be allowed to make their selections from our central headquarters office at 478 Davis Street.
>
> Collection point: Your neighborhood fire station
>
> For further information, listeners may call 123-4567.

Thank you for your help in spreading the news about these available school supplies for needy families.

For further information: Contact publicity director Lester Parrett at 555-5555.

• PLACING CLASSIFIED ADVERTISEMENT •

Dear Manager of the Classified Ads:

Please place the following ad in the Sunday edition of the paper in the section "Used Cars":

1996 Buick Regal: 12,000 miles. Excellent condition. $17,000.

Call 344-9987 after 7 P.M. or any time on weekends.

I've enclosed a check for $35 for the ad to run Sunday only. I understand that if I want to continue the ad on Sundays, I can phone by noon the following Friday and run it again for only $30 on subsequent insertions.

My work number for any questions you may have is 555-5555.

Sincerely,

• ENTERING CONTEST •

Dear Ms. May,

Please consider the enclosed poem, "The Battle Flag," for the *Star & Ledger*'s Independence Day poetry contest.

My poetry and essays have previously appeared in the monthly newsletter of Trinity Episcopal Church and in *Paging All Readers*, a publication of the Greenville Public Library.

Thanks for this wonderful opportunity to share my poetry and patriotism with fellow readers of the *Star & Ledger*.

Sincerely,

• REQUESTING CONTEST RESULTS •

Dear Ms. May,

I was disappointed that my poem didn't win the *Star & Ledger*'s Independence Day poetry contest, though I really enjoyed the winning entry ("On the Delaware," by Lisa Phan).

Could you send me a complete list of the runners-up? As your instructions request, I'm enclosing a self-addressed stamped envelope.

Sincerely,

• REQUESTING FREE ADVERTISEMENT •

Dear Ms. Sanchez,

I'm writing to request a free advertisement for the Second Methodist charity car wash in the *Brookline Gazette*. Enclosed find ready-made ads in eighth-, quarter-, half-, and full-page sizes.

We wish we were in a position to purchase an ad, but all proceeds from the car wash go to our mission in Costa Rica, and we have no ad budget. If you are able to find space for us, we'd be deeply appreciative.

Thanks for your consideration, and keep up the good work at the *Gazette*. I know of no other community paper that does such a fine job of keeping its readers informed about local issues and events.

Sincerely,

• PLACING PROFESSIONAL ANNOUNCEMENT •

Dear Editor:

Please place the following announcement in your "Bulletin Board" section of the business journal supplement that runs every Tuesday:

> The American Society for Training and Development will hold its monthly meeting February 16, at a new location: the Hilton at Lamar Avenue. The meeting will begin with cocktails and registration at 6:00 P.M., followed by dinner at 6:30 and a speaker at 7:30. Charge for members is $25; for nonmembers, $35. For registration, call 444-6666 by noon of the meeting day.

Thank you for this placement.

Sincerely,

• REQUESTING SYNDICATED CONTENT •

Dear Ms. May,

I've been a subscriber to the *Star & Ledger* for six years, and I admit that the first thing I turn to each morning at breakfast is the comics page. I've always appreciated the good mix of serial and funny comics found there (and the absence of *Prince Valiant*, one of my all-time least favorite comics).

My only complaint is that the *Star & Ledger* doesn't carry *Jackbird*. As you surely know, the creator of *Jackbird*, Timothy McShane, lives right here in Hathawa County, and his comic is syndicated in more than eighty papers nationwide.

Would you consider adding *Jackbird* to the lineup of syndicated comics currently offered in your newspaper? I know many of my fellow readers would enjoy McShane's wry sense of humor and take pride in the fact that the strip is produced locally.

Thanks for your consideration,

• PROTESTING CANCELLATION OF COLUMN/COMIC STRIP/PROGRAM/SERIES •

Dear Ms. Redus:

I am very disappointed about your decision to cancel Hal Boston's column on employment and job searches. Isn't it bad enough that so many of your readers have been "canceled" from their jobs and employers? Must you add to our dilemma by eliminating a very good source of job search tips and strategies?

Won't you please reconsider your decision to cancel Boston's column?

Certainly, you are aware that the unemployment rate in this state stands at 8.5 percent, according to a front-page story your paper ran two weeks ago. And many job seekers cannot afford to buy all the job-hunting books from their local bookstores. Boston's column on current trends in résumé writing, interviewing techniques, and compensation fills a big gap in the knowledge base of so many who've been with one employer for much too long to understand the complexities of the job market.

Not only does the column speak to the needs of the unemployed, but it also serves to make large corporations aware of the recruitment tactics and compensation packages offered by their competitors. My wife, a human resources specialist for a large oil company, also finds the columns up to date in their recommendations and information about trends in the HR field.

No, Hal Boston is not my brother-in-law. But I am a devoted fan, and I do hope you'll continue to carry his column in the weeks to come. I need to spend my time finding a new job, not a new newspaper.

Sincerely,

• Objecting to Cartoon/Ad/Program/Series •

Dear Mr. Seitzer:

I strongly object to the new 30-minute sitcom *Free for All.* Although the basic premise of the show holds promise, the situations and dialogues of the characters constantly attack marriage and religious commitments. I find these opinions outside the mainstream of American lives and morally objectionable.

Worse, this program is aired in prime time, when impressionable children and teens are most likely to be watching.

I strongly urge you to drop this program from your lineup and return to programs that strengthen rather than destroy the moral fabric of our country. By a copy of this letter, I'm also making my opinion known to the corporate advertisers sponsoring this program.

Sincerely,

• ADVERTISER COMPLAINT •

Dear Ms. May,

For ten years, my restaurant, India Palace, has been a regular advertiser in the *Star & Ledger*'s Dining Out section that appears in each Friday's edition. With three locations in town, we serve more Indian food to more of your readers than any other Indian restaurant in town.

That's why I was so disappointed when I read reporter Pete Nichol's roundup of Indian eateries in the December 11 edition and saw that India Palace was not included. Though he never came out and said so, Mr. Nichol's focus—perhaps his bias—was toward the more expensive Indian restaurants in town. Here at India Palace, we pride ourselves on being able to offer good food at a reasonable price, but we seem to have been penalized by Mr. Nichols for that approach.

I understand, of course, that being an advertiser doesn't entitle me to editorial favoritism. I'm not asking for any special favors. All I'm asking is that when you run such a story, you at least give India Palace the credit it deserves.

I can't tell you how many of my customers have come up to me, dismayed, wanting to know why Mr. Nichols omitted India Palace from the story. I hope that such oversights will not occur in the future. If they do, I will have to seriously consider a better use of my advertising dollars.

Sincerely,

• Complaining about Sports Coverage •

Dear Mr. Reese,

You can imagine my frustration when, after I enjoyed three innings of the Reds game on Saturday afternoon, your affiliate cut away to cover the Cardinals game.

No doubt there are demographic studies indicating that your broadcast area includes more Cardinals fans than Reds fans, and no doubt it's that greater number of Cardinals fans that your advertisers want to reach.

That said, I strongly disagree with your policy of cutting away from games in progress, regardless of the regional appeal of one game versus another. Like many diehard sports fans, when I sit down to watch a game, I'm making a commitment to watch the whole thing, and I expect an equal commitment from the broadcaster.

If your station is unable to make that commitment in the future, I'm perfectly willing to turn off the TV and listen to the radio instead. How might your advertisers feel about that?

Sincerely,

• REQUESTING EDITORIAL CORRECTION •

Dear Ms. May,

I'm writing with two corrections in the story about bass fishing that appeared on page E-6 in the Sunday, August 12, edition of the *Star & Ledger*.

In the third paragraph, the story states that Mike Levy won the 1995 Bass Master tournament at Lake Pillory. In fact, Mr. Levy won the event in 1985 (as the enclosed 1985 news clipping attests).

Also, the man identified as Mike Levy in the photograph is actually Denis McCoy, a longtime fishing associate and friend of Mr. Levy. I know, because that's me.

I hope you will see fit to print these corrections at your earliest convenience.

Sincerely,

• Requesting Editorial Retraction •

Dear Ms. May,

I'm writing to request a retraction of the story about Loren Jones that appeared on the front page of the Metro section in the Tuesday, August 14, edition of the *Star & Ledger*.

Despite the fact that my grandmother, Mrs. Jones, was never convicted of any wrongdoing, your reporter alleges that she was guilty of income tax fraud between 1993 and 1997. The story further implies that, thanks to her position in the state government, my grandmother was able to avoid scrutiny of the treasurer's office. However, nowhere in the story is evidence offered to substantiate this claim.

My grandmother is no longer here to defend herself, but I will not see her defamed in this fashion. Please publish a complete retraction of the story at the earliest opportunity and reprimand reporter Jessica Givens for her reliance on hearsay, rumor, and unnamed sources.

Sincerely,

• COMPLAINING TO PROGRAM'S SPONSOR •

Dear Ms. Griffin:

I was shocked to see your Gotchas, one of my favorite snacks, advertised during the broadcast of *Free for All.* My family and friends strongly urge you to reconsider that sponsorship and advertising decision.

We find the program particularly objectionable because it continually pokes fun at marriage and religious commitments. And we're surprised that a reputable company such as yours, which aims to reach the family market, would become associated with such a program.

If you cancel this advertisement and can persuade other sponsors to do the same, perhaps the TV network will be forced to drop the sitcom. The typical American household will certainly be the winner in that scenario.

We strongly urge you to consider this request so that we can continue to buy Gotchas in good conscience.

Sincerely,

• Supporting Editorial Position •

Dear Mr. Trang:

We applaud your position to repeal Legislative Bill H3889, commonly known as the Sit-Down Tax, and we thank you for highlighting this important issue in recent editorials.

Two years ago when they passed this bill, our state representatives focused on the least effective and most objectionable way to raise revenue. The intent of the bill was to rid our streets of the homeless, but the real effect of this bill has been to drive the homeless into shelters that are overcrowded and now dangerous themselves.

Thank you for investigating the far-reaching results of this law and bringing it to the attention of our lawmakers and our citizens.

Sincerely,

• CANCELING SUBSCRIPTION OVER POLITICAL ISSUE •

Dear Editor:

Please cancel our subscription to your newspaper, effective immediately. Although we've been subscribers for more than ten years, this past Sunday's editorial in support of redrawing our school district lines angered us to the point of taking drastic action.

My family and I, as well as those families I've spoken with in the community of Lakeview, oppose such gerrymandering of the school district on moral grounds. From the gist of the editorial, it is clear that the very few, but vocal, proponents of that action have racial discrimination as their primary purpose. That observation becomes very evident as one reviews the proposed new district lines, as mapped and distributed by the Lakeview Board of Education.

We believe that children need personal interactions with people of all races and economic conditions to teach them appreciation for the various cultures represented in our society. To redraw the lines solely to ensure that the races are kept separate smacks of the 1950s.

Frankly, we are shocked that your newspaper has taken such a stand. We hope you'll reconsider this position and take to higher moral ground with those readers who look to your newspaper as their only source of information.

Sincerely,

• SUBMITTING TO EVENT CALENDAR •

Dear Mr. Kim,

Please consider the following for a listing in the Datebook section of *Mt. Carmel Monthly*'s July issue.

What: Mt. Carmel Botanical Society 10th Annual Flower & Garden Show

Where: Mt. Carmel Botanical Society, 734 Pickle Lane

When: Saturday, July 11, 9 A.M. to 4 P.M.

Admission: free

For more information: Contact Mary Peters, president, 555-5555

In addition to an extensive display of plants and flowers—including the winners of our annual competition—we'll also have a plant sale with proceeds benefiting the Botanical Society's program to beautify highway medians in and around Mt. Carmel.

If I can provide you with any additional information for the listing, please let us know.

Sincerely,

• SUGGESTING STORY FOR COVERAGE •

Dear Ms. Ortiz:

I frequently travel out of the Dallas–Fort Worth airport and have few, if any, options for transportation home to the nearby city of Euless. It seems that taxi drivers think the minimum fare of $14 out of the airport is "peanuts" and often drive off and leave passengers standing on the curb when they discover their destination.

I, as well as several other Euless and Grapevine passengers, have been harassed, cursed, and detained by cabbies waiting on another, more profitable passenger to join me before they would agree to drive me to my destination. And after the shuttle services stop running at night, late travelers have no other options to get to their nearby homes.

When I've phoned and written the various cab companies (letters enclosed) to complain about their drivers refusing to accept a passenger going to Euless, the company officials all insist that their drivers are "required" to take passengers anywhere as long as they collect the minimum fare. But the company officials' statements to that effect do not ensure that their drivers comply. To my knowledge, they've taken no action to ensure that their cabs provide service to Euless.

I've also written our mayor (as suggested by one cabby) to petition the city to raise the minimum fare to ensure service to the community. To date, the mayor's office has not responded and no action has been taken.

I and my fellow midcities frequent flyers urge your help in investigating this frustrating, not to mention unsafe, situation.

Sincerely,

• Requesting Coverage of Event •

Dear Mr. Kim,

In July, the Mt. Carmel Botanical Society will be hosting its tenth annual flower and garden show. As a fan of your magazine's "Green Thumb" section, I thought this event might be of interest to many of your readers. Would you be interested in doing a story on the show?

There are several possible angles. Our annual competition includes many longtime rivalries among local gardeners. I'd be happy to put you in touch with two women who have been duking it out in the iris category for years. Your readers might be surprised to learn the lengths these contestants go to in order to capture the blue ribbon.

The Botanical Society's program to beautify highway medians in and around Mt. Carmel also offers a possible angle. No doubt most of your readers are familiar with the beautiful plantings at the main interchange just south of town. What used to be a garbage-strewn eyesore is now an inviting gateway to the metro area. Interestingly enough, the Botanical Society fought a long battle with the city council over this program—one that's still not over. An inside look at the politics surrounding such a seemingly innocuous program might make for interesting reading.

A third possible angle could involve Dora Spitz, a seventy-year-old gardener and charter member of the Society. What makes Dora's story unique is that she's blind. That's never kept her out of the garden, though, and it's never stopped her from winning at least one category every year since the show's inception. I've spoken with Dora, and she's more than willing to be the subject of a profile.

I hope you'll consider covering the show. If you'd like to discuss any of the above story possibilities or others, please call.

Sincerely,

• SUGGESTING EXPANDED COVERAGE •

Dear Ms. May,

As a ten-year resident of Greenville's east side, it has always troubled me that the *Star & Ledger* publishes special weekly sections for every part of town (Metro North, Metro South, and Metro West) except the east side.

I assume the absence of a weekly Metro East section has something to do with the economics of advertising—the fact that many of the city's poorest residents live on the east side, and the fact that we don't have the high-end restaurants and retail shops found elsewhere in the city.

Nevertheless, newsworthy happenings still occur here, and as the city's sole daily paper, the *Star & Ledger* has an obligation to cover that news in the same fashion that it covers news in other parts of the city.

Furthermore—though your editors seem not to have noticed— the east side is in the midst of an economic recovery. Eastland Mall has boosted its occupancy rate by more than 30 percent in the past two years, and new housing developments dot Macawber Boulevard between the mall and the highway interchange.

It is my sincere hope that your editorial staff will see fit to expand your coverage of the east side in the form of a Metro East section.

Regards,

• Offering Editorial Content •

Dear Ms. May,

Please consider the enclosed essay for publication in the *Star & Ledger*.

As a longtime subscriber, I've always enjoyed the local, first-person essays that appear in the *Star & Ledger*'s Focus section each Sunday. However, it wasn't until the city began considering another property tax increase that I felt moved to put in my two cents.

I think my essay deserves special consideration because, unlike other essays you've published on the topic, mine argues in favor of the tax increase. I think it's high time the residents of Greenville acknowledge the value of services provided by the city and recognize that those services don't come cheap.

Please note that I don't consider myself a writer, and should you choose to publish this piece, I would welcome the guidance and input of your editors.

Thank you,

• VOLUNTEERING EDITORIAL SERVICES •

Dear Ms. May,

I'm writing to offer my services as a book reviewer for the *Star & Ledger*.

As a longtime subscriber, I've noticed that you often use local writers to review books. I've always preferred to read the opinions of fellow Greenville residents as opposed to the syndicated book reviews out of New York, which often consist of little more than plot summary and don't reflect a "Greenville sensibility."

For the record, I've read at least a book a week for most of my adult life and have a broad range of interests that encompasses fiction, nonfiction, and poetry. To give you a sense of my work, I'm enclosing two sample reviews of recent hardcover releases.

Thanks for your time and consideration.

Sincerely,

• Volunteering for Community Panel •

Dear Ms. May,

I'm answering your call for volunteers to serve on the *Star & Ledger*'s readers' panel.

Though I've been a resident of Greenville for only five years, I read the paper from cover to cover every day and follow local politics closely. Furthermore, I've lived in eight cities over the past twenty years and have developed, I believe, a good sense of what makes a first-rate daily in terms of balance, coverage, and a paper's ability to reflect the particular concerns of its readers.

Please send me your application questionnaire. Should you choose me for the panel, I would look forward to sharing my views with your editorial board at the monthly roundtables.

Sincerely,

OPINIONS AND POLITICS

Only those who communicate with their elected leaders have the right to complain when events don't suit them. Change comes from persistent, clear communication from the communities that cast the ballots.

So to grab attention and get action, describe yourself as a voter, supporter of the cause, taxpayer, citizen, business executive, organizational spokesperson, industry leader, or some other label that underscores your leadership role and intention to influence others.

> *"I'm writing because, as a teacher and coach, I see every day in the classroom and on the court and hear from parents that..."*
>
> *"I'll be addressing those leaders in my industry at an upcoming seminar and want to be able to summarize your position about..."*
>
> *"As I travel around the state speaking on community college campuses, I often discover that..."*

Refer to the political issue or legislative bill by its popular title or by a number or referendum. Use any such number or title in a reference line above the body of the letter as well as in the body of the letter itself.

State specifically the action you want from your readers. Do you want them to vote for or against? Do you want money or an investigation? Do you want them to fund or stop funding a cause? Do you want them to introduce a bill or kill it in committee? Then elaborate on the reason behind your opinion or request for action.

When your expertise will grab attention, use it. Expand on your credentials or experience with regard to a position on a technical issue.

"As a biochemist with 15 years of research in..."

"As a parent of four teenagers in our school system..."

"As a volunteer having served in a number of positions in this industry during the past 20 years..."

Expand your clout by letting readers know of your intention to make others aware of their position, reply, or action (or inaction).

"I will be publishing your statement in a monthly letter to our members."

"We will be including your views in announcements we send home with our students."

"I plan to incorporate your response in my speech to the officers of our group."

Remember that politicians focus only on one issue at a time. So focus your comments on only the most pressing matter; save other issues and problems until later letters.

Finally, nothing motivates people for a repeat performance more than recognition and gratitude. When you appreciate a politician's or community leader's efforts or position, say so and be specific about the commendation. Performance rewarded is performance repeated.

• TO THE PRESIDENT—SUPPORTING BILL OR ISSUE •

The Honorable President of the United States
1600 Pennsylvania Avenue
Washington, DC 20510

Dear Mr. President:

Building a strong armed forces to ensure peace in the new millennium in a global marketplace will be the primary challenge of your presidency. You have campaigned hard on this issue and won my support. That support this past year took the form of monetary contributions to your campaign fund, attendance at political rallies, telephone canvassing, and public speeches as a member of my local city council.

A strong armed forces means that our country can respond to aggressors who determine that they will unexpectedly invade their smaller neighbors and rape the natural resources of the land. A strong armed forces means that our country can protect its own citizens who wish to live or travel abroad. A strong armed forces means that foreign demagogues will consider the cost and loss before violating human rights of their own citizens. Finally, a strong armed forces ensures that our economic interests are protected around the world.

I urge you not to let this issue take a back seat to other domestic problems and issues put before you by special-interests groups. My family, coworkers, and civic colleagues will be keenly aware of your leadership as the military funding bills are presented to Congress during your new term.

Thank you for your past years of service to the country.

Respectfully,

• TO LEGISLATOR •

Congratulating on Passage of Legislation

The Honorable Robin Fernandez
Texas Senate
Austin, TX 78710

RE: S7898-88

Dear Senator Fernandez:

We want to offer our congratulations on the successful passage of the recent tax bill to raise revenue to improve our state highway system. When things don't go well, I'm sure you hear from your constituents loudly and frequently, so we wanted you to know that we are pleased with your sponsorship of the bill and your skillful guiding of that bill through the Senate.

With the outspoken special-interest groups crying "foul" about the speed limits, you faced incredible odds against getting your message to the citizenry. The effort you spent in calling press conferences, from which excerpts were aired in prime time, certainly helped voters understand the real issues.

Keep up the good work on the behalf of all the citizens in our state.

Sincerely,

• To Legislator •

Opposing Bill or Issue

The Honorable Dolores Fregosi
U.S. Senate
Washington, DC 20510

RE: HR 98989

Dear Senator Fregosi:

I strongly oppose the idea of federally funded day-care centers built in corporate environments around the country. If the bill now before Congress (HR 98989) passes, this day-care system will cost taxpayers an estimated $8 billion annually, according to a recent article in *Time* magazine.

Am I antifamily? Am I anti-working mothers? No. I'm a single parent with two small children of day-care age. Despite the "convenience" of dropping my children off every day as I go to my management job with a large oil company, I fear the government intrusion into our free-enterprise system. If the government built such day-care centers on corporate sites with the proposed tax credits, the next round of regulations would involve the government telling the corporations how much tuition to charge their employees and then helping them formulate "policies" about sickness, discipline problems, and "bridging" from one corporation's day care to another after termination of employment. In other words, the intrusion and complexities will grow.

Would you please let me know how you plan to vote on this issue? As a manager of the human resources function in our corporation, I will be updating our employees about your comments and voting record on this important legislation.

Sincerely,

• TO LEGISLATOR •

Protesting Tax Increase

RE: State Senate Bill S9399932

The Honorable Gene L. Cornwall

Dear Senator Cornwall:

As a long-time worker in your past election campaigns, I strongly protest the proposed 3-cents-a-gallon increase in gasoline taxes now under consideration in our state legislature.

This tax unfairly penalizes commuters who live in small towns and must drive to the larger metropolitan areas for work. Instead, I propose an increase in the luxury tax to raise the revenues we need in the state. Such a tax would place the burden of the tax on those who can best afford it, as evidenced by their purchase of luxury cars, furs, and recreational vehicles.

I urge you to vote no when this bill comes up on the senate floor. Please respond to me about your views on this tax issue.

Sincerely,

• To Legislator •

Asking for Help

The Honorable Calvin Dernier
U.S. House of Representatives
Washington, DC 20510

Dear Congressman Dernier:

Congratulations on your recent reelection. You have an excellent record of supporting the concerns and needs of the elderly. That's why, during your campaign, three of my letters to the editors of our local newspapers were published, stating why I urged voters to support you in your reelection efforts.

Now that you've achieved your mission, I'd like to ask your help in achieving mine. My 70-year-old mother (diabetic, confined to a wheelchair, and a recent widow) is having great difficulty in finding an apartment on the HUD-approved and subsidized list. It seems that all apartment complexes in our city of Edmonton have waiting lists, and their managers estimate the wait for an apartment to be six to 12 months.

Specifically, the Elrod Apartment Complex, located at 477 Center Street and managed by Curt Bush, is refusing even to add my mother's name to the list because of the long wait. I might add that Mr. Bush has been rather surly, stating blatantly that he tries not to rent to anyone who needs wheelchair access to central areas because of the "traffic" problems on the sidewalks.

I'd appreciate your help in providing a list of all HUD-approved housing available in our city and investigating the Elrod Apartment Complex specifically to ensure that this manager complies with government regulations with regard to unbiased award of the apartments to future tenants.

(Continued)

Enclosed is my mother's application, including the financial information required.

Please respond to me at the above address and phone number. Thank you for any help you can provide in finding my mother HUD housing.

Sincerely,

• To Legislator •

Supporting Campaign for Office

Dear Mr. Metty:

We are behind your bid for Congress 100 percent. Thank you for your stand on returning order to our classrooms by giving teachers and school administrators the laws they need to earn the respect of their students and to create a learning environment.

Second, we believe in your stand against forbidding public prayer in the classroom and think your pro-life position for the unborn will help rebuild the moral fiber in our marriages and family. We strongly reaffirm the separation of church and state, and we value human life in all forms.

Would you send us your literature summarizing your stand on these issues, as well as your position on other issues facing our country? We plan to duplicate and distribute copies of your campaign platform to our church groups and to the 1100 employees in our business.

If you need additional volunteers for telephone canvassing in the evening hours, please have someone on your staff contact us. We look forward to working with you at the grassroots level to change the future of our country.

Sincerely,

• TO LEGISLATOR •

Regretting Election Defeat

Dear Mayor Pagnozzi:

We are deeply disappointed by last week's vote and regret that you will not be serving another term as our mayor. As you make your plans to leave office, we want you to know how much we have appreciated your leadership.

Specifically, we want to highlight the many accomplishments of your past two terms: the expansion of our park system, the revenue-generating arrangement for summer youth activities, the excellent condition of our once pothole-filled streets. The most significant accomplishments have to do with your positioning the city to attract major corporations here. As a result of your work, we've seen numerous corporations (Wal-Mart, JCPenney, Honeywell, and Steinmart) move into our city limits, thereby significantly expanding our tax base.

The citizens of Harrisburg owe you a great deal. Thank you for your service to the community these past eight years.

Sincerely,

• To Legislator •

Supporting Bond Issue

Dear Representative Santovenia:

As a well-informed citizen and resident of Minnesota, I favor the construction of the TGV train between Foster and Mackentown. No doubt the completion of such an undertaking will save Minnesota residents an infinite sum of money in the long run, not to mention prevent an inestimable number of highway fatalities, as well as aid the protection of the environment.

I am confident that you will continue to champion the construction of the TGV despite others who may shortsightedly protest it. I would like to congratulate you for standing firm so far, and encourage you to persist in your efforts.

I, myself, am well acquainted with traveling Highway 287 between Foster and Mackentown on a regular basis. My family lives in Foster, and when I was a college student at the University of Mackentown, it seemed as though I was always driving that expanse of road. I saw countless accidents and was even in a minor one myself. I now occasionally travel this route on business, and in addition to my personal safety, I have become increasingly concerned with the environmental damage caused by the heavy traffic that frequents this highway.

The TGV could eradicate these problems, which will only worsen as Minnesota's population grows. Support this objective, and you will win my reelection vote.

Your loyal constituent,

• REQUESTING INFORMATION ON RUNNING FOR OFFICE •

Dear County Election Commissioner,

After years of being frustrated at all the gridlock in local politics, I've decided to do something about it. Next fall, I plan to run for city council as an independent candidate. Please send me instructions on how to file for office as well any required forms and petitions.

Sincerely,

• REQUESTING POLITICAL INTRODUCTION •

Dear Jim,

I've decided to run for city council next year and would really appreciate your help. In preparation for my campaign, I'm hoping to consult with a few key people who know the local political scene. Would you be willing to arrange a meeting for me with Councilwoman Janet Alderman?

Councilwoman Alderman has long been a hero of mine, and her commitment to nonpartisanship and compromise has inspired me to build my platform on those very same themes. That said, I know that you and Janet have been friends for years, and the last thing I want to do is jeopardize that friendship. So if you're uncomfortable arranging an introduction, I completely understand.

Thanks for your time and consideration.

Regards,

• REQUESTING POLITICAL ADVICE •

Nick,

I've recently decided to run for city council next year and was hoping you could advise me as I begin putting my campaign together. I'm especially interested in any thoughts you have on the electability of an independent candidate in a town so thoroughly dominated by partisan politics. Over the years, your views and opinions on the local political scene have greatly influenced my own, and I can think of no person who could provide more trusted guidance than you. If you're inclined to help out a like-minded political neophyte, I hope you'll give me a call.

Regards,

• Invitation to Join Campaign •

Dear Alice,

I've recently decided to run for city council next year and would like for you to serve as my election chairman. I believe the council needs somebody like me, but in order to get there, I need somebody like you: smart, committed, energetic, and resourceful.

My main goal is to help break the gridlock that has crippled the council these past two sessions, and to that end I'll be campaigning on a platform that emphasizes nonpartisanship and compromise. If you feel as passionately about transforming our city council as I do, I'd be grateful for your help in the campaign.

Give me a call if you're interested so we can get together to discuss the details.

Regards,

• ENCOURAGING VOTER TURNOUT •

Dear Constituent,

On November 7, I'll be running for city council as an independent candidate. My main goal is to break the partisan gridlock that has crippled the council for the past four years.

If you feel as passionately about transforming our city council as I do, I'd be grateful for your vote on election day. Working together, we can once again make our local politicians serve you, the citizens of Collinwood—and not the other way around.

Sincerely,

PARENTAL CONCERNS

Rearing children means having to say you're sorry, having to express appreciation, having to offer explanations, and having to request action by or information from schools, sports clubs, and governmental agencies.

In these various situations, you'll need to summarize your commendation, complaint, request, or permission in a sentence or two at the beginning of the letter.

"I'm writing to suggest an investigation into why..."

"I need some information about your plans to..."

"I want to commend you on the way in which you have..."

"We're having difficulty understanding your recent policy to..."

Be specific when requesting corrective action or resolution of a problem.

Remember to use your child's full legal name in any reference, especially if the last name differs from yours. For formal matters, include this information in a reference line. Also include dates of past or future attendance at the school and any other identifying information for quick recall and association, such as "enrolled in Mr. Turner's ESL classes in the after-school program."

And be sure to alert the school or religious officials to any potential danger and any precautions you are suggesting in relation to your child's safety or health.

In sensitive situations, make it clear whether the information you are supplying should be kept confidential from your child. Or state whether your child has been given the same explanation or instructions as you are giving the school or religious organization. For example:

"I have not told Susan that I was writing you about her condition."

"I'd appreciate it if you'd not mention to Susan our discussion."

"Thank you for being discreet in any action you take so that others will not isolate Susan for this condition."

"You may feel free to discuss this matter with Susan; she is aware that I will be contacting you about her grades and absences."

Don't take it for granted that a teacher, coach, or other leader would understand exactly how such matters should be handled with the child and others involved.

On the happy occasions when you are commending individuals, be specific; make sure they know what they did to get the good rating. Specific comments give readers time to reflect on and "enjoy" the details once again. Consider the "afterglow" following such specific remarks as these:

"Your thoughtfulness in remaining out on the curb until I arrived was very much appreciated."

"We appreciate the care you take in giving thorough instructions to the students who seem behind in the class."

"Thank you for wording your disciplinary action in such a tactful way before the class."

"Thank you for the inordinate amount of time such tournaments must require."

When the situation has become or could become a negative one, use a supportive and firm, but nonconfrontational tone. Commend the organization, if appropriate, for past actions, standards, concerns, and accomplishments.

"Thank you for investigating this situation and reporting back to me about the action you've taken."

"We hope these suggestions will eliminate the ambiguities in the ways the policies have been enforced."

"We're looking forward to a more rewarding semester in the spring."

"I'm hopeful that this clarifies our position with regard to Susan's absence."

Above all, keep in mind that a careless or carefully chosen word or phrase can drastically affect the treatment your children receive—and the situation in which they thrive or survive. Write with their future welfare in mind.

APPRECIATION

• TO COACH OR GYM TEACHER •

Dear Coach Trillo:

We want to express our thanks for making our son, Turk Sutcliffe, feel a part of the basketball team this year. If you recall, Turk transferred into the district in late October just after you had officially ended tryouts. You agreed to make an exception and let him try out for the team the following week, and fortunately you selected him for the starting lineup. That exception, in itself, could have created jealousies among other students.

We, as well as Turk, feared that might be the case. But as the season began, you planned some very important team-building "bonding" experiences for the boys as you traveled to various tournaments to scout the opposition. Those trips especially gave the team members a chance to get to know Turk quickly one on one off the court. Those opportunities made the transition much easier for him in the new school.

By the way, I might add that his grades have reflected a comfortable adjustment as well.

As you may have guessed, changing schools in the middle of the year is never a good situation for any student, but for an athlete it can be disastrous. Such was not the case for Turk this year, thanks to you. We do appreciate your constant encouragement, your competent coaching, and your efforts to see that the college scouts take a look at your athletes. What more could parents ask?

Sincerely,

• To Private Instructor •

Susan,

Lenny has been taking swim lessons for three years, but it wasn't until he enrolled in your class that he finally conquered his fear of water. I really appreciate your being so patient with him and working so hard to boost his confidence. The additional instruction you gave him after class really made a difference. Lenny is already looking forward to taking your Level 4 class next summer.

Cordially,

• TO TEACHER •

Dear Ms. Palmeiro:

We so much appreciate the special attention you have given to Keith while he has been hospitalized off and on throughout the year. As you know, such extended absences can play havoc with a child's relationships with other students, and you have been particularly sensitive to making Keith feel a part of the group when he was able to be in class.

Specifically, I want to thank you for the several occasions when you gave the other children time to make cards and write notes to Keith. Not only were you teaching your fourth-graders penmanship and writing skills, you were teaching them to care about other people. That, I'm sure, is a direct reflection of your own personal commitment to your students.

And what a wonderful idea to videotape their class parties and special days to send home for Keith. Although he sometimes watched through tears of disappointment that he could not be part of the festivities, those tapes kept him in touch with his friends during a very difficult time.

I'm sure teachers hear complaints from time to time, but I wanted you to know that we in our household and neighborhood are certainly singing your praises. Thank you so much for your dedication.

Sincerely,

• To Parent of Child's Friend •

Juanita,

I just wanted to thank you for seeing that Roscoe had such a wonderful time at Cynthia's birthday party. It's not easy being the youngest child at a party, especially when all of the other children are at least two years older and considerably bigger. By giving Roscoe a little extra "help" with the piñata, you really made him feel like he belonged with the big kids. He told me he had even more fun at Cynthia's party than at his own!

Cordially,

• TO BABY-SITTER •

Dear Kelly:

Just a note to let you know how much we appreciate the care you're providing to Jason and Jaylee. When my husband drops by to pick them up each day after work, they jump in the car so full of enthusiasm and so excited to tell him about the day's activities.

Many baby-sitters envision their jobs as simply to meet the physical needs of the kids and ensure the children's safety while under their supervision. You, on the other hand, have shown so many evidences of understanding and providing for the kids' mental growth and emotional development. The "art" projects, the games, the snacks, the story times—all these special activities require supplies and extra time for preparation and cleanup, not to mention patience.

Thanks so much for all your extra efforts with our children. When they're happy, we're happy.

Cordially,

• To Daycare Facility •

Dear Ms. Gore,

Thanks so much for making the After School Club such a welcoming and stimulating place for Cleo. Since you introduced him to word puzzles, he's become a real whiz. And I've also noticed he's much more interested in reading, thanks to some of the books you've recommended. Sometimes I even think he learns more at daycare than he does during school. That's a very comforting thought for a working mother who misses being home in the afternoon with her son.

Regards,

• MEDICAL •

Dear Dr. House,

Arthur was more than a little wary about his checkup last week, but you did a beautiful job of putting him at ease. When you handed over your stethoscope and let *him* examine *you*, I knew he was in the hands of a doctor who really understands children. He has certainly never taken a shot so well—much less two! Thanks for taking the time to make Arthur feel good about going to the doctor's office; you not only did him a favor, you did a favor to all the future doctors in his life.

Sincerely,

• To Neighbor for Watching Child •

Sue,

Thanks so much for watching Rebekah after school these last few weeks while I conducted my job search. As we discussed, I didn't want to select a day-care center and make permanent arrangements until I knew for sure whether we'd be staying in this neighborhood. Now that I've found a job so close by, I will, of course, enroll Rebekah in Kindercare down the street.

Your baby-sitting help gave me just the freedom I needed to schedule interviews and do the necessary library research on the companies I wanted to approach for a job. I left home every day with peace of mind in knowing you would keep Rebekah safe and happy. Please let me know when I can return the favor. I'll be eagerly looking for that opportunity.

With gratefulness,

COMPLAINTS

• To Coach or Gym Teacher •

Dear Ms. Burnell:

We appreciate your physical education goals; you have succeeded in making your students aware of the importance of regular exercise and proper diet to their overall health and appearance. I'm writing, however, to call your attention to a frustration for the girls in Periods 1 to 5: They are having difficulty getting showered and dressed and to their next class before the tardy bell rings.

I can imagine that you have some students who take advantage of every opportunity to "lolligag" between classes, talking to boyfriends in the hall or sharing their weekend adventures with classmates. But for other students who are making an honest effort to get to their classes on time (without receiving penalty points for tardies), they need the full eight minutes after gym class to dress for their next class. On three recent occasions (January 5, 15, and 18), my daughter, Elena Rousch, says they had less than three minutes after the time you dismissed them to make their next class.

On January 18, her science teacher deducted 15 points from her test grade because she arrived to science class five minutes late, after being dismissed late from gym class.

Would you please give careful attention to finding a way to complete the class exercises so that the girls are dismissed when the bell rings? I'll appreciate your efforts in alleviating this stressful situation for those girls trying to be prompt students. Thank you.

Sincerely,

• To Private Instructor •

Dear Ms. Lynn,

Corrine's confidence at the piano has grown exponentially since she began taking lessons with you, and not only does she feel better about her playing, her playing itself is much improved. I worry, though, that 90 minutes of practice a day is a bit much. Her grades have begun to suffer, and I think it's because she's spending less time on homework and more time on the piano.

The last thing I want to do is squelch Corrine's interest in music, which is why I'm turning to you, the person she most trusts and admires when it comes to the piano. Would you be willing to assign her less practice time? It probably wouldn't hurt if she also heard from you how important schoolwork is. I look forward to us working together to make sure Corrine reaches her full potential as both a scholar *and* a pianist.

Sincerely,

• TO TEACHER •

Dear Mr. Hayes:

I want to make you aware of the difficulty my daughter, Callie Gossage, is having finding library resources to complete her research papers for your Period 6 history class. The requirement to have ten books and 15 articles as sources for the paper demands that students go outside the school library to find other resources, and that has posed an undue hardship on the family because of our work schedule and transportation situation.

I have a suggestion: Would you consider putting some of the more popular resource books and periodicals on reserve in the library so that all students have equal opportunity to use them during their study periods and before and after school hours? For students like Callie, that is the only time they have available in any library.

I understand that some students may wait until the last minute to try to locate reference materials and then complain that all available books are already checked out of the school library. But with the Period 6 students, that often is the case. By the time this class group meets and receives your assignments, students from other periods have already checked out all available sources in the school library.

Callie understands you to say that they should be able to use their own home computers for online research, but all students, I fear, don't have home computers with Internet access. Callie doesn't. And although Callie is old enough to drive, she doesn't have her own car. Both her father and I have to make alternative travel plans to allow her use of the car in the evenings. During the weekends, she works at her part-time job.

(Continued)

Callie and I would very much appreciate your attention to resolve this issue. And thank you for your commitment to preparing your students for college and teaching them to express themselves adequately in writing.

Sincerely,

• TO PRINCIPAL ABOUT TEACHER •

Dear Mr. DeVille:

I am writing for your intervention in a matter involving my son, Bret Hurst, and his English teacher, Nancy Platt. Bret continually brings home excellent English grades, yet he doesn't seem to understand the grammar and writing rules he is supposed to be learning in Ms. Platt's class. I'm concerned that her instruction is inadequate and that her review and grading of compositions is cursory.

I'd like to request that Bret be moved into another English class for the remainder of the year. If it is necessary for me to discuss the matter with you in person, please phone me (555-5555) to schedule a meeting time most convenient to our mutual schedules.

Let me explain why I am concerned about the English class: First, the test questions themselves contain misspellings and grammatical errors. (I've attached two such tests with the errors circled.) Second, Bret's compositions contain misspellings and grammatical errors that have gone unnoticed and uncorrected. (I've also enclosed two such essays for which Bret received As.) I realize that teachers do not routinely mark all errors on a composition, but instead focus on two or three skills or grammatical rules for each effort. But as you'll notice from what I've marked, a ninth-grade student should certainly be made aware of sentence fragments and misspellings in a paper, even if the student is not penalized for those errors.

Thank you for considering this change request for Bret. His writing skills are extremely important to his future, and I want to ensure that he has a master teacher.

Sincerely,

• To Principal about Disruptive Student •

Dear Principal Dawson:

The after-school wait for the second bus has become an ordeal for my daughter, Jean Schumacher. Another student, Mike Ruffin, who also waits for the second bus to Hogan Town, has repeatedly hit her, teased her, and generally made her life miserable for the past three months.

During the last incident, on Monday, November 6, he struck her with a baseball bat, attempting to "bat" her books out of her arms. As a result, she missed her bus trying to collect school papers that went flying across the lawn, and came home with bruises. Although the bruises were not serious enough to seek medical help, this situation needs your immediate attention.

I'm requesting that you observe Mike Ruffin's behavior, and if changes don't occur, that he be restricted from riding the same school bus as Jean.

If you asked Mike Ruffin whether he intended to assault my daughter, I'm sure he would say no. His antics, according to him, are all in fun. And giving him the benefit of the doubt about the incident with the bat, I know that he didn't intend to strike Jean's shoulders, but only her books. Nevertheless, his attempts to tease have gotten out of hand.

Please let me know what action or precautions you've taken about the situation. Jean wants to "handle" the situation on her own, because she fears being labeled a "tattler." Therefore, I'd ask you not to let her know that I've requested your help to correct this situation. Thank you for your commitment to provide a safe school environment.

Sincerely,

• TO PRINCIPAL PROTESTING UNFAIR DISCIPLINARY ACTION •

Dear Mr. Peacock:

My stepson, Frank Templeton, was recently disciplined with in-school suspension from January 6 to 16 for leaving campus without permission on January 3. I think that once you review the details of the situation more carefully, you will agree that this action is unwarranted and unfair.

On behalf of my son, I respectfully request that this decision be reversed immediately. Otherwise, I will be forced to appeal to the school board for a ruling.

Once again, let me explain the situation from our perspective. Your memo to the parents about the new restrictions on leaving campus was dated and sent home with the students on December 18. Your announcement of the change in policy was made to the students over the public address system on December 17 and 18. However, my stepson did not attend school after December 16; we left town early to be with our family in Canada during the holidays. His first day back at school was January 3—the day he left campus for lunch with his brother, who works nearby, as he has done on and off for the past two years.

Yes, Frank may have heard other students complain about the rumor of the new campus restrictions before he left town, but he had forgotten about the restrictions during the intervening holidays. We, as parents, never received the notice sent home on December 18 because of our trip to Canada.

We believe the in-school suspension is unduly harsh, particularly in light of the fact that Frank has not had past difficulties in following school rules. I understand your position in wanting all

(Continued)

students to know that you intend to enforce the new policy, but "making an example" of Frank will build more animosity than compliance.

I've written rather than phoned to let you have a few moments to investigate and verify the facts as I have stated them. I can assure you that Frank and I will keep the details of your review of his situation confidential so as not to create any loss of face about a reversal in the situation. Would you please phone me today at my work number (555-5555) to let me know of your decision?

Sincerely,

• TO DAYCARE FACILITY •

Dear Ms. Gore,

I'm writing regarding the level of supervision offered at the After School Club. My son, Cleo Pickens, has been enrolled there since the beginning of the semester. In that time, he has come home with a sprained ankle, a mild concussion, and numerous scrapes and bruises. One of his friends, Darrin Jackson, suffered a broken arm, and another friend, Billy Hatcher, sustained a cut on his foot that required fifteen stitches.

I know young boys like to play hard, and I know you and your staff can't be there to catch every child every time he or she falls. I also know that your staff size meets the minimum requirements set forth by the state.

I nevertheless would like to see you improve the level of supervision you provide, especially for outdoor activities. As one of Connerville's more expensive after-school daycare centers, the After School Club could certainly afford to hire at least one more staff member to help keep a closer eye on the children.

Would you be willing to meet with me and the parents of Darrin and Billy to further discuss this matter? I can be reached during the day at the work number below, or we could set up a meeting when I come to pick up Cleo after work on Monday.

Regards,

• MEDICAL •

Dear Dr. Foote,

I've always appreciated the high level of dental care you provide for my family. You seem truly committed not only to keeping our teeth healthy, but to making sure our visits to your office are enjoyable as well.

That's why I'm writing to you about my son, Donald Calloway, and his annual cleaning and exam on March 11. Donnie had a new hygienist, Maria, and the experience was not a positive one. In addition to flossing Donnie's teeth so roughly that he cried, Maria was impatient and rude, repeatedly telling Donnie to stop whining and act his age.

I'm sure that cleaning a child's teeth is trying work, but I think a hygienist should at least be professional and patient. I'm writing to ask that Donnie and my daughter, Clara, be assigned a different hygienist in the future and that Maria receive whatever training is needed so that she can work more effectively with children.

Thank you,

• TO PARENT OF CHILD'S FRIEND •

Juanita,

I was so sorry to hear things didn't go well for Roscoe at Cynthia's birthday party. I know you must have had your hands full with twelve ice-cream-fueled kids running around. That said, it's never easy being the youngest kid at a party, and I think Roscoe would have benefited from just a little help finding his place among the older children. Not being able to reach the piñata left him feeling especially small and embarrassed.

Will you do what you can to make him feel more comfortable next time he's over? He really looks up to Cynthia and wants so badly to fit in with her circle of "big kid" friends.

Sincerely,

SCHOOL

• NOTIFYING SCHOOL OF CHILD'S RIGHTFUL GUARDIANS •

To School Officials:

This letter is to inform you that we, Tim and Kiana Boudreau, are the legal guardians of your third-grade student, Tate Allen, assigned to Mr. Zindler's homeroom class. The custody suit between Tate's estranged father and us has at last been resolved in our favor.

With this letter, we are alerting you to the possibility that his father or another family member may make an effort to contact him during the school day. We ask that you continue to enforce your policy of a child's release only to the legal guardians in all cases.

Thank you for your efforts to enforce these policies, which make the lives of your students safe and less stressful for all concerned.

Sincerely,

• REQUESTING MEETING WITH TEACHER •

Ms. Ryan,

I would like to schedule a meeting with you to discuss Joanna Morgan's progress in your class.

I understand from calling the school office that your conference period runs from 3:30 to 4:15. Tuesday or Thursday afternoons will work best for me, but I can arrange to meet you another day of the week if that is necessary. Please leave a message on my home recorder (555-5555) suggesting a convenient meeting time. Thank you.

Sincerely,

• REQUESTING CLASSROOM VISIT •

Dear Dr. Carpicke,

My wife and I would like to visit one of your Early Childhood 2 classrooms. Our daughter, Penelope Anderson, is applying for admission to the EC2 program in the fall.

Would it be possible for us to come one morning during the week of March 5–9? We've heard wonderful things about your teachers and students, and seeing them in action together will help us make an informed choice when admissions decisions are announced next month.

Sincerely,

• REQUESTING INFORMATION ABOUT PRIVATE SCHOOL •

Dear Ms. Langley:

I'm considering enrolling my children in St. Thomas's for the upcoming fall semester. Marie Ella will be entering the third grade, and Darnell is in the fifth grade. Having recently moved to the area from Boston, I'm afraid I have very little information about your school, its accreditations, and its academic standing in the community.

Would you please forward to me a packet of information, including tuition costs, required immunizations and other medical records, bus transportation options, accreditations, and extracurricular activities available to students? If you have information about parents' support organizations, that would be helpful as well.

We're looking forward to learning more about your school.

Sincerely,

NOTES OF ABSENCE AND GYM EXCUSES

• EXPLAINING CHILD'S ABSENCE •

Illness or Injury

Dear Ms. Greenaway,

Please excuse Sissy's absences on March 2 to 4. She had a bad case of influenza, and her doctor suggested complete bed rest. We'll appreciate your permitting her to complete any assignment she has missed and giving her study time before she has to take any tests over topics discussed during her absence.

Thank you,

• EXPLAINING CHILD'S ABSENCE •

Death in Family

Mr. Caldwell:

Archie Corando has been absent for the past three days (May 6 to 8) because her grandfather passed away. I ask your understanding and patience in the next few days if she seems distracted and fearful. I'll also appreciate any help you can give her in making up her work. Specifically, she was concerned about her math grades and missing your in-class explanations of the word problems. Thank you for your extra help during this time.

Sincerely,

• EXPLAINING CHILD'S ABSENCE •

Family Business

Dear Ms. Hendricks:

Evan Riley, in Tony Wilk's homeroom, missed school on Friday (September 6) and Monday (September 9) to accompany both my wife and me on out-of-town business.

We respectfully request that you excuse his absence on this occasion. We are very mindful that regular attendance is important to a child's overall school success. But we decided that since we are so close to the beginning of the school year this brief absence would have minimal effect on Evan's ability to keep up with his class.

My wife had the opportunity to attend a convention in Orlando as part of her work assignment, and we decided to take the entire family along and complete the handling of my father's estate. As executor of his will, I have had many obligations since his recent death and very little time to be out of town to attend to the matter.

We hope you'll agree to excuse our son's absence to accompany us out of town. Thank you for your commitment to academic excellence for all our students.

Sincerely,

• EXPLAINING CHILD'S ABSENCE •

Vacation

Dear Mr. Trujillo,

Penelope Anderson will be absent from your second-grade class during the week of October 12–16 for a family reunion in Austin, Texas.

I'm writing to ask that these missed days be counted as excused absences. Though I recognize the value of regular attendance, I think it's important that Penelope spend time with her family members, many of whom she sees only once every few years. (Some are coming from as far away as Alaska and London.)

In addition to her making up any missed work, I've suggested that she research and compile a family history during the reunion. If you'd like to make this a formal assignment, I'd be happy to see that she reaps the full educational benefit that such a family gathering can provide.

Sincerely,

• ALERTING GYM TEACHER TO CHILD'S PHYSICAL LIMITATIONS •

Dear Mr. Halsey:

Stefan Beers has been assigned to your Period 2 physical education class, and I wanted to let you know of his physical limitations, which may not be obvious from immediate observation. He suffers from chronic asthma and has severe attacks after long periods of physical exertion. However, he hesitates to call attention to that condition for fear of being teased by the other students.

When you observe that he is becoming short of breath, please permit him to stop exercising immediately. His attacks after such exertion have required hospitalization and oxygen tanks on several occasions. (Enclosed is a letter from his physician attesting to this condition and his limitations.)

Thank you for being mindful of Stefan's condition during your PE classes and handling the matter discreetly.

Sincerely,

• EXCUSING CHILD FROM GYM FOR ILLNESS OR INJURY •

Mrs. Earp:

Would you please permit Joelle Munich (Period 5) to "sit out" during the dance routines for the rest of this week? She twisted her knee in a ski accident over the weekend and is still having some swelling. The doctor assures us that it's only a pulled muscle that will heal with time and rest. Thank you for your attention to her condition. She enjoys your class very much.

Cordially,

SPECIAL CIRCUMSTANCES AT SCHOOL

• DIETARY RESTRICTIONS •

Dear Dr. Carpicke,

I'm writing regarding the special dietary needs of our daughter, Penelope Anderson, who is enrolled is Mrs. Tucker's Early Childhood 2 class.

Penelope was recently diagnosed with a peanut allergy. As you may know, even trace amounts of peanut can cause an allergic person to experience symptoms ranging from mild swelling to vomiting and nausea to death.

We'll be preparing bag lunches for Penelope so you and your staff needn't worry about providing special meals. Also, Penelope is aware of her condition and knows to avoid peanuts.

However, avoiding peanuts isn't always easy, as they are sometimes identified on food labels under different names such as "hydrolysed vegetable protein" or "groundnuts." I'm asking that you exercise extreme caution in situations where Penelope comes into contact with food, whether it be from other students, during snack time, or on field trips.

I'm enclosing an information sheet detailing other symptoms of an allergic reaction, treatment procedures, and emergency contact numbers for my wife and Penelope's grandparents.

Thanks so much for your help in keeping our daughter safe and healthy.

Sincerely,

CC: Angelina Tucker

• HEARING IMPAIRMENT •

Dear Dr. Carpicke,

My daughter, Penelope Anderson, a student in Mrs. Tucker's Early Childhood 2 class, was recently diagnosed with moderate hearing loss in her right ear.

After consulting with her doctor and an audiologist, we've decided not to fit her with a hearing aid. As you know, her language skills are exceptional, and unless her hearing loss worsens, her impairment should be no problem in school.

However, I do hope you and Mrs. Tucker will take a couple of simple steps to accommodate Penelope. She will be better able to hear if she is seated at the front of the room with her good (left) ear toward the center of the classroom and away from the window, where traffic and playground noise could be distracting.

Also, to protect her good ear, I ask that you keep Penelope away from sustained loud noises such as mowers, electric hand dryers, and the like. And, finally, if you see any sign of Penelope's struggling in school, we'd appreciate your notifying us immediately.

Obviously, we are saddened by Penelope's hearing loss, but we're optimistic that, with a little assistance from her teachers and from us, the impairment will not hinder her learning.

Sincerely,

CC: Angelina Tucker

PHYSICIANS AND MEDICAL ISSUES

Sooner or later in the typical family, health care becomes a concern. For ourselves, our children, or elderly relatives, we'll need to handle medical records, offer or request explanations about hospital or physician treatment and billing, or express appreciation or displeasure about medical services received. Despite all the health-care revisions in the past few years in our country, the paperwork has not disappeared.

So when handling medically related correspondence, use a reference line, including the patient's full name and address, and any account or billing number.

Begin by summarizing your commendation, complaint, or request in an opening sentence or two. For example:

> *"I want to thank you for the excellent emergency room procedures that saved my daughter's life."*
>
> *"I want to protest the way you handled..."*
>
> *"I'd like to suggest a change in policy in situations where..."*

Then state any follow-up action or response you expect and be specific.

> *"I expect to see a corrected invoice."*
>
> *"I'd like to have the nurse instructed to..."*
>
> *"Would you please detail the necessities of these procedures to me?"*
>
> *"Will you or will you not contact the insurance company on my behalf?"*

Give full details as to admission dates, treatment dates, medication, or fees under discussion. And provide any related insurance information: group or member number, and address and phone numbers for filing claims or verifying coverage or payments (limitations and deductibles). When relevant, state who other than the patient is responsible for the patient's billing. For example, if you are writing about a minor child's care, be sure to include the legal guardian's name and contact information.

In our country, we are blessed with the best health care in the world. Don't let the associated paperwork details discourage you from expressing appreciation when it is due. Commend those who serve you well.

• LETTER TO DOCTOR IN ADVANCE OF APPOINTMENT •

Dear Dr. Tavel,

I'm looking forward to seeing you for my annual physical on May 11. There are several health issues I'd like to discuss. I don't want to forget anything once I'm at your office, so I've prepared a list of questions:

1. Last year, you were concerned about my white blood cell count. If my tests show no improvement this year, what should be done to address the problem?

2. At what age should I consider a prostate exam? Though there is no history of prostate cancer in my family, I know it's a common cancer among men and would like to stay on top of the situation.

3. I've put on five or six pounds in the past year despite jogging two miles daily. Do you have any specific exercise or dietary recommendations to help me control my weight?

4. My left knee has been giving me trouble. Sometimes, when I'm climbing stairs, the knee feels loose, as if it might slip out of joint. Though there's no pain, I'm concerned. What might be the problem?

Could you please review these questions in advance so that we can discuss them next month?

Regards,

• AUTHORIZING RELEASE OF RECORDS •

RE: Patient Kyle R. Sherlock, Jr.

Dear Dr. Narrows:

With this letter, as parent and guardian, I'm authorizing your office to release medical records for my minor son, Kyle R. Sherlock, Jr., with regard to his recent back injuries.

Please send those records to the office of Dr. Guillermo Canseco, P.O. Box 3889, Atlanta, GA 30339.

My health insurance requires that we have a second opinion before extensive surgery, and Dr. Canseco is providing that opinion. He does not want to order X rays unnecessarily, as long as those your office has completed provide adequate detail to make his recommendations.

Thank you for sending these records promptly.

Sincerely,

• GRANTING TEMPORARY EMERGENCY MEDICAL CARE AUTHORIZATION •

RE: Patient Biff C. Upton

To Whom It May Concern of the Hospital/Medical Staff:

By this letter, I am authorizing my brother-in-law, Barry McGwire, residing at 489 Wolfroth Lane, Waterloo, IA 50701, to obtain and approve all necessary *emergency* medical care for my father, Biff C. Upton, while I am out of the country on business next month.

This authorization covers emergency medical care only, between the dates of April 6 and April 16, 20—.

The required, notarized signature is provided below.

Signature _____
                Tom C. Upton

• GRANTING PERMISSION TO DISPENSE MEDICATION •

Dear School Nurse,

My daughter, Jean Thibodeaux, has recently been diagnosed with ADHD by her physician, Dr. Mary Tyler, who prescribed Relaxon. I'm enclosing a month's supply of pills to be kept in your office in accordance with school policy.

Dr. Tyler has instructed that Jean take one pill daily after lunch. Please see that she swallows the pill before she leaves your office. If you have any questions or concerns, I can be reached at 333-3333.

Thanks,

• Requesting Information about Prescriptions during Vacation •

re: Policy 3967294

Dear Mutual Insurance,

Under the terms of my health insurance policy, the prescription for my kidney medicine can be refilled only once a month. This spring, however, I'll be traveling in the Australian outback for six weeks and will be unable to refill the prescription there. How do I go about procuring enough medication to last me through my trip?

Sincerely,

• REQUESTING GENERIC PRESCRIPTIONS •

Dear Andy Pavelik,

Yesterday, my wife was in your pharmacy to pick up my monthly prescription of Xerex. When I saw the receipt for $26, I was quite surprised. Up to this point, you've been filling the prescription with a generic equivalent that costs only $10—the maximum amount covered by our insurance. I'm writing to ask that you use the generic for all future refills and notify us if it is out of stock or no longer available. Also, on my next visit, I would like to exchange the bottle of name-brand pills for the generics and a refund of $16.

Sincerely,

• Requesting Medical Excuse or Information for Employer •

re: Patient Melvin T. Fingers

Dear Dr. Moran:

I have been under your care for the past four months for ongoing foot problems, and will be returning to work as a deliveryman for Oppenheimer Furniture. I've requested a change in work assignments so that I can minimize time standing on my feet. I've asked that I be given a clerical job in the warehouse rather than continuing my duties of loading and unloading trucks.

I need a letter from you, summarizing the medical problems related to my feet and a statement as to the extent of this disability in performing my current duties, which require that I be on my feet all day. With this letter, I authorize you to release any test results or related documentation to substantiate your medical opinions and recommendations.

Please send your letter directly to my supervisor: Gus R. Tuttle, Oppenheimer Furniture, 47889 Overlake, Stanton, OH 44054.

Thank you for supplying this opinion promptly so that I can move ahead with my reassignment of duties. I appreciate your competent professional care in this situation.

Sincerely,

• DISPUTING BILLING ERROR •

RE: Patient Cassie A. Petrowski
   Case Number 3434387

Dear Hospital Administrator:

On September 30, I reported to your emergency room with a severe nosebleed. Although I went through the admission process, because of the busy nature of the hospital that evening, I received no treatment and finally left on my own accord. Today, however, I received a $120 bill for "treatment."

Please remove this erroneous charge from my account and credit card immediately.

During the time of admission, your admitting clerk did begin the paperwork procedure with me and my husband, collecting my insurance policy number and my credit card, saying she was unsure if she could verify coverage at that hour (1 A.M.).

The staff ushered me into a treatment room to wait "about 15 minutes" to see the doctor. We waited for almost three hours with no treatment whatsoever. When we inquired once as to why the delay, we were told that other patients had more urgent need of care and that the doctor would be in "shortly."

Finally, we were able to control the nosebleed ourselves and decided to leave the emergency room to go elsewhere. Neither a nurse nor a doctor ever spoke with us about the condition or treatment, or provided any assistance. I might add that we understand the necessity for treating patients entering the emergency room according to the urgency of their condition. But we do not understand the lack of common courtesy in informing us of what was going on during our long wait.

Then today we received a bill from your hospital for $120 for "services rendered for emergency room care." An attached note stated that should payment not be received from the insurance company within 30 days, your hospital would bill our credit card account.

Having never received any medical diagnosis or treatment on September 30, we do not believe we are responsible for any charges. Consequently, we are instructing our insurance company (by copy of this letter) not to pay any claims you may file on our behalf.

Yours truly,

• REQUESTING SPECIAL PAYMENT SCHEDULE •

RE: Patients Fern James and Cheryl James (daughter)

Dear Dr. Tavel:

Yes, your dental records are accurate; my unpaid balance has been $1400 for the past 60 days. I do intend to pay the total amount, but I am requesting alternative payment arrangements since losing my job recently. I'd like to pay $50 a month toward the balance until I secure other employment. Enclosed is a check for that amount this month.

We have been very pleased with the dental care you have provided for my daughter and me, and are embarrassed at the economic predicament we find ourselves in. I understand that the dental work we've had done is not an emergency situation, and of course we would not have had the work done had we anticipated the job layoff.

We hope this monthly repayment arrangement will be acceptable to you, and I will let you know as soon as I find other employment and can pay the full amount. Thank you for your understanding in this situation.

Sincerely,

• EXPRESSING APPRECIATION TO PHYSICIAN OR HOSPITAL •

Dear Dr. Redford and Hospital Staff:

As you may recall, my mother, Meredith Townsend, recently died while under your care at Carter Hospital. I want to express my heartfelt appreciation for the excellent care and the genuine concern you showed during her extended illness.

In any hospital, one expects competent medical care, clean rooms, nutritious food, and reasonably prompt service. We received all that, but much more. I want to commend you on your rather quick process in admitting patients to the hospital. Your staff had completed all the necessary paperwork from the information provided in earlier phone calls and we waited less than ten minutes to have my mother in her room. And that response was just a preview of the streamlined processes we experienced throughout my mother's four-week stay with you.

Not only did we find your response to our calls and questions prompt and receive accurate information about tests results, but your nursing staff went out of its way to elaborate on details of each procedure and test. Henrietta Berry, Sal Campanella, and Juanita Mesa particularly stand out in my mind because of their habit of stopping by my mother's room at the start and end of their work shifts to check on our needs. On three or four occasions, when mother was suffering so badly that I didn't want to leave her side, the nurses brought lunch to me when they returned from their own lunch breaks.

Please commend the nurses that I mentioned above and express the family's appreciation for their dedicated service.

(Continued)

I'm sure that when things do not run so smoothly patients let you know of their bad experiences, so I wanted to take the time to let you know of my complete satisfaction with the service you provide to the community. We will, of course, recommend your hospital to our friends.

Sincerely,

• Complaining about Medical Staff or Procedures •

Dear Dr. Brown:

I'm writing to make you aware of a routinely frustrating experience in dealing with your nurse, Dorothy Stern. Her tone is demanding, her questions during medical intakes are abrupt, and her manner of shouting confidential information down the hallway to other staff members becomes quite embarrassing. Not only has she been overbearing with me, but I've overheard such treatment and comments while she was attending to other patients as well.

On one occasion, a patient that Dorothy had belittled while still in the waiting room left your office in tears, vowing to go elsewhere for treatment in the future.

Although a talk between you and Dorothy may improve the abrupt tone and questioning, I ask that you make a more specific procedural change. That is, I suggest the policy that your staff does not discuss a patient's condition in the hallway within the hearing of other patients. Confidentiality is of utmost importance to most people nowadays.

Dr. Brown, I have appreciated your competent care in the past for my entire family, so I thought you'd want to know of this situation, which may be negatively affecting the reputation of your practice. Please phone me at your convenience (555-5555) to let me know you received this letter.

Sincerely,

• Terminating Poor Medical Service •

RE: Patient Elyse Julian

Dear Dr. Sherman:

My family and I will not be returning to your office for future medical treatment. Although we have been pleased with your professional competence, the new telephone screening procedures have become a real detriment to your practice and our confidence in receiving acceptable service. Consequently, we are asking that you forward all medical records for the family (Elyse Julian, Sandra Julian, Kathryn Julian) to us at the above address.

On several occasions during the last six months we've phoned your office about routine issues: a prescription refill, a request that X rays be sent to another doctor for a second opinion required by our HMO, a question about reaction symptoms to an antibiotic, a request for a prescription for motion-sickness pills for our recent cruise, and finally a call to schedule a routine exam.

In each case, we've been put off, put on hold, or put down. That is, return calls promised by nurses have never materialized. Questions to you have been answered by "Make an appointment." Prescription refill requests receive a "We're working on it" response, yet no follow-up.

I do understand the need for some screening procedures and for help in returning your calls on routine matters. But it has become virtually impossible to receive a response or generate action from your office with a single call within a day's time. We simply do not have time to make the necessary follow-up calls to your office to see a request through to completion.

I'm sorry we will not be able to recommend your services to our friends and family.

Sincerely,

• RENTING WHEELCHAIR •

Dear Capital City Medical Store,

My mother, Wanda Palmer, recently broke her leg and will need a wheelchair for the next six to eight weeks. She says any old wheelchair is fine, but I'd like for her to have the most comfortable model available. Could you advise me regarding price and availability? I need to have the wheelchair by Monday, when she's scheduled to be discharged from Tri-Health Community Hospital.

Sincerely,

• REQUESTING HANDICAPPED ASSISTANCE •

Dear Country Club Manager,

On Saturday, September 16, my wife and I will be attending a wedding reception in your main ballroom. My wife is confined to a wheelchair. Could you give me a call to discuss the building's most easily accessible entrances and bathrooms for the handicapped? I'm grateful for any steps you and your staff can take to ensure that her visit is a smooth one.

Sincerely,

• REQUEST FOR HANDICAPPED PARKING INFORMATION •

Dear Collingwood Police Department,

My mother, Wanda Palmer, recently broke her leg and is on crutches, but she refuses to let the injury keep her away from her '68 Mustang convertible or her weekly bingo game.

I'm writing to inquire about the availability of a temporary handicapped parking permit. Attached is a note from her doctor, verifying the extent of her injury. Please send the necessary paperwork to the address below.

Sincerely,

• REQUEST FOR PHYSICIAN TO VERIFY HANDICAP •

Dear Dr. Conroy,

Thanks for the wonderful care you've provided my mother, Wanda Palmer, since her fall. I'm trying to arrange for a temporary handicapped parking permit for her to use until she's off crutches. Could you please provide me with a letter verifying the extent of her injury? The Collingwood Police Department requires that such a letter accompany all applications for handicapped parking permits.

Regards,

• REQUESTING LARGE PRINT BOOKS •

RE: Membership 6788774

Dear Romance Book of the Month Club,

I'm enjoying my membership as much as I did the day I joined fifteen years ago, but as I get older, it's harder for me to read all that small print. I'm writing to request that you begin sending me large-print books. If a large-print edition is unavailable for the main selection, I'll happily take one of the large-print alternate selections.

Thank you,

• INQUIRING ABOUT MEDICAL FACILITIES •

Dear Ronald Peterson,

My wife and I are interested in signing up for one of your African safaris next spring, but because of health issues, we're nervous about being too far from modern medical facilities. She's 54 and suffers from diabetes; I'm 60 and am prone to upper respiratory problems.

Could you tell me about the medical facilities and staff at your base camp? Also, what do you do when there's a medical emergency that requires treatment not available there? I'm particularly interested in any details you can provide that might pertain to our particular health conditions.

Sincerely,

• REQUESTING INFORMATION FROM RESEARCH ORGANIZATIONS •

Dear Director:

I've recently been diagnosed with diabetes and have been referred to your organization for information to help me deal with the condition.

Would you please provide any information you have available on dietary and exercise issues, causes, hereditary concerns, and any preliminary data on ongoing research regarding a cure? In other words, I have all the typical questions anyone might have who has had no previous experience with the disease among family or friends.

Thank you for your continued work on behalf of those stricken with diabetes. I'll appreciate any information you can provide for my own treatment and care.

Sincerely,

• REQUESTING INFORMATION ABOUT PROGRAM •

Dear WFNR,

Recently I heard an advertisement on your station for Illinois Reading and Information Services (IRIS), a service for the print-impaired. Could you send me more information about the program and an application form? Attached is a statement from my doctor verifying my visual impairment. I am especially interested in receiving broadcasts of my local paper, the *Daily Mirror*, which I haven't been able to read in years.

Sincerely,

SYMPATHY AND CONDOLENCES

People often put off writing sympathy notes until they become embarrassed at not having written. It's not that people are uncaring in such situations; it's more often that they're saddened and unsure about how best to express these deep feelings in the face of sorrow or tragedy. But in just such situations, friends and family have the greatest need to hear from us.

Determine that you will not leave your family and friends bewildered about your lack of concern. Express your regret and sorrow at hearing of the death, illness, accident, divorce, or other misfortune. Begin your letter or note with straightforward comments like these:

> *"I was so sorry to hear that…"*
>
> *"I feel overwhelmed that…"*
>
> *"We were so sad to hear…"*
>
> *"I'm shocked and saddened by the news that…"*
>
> *"I want you to know how sorry I feel about…"*
>
> *"I want to express my sympathy at the loss of your mother."*

One of the deepest needs of survivors in times of grief is the opportunity to talk about the loved one or the misfortune. Mention something you remember about the individual or recall something you've heard others say. In the case of other misfortunes, let the reader know you understand the extent of the loss and the painful situation:

> *"I know you depended so much on your father's advice. He was so knowledgeable about…"*

"I know you had wanted a baby for such a long time."

"Sharon was such a devoted wife. I recall fondly the many times she laughed at all those jokes you used at our annual roasts."

"The boys adored their father. Many, many times I've sat and listened to them talk about their camping trips and how their dad always…"

If possible and if you're sincere, offer to help in some specific way. Vague offers ("Call me if you need anything") sound empty and insincere. Can you baby-sit? Are you willing to make a donation or cover some necessary expense? Do you have some extra time to take on some of the family members' responsibilities for a few days or weeks?

In the case of divorce, be sensitive to feelings and circumstances of which you may be unaware. Express your confidence that the individual has made the correct decision and offer your emotional support. Consider the following comments:

"I don't want to add to the problem by prying, so I'll not plan to phone unless you want to talk about it."

"I know you have made the best decision for all involved."

"Sometimes you have to act even when the road ahead doesn't seem totally clear."

"We know you made this decision with much prayer and forethought."

"We will be here to offer our support in the days ahead."

"Our home is open to you. Call on us when you feel like chatting about it. What's a few tears between friends?"

Finally, don't worry about polished wording. In fact, expressing your feelings in your own words, even awkwardly, sounds most sincere. Your comments should sound like your spoken words, as if talking with the reader face to face. And, of course, write the letter yourself on your own stationery or card. This is not a chore to be delegated to someone else. Your letter must come from your heart.

• DEATH OF CHILD •

Mercedes and Luis:

The news of Audra's accident has shocked and upset us beyond expression. It seems just like yesterday that we all played at the beach together and cooked hamburgers in your backyard. Being so far away from you during this tragedy makes us feel so help- less. We can only imagine how devastated you must feel.

I know the darkest days are before you now as you try to go through the motions of living. Please know that we are as close as your phone. And if you find the need to get away momentarily from the visible reminders, we would love to have you visit us here as long as necessary.

We know that only God can comfort your heart in times like these. You are in our prayers hourly.

Sincerely,

• DEATH OF PARENT •

Samantha:

When I phoned the office today, Mark Bolen told me that your mother had passed away yesterday after a long illness. Although I know she was elderly, losing a parent is never easy. Death always leaves an emptiness and brings solemn reflection on the meaning of life and family.

Many times I've heard you talk fondly of your mother and joke about how she cajoled you into eating healthy and begged you to get more sleep. And from what I know about you, I can imagine that you returned her love and concern openly.

If I can pick up any of the slack at the office while you're away handling your mother's affairs, let me know. I'd be pleased that you considered me friend enough to help you through this tough time. My thoughts are with you.

Sincerely,

• DEATH OF SPOUSE •

Elizabeth,

I want to express my deepest sympathy in the loss of Daniel. Marriage being the closest bond people experience on earth, I know you must feel desperately lonely and empty right now.

Even as casual friends, Johnnie and I noticed and often remarked how devoted Daniel was to you. And your children seemed always to love and respect him for the guidance he gave them through their teen years. You all were very fortunate to have such a loving husband and father to share your lives.

We will be praying that you'll find comfort in knowing that you did all that was possible to make Daniel's last few weeks so very meaningful for him. God's peace to you.

Sincerely,

• DEATH OF ANOTHER RELATIVE •

Dear Enrique,

I just wanted to write you a brief note to tell you how sorry I was to hear about your brother's accident. No one is ever ready or prepared to accept such tragic news. I've heard you so often tell about your hunting trips and golf outings together and how very much you enjoyed each other's company. Memories of those times, I guess, will be even more precious to you as the years go by.

Please accept my sincere condolences. I am sorry.

In deepest sympathy,

• MISCARRIAGE •

Missy and Leon,

I want to express my deepest sympathy for the loss of your child. Even though he never made it into the world, you still managed to be wonderful parents to him. Missy, I so admired the care you took with your diet, and Leon, I'll never forget the gentle way you spoke to him when he started kicking during the pool party last month. The miscarriage can never undo the loving care you provided for your baby. Please know that our thoughts and prayers are with you.

Sincerely,

• DEATH OF PET •

Margaret,

No one but another pet owner would understand what you're going through with the loss of Chowder. She was such a strong, loving dog, and I know she gave you hours of pleasure, company, and protection.

I know you must still be upset about someone's leaving the gate open so that she wandered out into the street. So thoughtless.

Well, you can find other protection for yourself and your home, but you can't just replace the pleasure and company Chowder provided quite so easily. Dogs are intelligent creatures, and they can form bonding relationships. I'm sorry for your loss.

Sincerely,

• PERSONAL FAILURE •

Example 1

Eduardo,

I was so sorry to hear that the bar exam got the best of you—as it does to so many capable people. I know how hard you've studied and how much you've sacrificed to realize your dream of becoming an attorney. Fortunately, there will be other chances to take the exam, and I'm sure a man of your dedication and determination won't let this one setback stop you.

In the meantime, I'd be happy to help you prepare for your next try, whether you need a study partner or just someone to watch the kids while you're at the library. Please hang in there—and do let me know how I can help.

Sincerely,

• PERSONAL FAILURE •

Example 2

Mike,

I want you to know how sorry I was to learn about your ankle. All athletes face injury sooner or later, but to suffer one in the middle of your first marathon seems a particularly unlucky break. I'm sure you must be very disappointed, but in my eyes, the fact that you didn't finish the race in no way diminishes your accomplishment. Just watching you hit the streets every morning at 5 A.M. to train was an inspiration to me. Here's hoping you have a speedy recovery and better luck next time.

Regards,

• LOSS OF HOME OR BUSINESS IN DISASTER •

Dear Kenneth and Marisa,

I was horrified to see and hear on the news what the tornadoes did to your hometown. And then when Clare Bettendorf told me about both your house and your place of business being destroyed, I just could not imagine the discouragement and hardship you're experiencing.

Of course, by now, I'm sure you've made emergency arrangements for immediate housing, but surely there must be something we can do to help with the business end. As you may know, my staff specializes in custom software for accounting firms. Would you have use for a consultant on site to get you up and running again? I'd be happy to make one of our senior people available to you at no charge for 3 or 4 days if that would help get you operational quickly. Please call me at (555) 555-5555 to let me know the specifics of your setup, and I'll schedule someone to visit your site.

Of course, I'm sure you're feeling quite a loss on the home front also. And items destroyed with a home can never be replaced. You must feel devastated about that. But then I know you two. You've got a strong faith, a solid determination, and a commitment to your kids to pick up the pieces and move on with life.

Our prayers are with you. And please give me a call about scheduling one of our software engineers.

Sincerely,

• FAILURE OF BUSINESS •

Dear Zachary:

When I phoned last week, I of course heard your tape that your number is no longer in service. Thinking I'd confused the number some way, I did a little investigating and discovered that your plumbing supply shop had closed its doors for good. Frankly, I was very sorry to hear that.

Although I don't know your specific situation, I am reading more and more articles and hearing frequent TV reports that small-business closings are a phenomenon across the country, thanks to the superstores spreading like wildflowers. Competition is fierce. But whatever your reasons, I know you made the decision with much thought and careful analysis.

Still, there must be some sadness in closing that chapter in your life. But after each ending, there's a new beginning. Another battle to fight and win. Another experience to initiate and grow from. I know with your solid decision-making skills and your willingness to work long hours you've probably already headed down another road. I wish you the best in whatever you undertake next.

Sincerely,

• FINANCIAL RUIN •

Art,

I was so sad to hear about your financial difficulties. Deciding to file for bankruptcy is never easy, even when there are no other options left. I don't think I've ever told you, but Meg and I went through the same thing years ago. I won't say the road back to financial stability is a smooth one. I can say, though, that it's a lot smoother if you're willing to let your friends help you out. We'd be happy to lend you money, cosign for a loan or credit card, or let you stay with us until you're back on your feet. Won't you stop by for a visit soon?

All our best for a smoother road ahead,

• LOSS OF JOB •

Coworker

Erin,

All of us here in the marketing department were truly shocked when you were laid off. It seems like just yesterday that you were coaching me on the Morgan account and keeping us all loose with your endless store of duck jokes. (Really, I had no idea how funny ducks were until I met you.) Suffice it to say, it's way too quiet around here without you.

If I can help you in any way with your job hunt, just say the word. I've got friends in the marketing departments at Peabody Associates and the Triad Group, and I'd be happy to serve as a personal reference, arrange an introduction, or write a letter of recommendation. Please know that you're in our thoughts and hearts every day.

Sincerely,

• LOSS OF JOB •

Friend

Erin,

When you told me you'd been laid off, I could hardly believe it. After fifteen years of dedicated service, you certainly deserved better. I'm just sorry you have to deal with such a headache at this stage of your career. If I know you, though, you'll land on your feet soon enough. Until then, how about letting me buy dinner on Girls' Night Out?

All the best for the new job ahead,

• GET WELL SOON TO CHILD'S TEACHER •

Dear Ms. Willingham:

Carrie tells me that you are going to have extended surgery and will be recuperating for at least the next two months. These things never happen at a convenient time, do they?

I just wanted to wish you a speedy recovery and to let you know how much the children—and their parents—will miss you while you're convalescing at home. Particularly, the children have enjoyed your most recent unit on the galaxy. Carrie has been unloading facts and "mysteries" on us just about every night at the dinner table. We do so much appreciate your dedication to the children and your commitment to stay up to date in your field. The little extra handouts and current discoveries that you add to the class activities I'm sure are not in the textbook and are the result of many after-school hours spent in preparation. Thank you for that extra effort on the behalf of our children.

We're wishing you a very nice rest and full recovery.

Sincerely,

• TERMINAL ILLNESS •

Friend or Relative

Ricky,

The news about your diagnosis has upset the family and me very much. No one ever expects something like this, and there's simply no way anyone can prepare and brace for such a shock.

I was just writing to let you know how much we care. Every time I've picked up the phone to call you, I've become too emotional to put my feelings into words. Therefore, I decided to write so at least you'd know that it was not lack of concern that prevented my contacting you.

I know you must have heard it all before, but it's still true: Medical miracles happen every day—with new equipment, new treatment, new drugs. We're praying that will be the case in your situation.

We will be thinking of you and will be in touch as you begin your treatment.

Sincerely,

• TERMINAL ILLNESS •

Acquaintance

Dear Trina:

We were so sad to hear from mutual friends (Hal and Linda Chabon) about your illness. I understand that you have been going for testing off and on now for several months. I suppose after such a long ordeal, you're at least somewhat relieved to have some closure on the extensive testing and to know what has been causing the pain.

I wanted you to know that you are in our prayers continually. We've offered your name to our support group, and others too will be remembering you in this way. Only God can provide direction and comfort in times like these.

Please call on us if we can help with some of your responsibilities with the youth group. I know you yourself have served as sponsor to so many events, but we'd be happy to cover some of the upcoming summer outings for you. You can reach us at home (444-4444) or at work (Bob at 333-3333; Mandy at 666-6666).

Sincerely,

• CANCELED WEDDING •

Eric,

Your mother just called to tell me the wedding is off, and I wanted to say how sorry I am that things between you and Tina didn't work. I'm sure the two of you had good reasons for making the decision you did. But even so, I know it must have been difficult, particularly with all of the pressures and expectations that inevitably surround such a big wedding. You've been there for me through two rocky marriages, and I hope you'll let me be there for you now. If you need somebody to talk to, call me anytime, day or night.

Your friend,

• TO PARENTS OF SOMEONE GETTING DIVORCED •

Dear Finn and Renata:

Someone mentioned to me that Elrod and Jane had recently decided to go their separate ways. I know that must be shattering news to you, because you always spoke so highly of your daughter-in-law and loved her like your own daughter.

Although many people don't realize it, I think divorces are almost as difficult on the parents as on the two involved. There are the future plans unfilled, the relationships with the grand-kids to consider, the financial hardships that sometimes arise during the readjustment period—not to mention the loss of a close relationship (Jane in this case) important to you both.

I just wanted you to know that we are thinking of you during this difficult time.

Sincerely,

• To Friend or Relative Getting Divorced •

Dear Sally,

Ed Topham dropped by my office last week and during the course of our discussion mentioned that you and Roy were getting a divorce. I just wanted to let you know that I'm sorry things didn't work out between you two.

Life certainly takes unexpected turns. And divorce, at least from what other friends have told me, can take the sharpest turns of all. I don't want to pry and don't need any details that you don't feel comfortable sharing. I just want you to know that I'll be thinking about you as you make the adjustment.

I'd like to get together for dinner when I'm in Boston next September. I'll phone as soon as my plans become firm and see if you're available for an evening.

Sincerely,

• CRIMINAL CONVICTION •

Hayden,

I was shocked beyond belief to learn of your conviction. I don't know what went on in the accounting department and—unless you want to talk about it—I don't really care. All I know is that it seems you're the fall guy for the higher-ups, and it's an all-too-familiar story that breaks my heart, especially since this time the guy on the short end of the stick is my buddy.

I'm guessing (and praying) you'll only get a few months, but no matter how long you're gone, I'll be there for Caroline and the kids. Let's get together before your sentencing date and figure out how I can best help you and your family get through this difficult time.

Your friend,

• Victim of Crime •

Theodore,

I was so shocked and sorry to hear about the holdup. How one man can shoot another over $20 is something I'll never understand, and it seems especially unfair considering all you've done to make the Quick Mart such a credit to our community. I hope the guy got a good look at the pictures of all those Little League teams you've sponsored, and I hope that memory keeps him awake at night—at least until the police can track him down. Mostly, though, I'm just glad you're alive. If you're up for visitors yet, please let me know. I promise to bring the latest issue of *Sports Illustrated* instead of flowers.

Get well,

THANK-YOUS

Gifts, hospitality, help, encouragement, notes written to us—all are occasions for expressing gratitude to our friends and family.

No need to waste time before getting to the point. Your thank-you comments should not sound like an afterthought at the end of a phone conversation or a routine letter. Instead, be direct and purposeful with your comments. Thank the reader immediately for the kindness or gift.

Then elaborate on why the note, occasion, or kindness was particularly meaningful to you. Be as specific as possible. Instead of "You saved me a lot of time," try:

> *"Your help before the party saved me hours—the trip to the party mall, the trip to pick up the extra costumes, your stuffing the mailers."*
>
> *"Your note was particularly special because..."*
>
> *"You made me feel so special in the way that you..."*
>
> *"How could you possibly know that I so much needed to hear from you about this..."*
>
> *"The party was delightful—I was so shocked that you'd taken so much trouble to find out the addresses of all my special friends."*
>
> *"You obviously spent an incredible number of hours and mind-boggling emotional effort on..."*

Don't let clichés roll off your pen; it's not the polished formal statement, but the heartfelt sentiment that makes your note most appreciated.

Be careful to avoid mentioning any negative outcomes or circumstances surrounding the situation. *Not:* "Too bad more people didn't show up to sample your great food." *Not:* "You were thoughtful to try to include everyone—even if things were a little cramped." Those comments, often unintentional, will detract from the overall feeling of satisfaction about the gift or deed.

A thank-you delayed is often a thank-you ignored. By the recipient, that is. Sincere comments suffer from delay. Write your thank-you notes and letters promptly.

• BIRTHDAY GIFT •

Gillian,

As much as I love cheese, I rarely buy exotic flavors for myself, so you can imagine how delighted I was when your gift arrived. A whole basket of the most delicious cheeses and gourmet crackers I've ever tasted! What a unique idea! You really know how to make a girl feel special. Now all I need is a good friend to share a snack and lazy evening of memories. What are you doing next Saturday?

Yours,

• MONETARY GIFT •

Dear Uncle Regis,

I just wanted to tell you how much I appreciated your (more than generous) check. All summer I've been saving up for a car, but it hasn't been easy on a busboy's wages. In fact, it was looking like I'd be spending another year riding the school bus. Now, because of you, I'll have my own car by this weekend. Thanks for the best gift ever.

Sincerely,

• BABY SHOWER GIFT •

Charlene,

The football sweats for Adam are adorable! With that suit and another couple of hundred pounds, he could be a wide receiver for the Detroit Lions! Thanks for taking the time to select such a cute gift. Nate tries to dress him in that outfit every time we leave the house; and of course, I have to remind him that the sweats aren't exactly appropriate attire for a christening and the like.

I'm planning to bring the baby to the office in a few weeks and hope to show him off to you then. Thanks for being so thoughtful.

All our best,

• CHRISTMAS GIFT •

Example 1

Dear Christian,

The fruit tray arrived today and tempted us all to a midafternoon snack. Your selection had so many different little goodies—nuts, candies, cookies—that even our finicky family eaters (I'll not name names here) dove in with delight.

Thank you for thinking of us in such a classy way. Our best to your household for a happy holiday season!

Sincerely,

• CHRISTMAS GIFT •

Example 2

Dear Mary Ann,

You did it again—you sent the perfect gift! How could you know how much I needed new towels? Everything we have is early marriage, circa 1990. The plum-and-green looks wonderful in both the master and guest baths. But then you know how I hate to save things for "company" use only. Big, beautiful, luxurious towels are a treat a woman needs almost daily, don't you think? Thanks so much. Hope you and the kids had a great holiday yourself.

Love,

• WEDDING GIFT •

Dear Cindy and Steve,

I'm thrilled with the crystal rose bowl. It fills the vacant spot on my étagère just perfectly and looks elegant. You're always so observant about gift giving; I assume you've overheard me talking about my collection and wishing for more. Thank you for taking the time to come to the wedding and help us celebrate our special day. We so much appreciate having special friends like you with us.

Sincerely,

• HELP DURING CRISIS •

Dear Veronica and Kishan,

I feel a little overwhelmed and crowded now by all the "new" in my life. New job. New apartment. New neighborhood. But the best "new" is a new perspective. I don't have to tell you how desperate I was feeling, still entangled in my relationship with Marc. When things started to go from bad to worse, I almost felt numb. That is, until you two came on the scene.

I just can't thank you enough for all the time you've spent with me. Calling everyone in your network to help me locate a new job here. Coaching me on the interview. Even neighborhood hunting all weekend. The hours and hours you've spent on my behalf seem like an incredible gift. And an investment—an investment in helping me start a new life.

How can you thank someone for all that? Please know how dear you've both become to me. Your love and concern feel like a warm blanket on those long nights as I adjust to my new life here.

With much love,

• HELP ARRANGING EVENT •

Lynn,

I honestly don't think I'd have been able to pull off the reception without you. Your choice of floral arrangements was exquisite; your table assignments were inspired; and your diplomatic handling of the caterer left me truly impressed. Thanks for all of your tireless work. I only hope that one day I'll be able to offer a huge favor in return.

Best,

• HELP MEETING DEADLINE •

Dear Cassandra,

Thanks so much for helping me locate a printer to handle such a rush job for the fund-raising gala at the hospital. As you know, printers can be contrary people when it comes to deadlines. Promise them anything and give them what you happen to get done—that's been the credo of the few I've worked with through the years on other projects.

But your solution in going with BFI Printing saved the day. I called Mitchell, used your name, and mentioned the previous projects you'd done with him—and he welcomed the business with open arms. I might add that he met our crucial deadline with a top-quality flyer.

Thanks for your time in digging through your basement files until you found his name and number. Thanks to you, another civic project with a happy ending!

With appreciation,

• SYMPATHY OR COMFORTING NOTE •

Example 1

Dear Holly,

Your note came exactly a month after mother's death. It was so comforting to know that you still have me in your thoughts. As you may have guessed, the hardest part of grieving starts after all the flowers have faded and after all the friends and family have gone home. When I came in from work that day to find your letter, it was such a lift. I'm blessed to have such a special friend.

Love,

• SYMPATHY OR COMFORTING NOTE •

Example 2

Dear Claudell:

Thank you for your kind expression of sympathy after my son's tragic accident. We can never prepare for the depth of despair that such a sudden death brings, and the connection of our coworkers and friends helps tremendously to ease us back into the mainstream of life—physically, if not yet emotionally. Thank you for your card and concern.

With appreciation,

• ENCOURAGEMENT AND SUPPORT •

Missy,

Just a note to let you know how much I appreciate all the words of encouragement to me during my year as president of the school board. As you well know, it's impossible to keep all the people happy all the time. So I just settled, thanks to your advice, for keeping some of the people happy some of the time.

Seriously, this has been one of the most difficult, although rewarding, years of my life. I can't thank you enough for giving me perspective on the big athlete-expulsion issue we had back in October. And your input about the outdoor sculpture at Lamar Junior High was totally on target; you helped me nip that one in the bud. Those long lunch hours with you helped preserve my sanity. And you do need a modicum of that (sanity) to run a school system these days!

I'm prone to become discouraged when I don't feel as though people understand the bigger issues or appreciate the complexity of a problem. And when I become discouraged, I'm always tempted to hand others the baton and let them lead the parade. You must have intuitively known that; otherwise, how would you have known just when I needed a reassuring comment, card, or smile?

Please know that I owe you a great deal of the credit for what turned out to be a successful term on the board.

Cordially,

• JOB WELL DONE •

Martin,

Who says nobody cares about quality anymore? Not only did you do a beautiful job on our bathroom, but you finished the renovations a week early and beat all of the other estimates by more than 25 percent. Amy is especially pleased with your meticulous tile work around the tub.

Working with such a diligent, capable, and honest contractor has been a real pleasure. We'll look forward to calling you for our next project.

Sincerely,

• For Good Deed •

To the gentleman in apartment 12C,

You were so kind to help me carry my groceries when the elevator was out of order yesterday. I'm guessing, based on your tuxedo, that you were on your way to a function of some sort, and probably in a hurry. That you would take ten minutes out of your evening to assist a complete stranger is quite remarkable in this day and age—especially considering I live on the sixth floor. Next time we meet, I'd like to learn your name. Mine's Thelma, and I'm much obliged to you.

Sincerely,

• FOR SHARED EXPERTISE •

Kelly,

After spending all day cajoling computers to work, you probably have more fun things to do than repair mine. I really appreciate your coming over last night to take a look at our modem. Obviously, your diagnosis was right on the money. If it weren't, I'd be schlepping my machine to the shop today instead of sending you this e-mail. You should have let me pay you for your time, but since you didn't, how about lunch tomorrow, my treat?

Best,

• FRIEND'S HONESTY AND ADVICE •

Dear Mark:

The conversation we had last weekend has continued to give me food for thought—in fact, I'm still "chewing" rather hard on your advice. It's not easy to hear the kinds of things you said to me about the way I'm living my life. Make your decision, go for it, and don't look back—that has always been my philosophy in life.

But when you took the time to point out how some of my decisions were affecting Sarah, I had to face my responsibilities there for the first time. You were right. Thanks for being the kind of friend you are—and having the backbone to say some hard things to get my attention.

Thanks again,

• STRANGER'S HONESTY •

Dear Mr. Simpson:

I'm still rather astounded to have my billfold back—with all the money and credit cards still inside. Believe me, I never in my wildest dreams expected to have someone ring my doorbell and hand me back that peace of mind I so carelessly lost.

What an incredible thing for you to do! And I'm flabbergasted about not only your honesty, but your willingness to take the time to deliver the billfold to my doorstep rather than simply call me to let me know I could arrange to pick it up.

You are a very special person, Mr. Simpson. If all the kids in the world had you for a role model, we would have no need of prisons.

With great appreciation,

• FOR ROMANTIC EVENING •

Percy,

What can I say? Even after all these years, you still surprise me. Thanks for a wonderful supper last night. The crème brûlée was an especially delicious touch. It reminded me of our trip to Quebec, the dinner at the hotel overlooking the river. I had a hunch then that you'd be the love of my life, and you know what? I was right.

xo

• FOR HOSPITALITY •

Edwina,

Staying with you and the girls was the highlight of my trip. Thanks so much for the Southern hospitality. Your veal cordon bleu was divine—as always—and I can't remember the last time I laughed as hard as I did the evening we spent on the porch reminiscing about our wild years in the Alpha Phi house. If you ever make it up to Detroit, my door is always open.

Love,

• FOR VISITING •

Tracy,

I didn't realize just how much I missed you until you got here. Thanks for spending Labor Day weekend with me and the girls. I know you had a lot of work waiting for you back at the office, but I was so glad you decided to stay the extra day so we could go to the museum. What a relaxing and fun afternoon that was.

I'll call you next week, and in the meantime, I'm finally going to look into flights to Detroit. Really.

Love,

VACATIONS AND TRAVEL ARRANGEMENTS

Alas, even fun and games require paperwork these days. There are maps, reservations, passports, cancellations, and complaints to deal with. But don't let the necessary preparation deter you from traveling in style and with confidence that your correspondence has paved the way for a delightfully uneventful (no surprises) vacation.

Summarize your travel plans in a sentence or two as an opener. (You will be safe to assume that your reader doesn't care about all the background and details spurring you to make the trip. Write only about your arrangements.) Jump right in with these direct openers:

"We plan to travel to your state next month and need..."

"I will be spending six weeks in your country..."

"My father will be traveling aboard your ship on August 9 to..."

Request information, reservations, confirmations, changes, or guarantees immediately, without fanfare.

"Would you please send confirmation that..."

"Please provide a confirmation number for our week's accommodations with you."

"What kind of guarantee do you provide in case of inclement weather?"

Repeat for verification purposes all dates, passenger names, group or member numbers, confirmation numbers, or record-locator numbers. And include any written documentation for previous arrangements or payments.

Mention any time frames and deadlines you have for making arrangements and decisions. Otherwise, you may find yourself in the unhappy predicament of having your bags packed with no place to go.

If you are commending a service employee, be specific in your praise. Specific praise sounds more sincere than general comments. Also, elaborate about why you are in a position to recognize excellent service (frequent travel, special needs not routinely met, and so forth). Consider these comments:

> *"I travel frequently overseas and seldom observe agents who are so good at..."*
>
> *"As a guest-relations supervisor, Mr. Maxwell has an uncanny way of identifying with those of us who are less outgoing and thus avoid the spotlight at such parties. I have been embarrassed on numerous occasions at other resorts. Not so with Mr. Maxwell in charge."*
>
> *"I spend more than 100 nights each year in hotel chains and, believe me, I know excellent service when I see it."*

You can travel confidently when you have tagged all the bases with your up-front correspondence. Time spent verifying the details before you leave home saves time and frustration on the road.

REQUESTS FOR INFORMATION

• Requesting Information from Resort or Hotel •

Dear Resort Representative:

My husband and I and our two children (ages six and 14) will be traveling to Corpus Christi the week of July 4 and would like some information about your resort before we make our final plans.

Would you describe your accommodations for our family (we prefer cooking amenities and a two-bedroom condo), availability for the week of July 2 to 9, and costs? Also, please state your policies on cancellations or changes and mention any deposits required. Would you include information on nearby recreational activities and their costs as well?

Please send your information packet to the above address as soon as possible so that we can make our final decisions. We look forward to learning about and possibly vacationing at your resort.

Sincerely,

• REQUESTING DINING RECOMMENDATION •

Dear Dining Editor,

Based on your website, I gather that *Columbia Monthly* boasts the city's most authoritative dining coverage. Next month I'll be in town for a convention and am looking for a great restaurant where I can entertain clients. It is important to me that the restaurant be local and not a chain with which my clients might already be familiar.

Could you recommend the top steakhouse in town as well as your overall pick for best restaurant? Thanks for any assistance you can provide, and I look forward to picking up an issue of your magazine when I'm in Columbia.

Regards,

• REQUESTING STATE ROAD MAP •

Dear Chamber of Commerce Representative:

Would you please send us a road map of Virginia so that we can select the most appropriate routes and activities as we vacation in your state? We'd prefer one that includes all the back roads, as well as enlargements of the metropolitan areas.

Any other information you can provide about lodging, attractions, or leisure activities would be welcome. Because we are in the midst of a move, please send the entire packet to my work address: 1357 Noel Road, Nashville, TN 37234.

Thank you for helping us as we make our vacation plans.

Sincerely,

• REQUESTING TOURIST INFORMATION •

Dear Columbia Tourism Bureau,

I'll be vacationing in Columbia with my family from June 12 to June 16. Could you send me information about tourist attractions in your city?

Also, my son recently broke his leg and will be in a wheelchair for the rest of the summer. Do you have any specific tourist recommendations for (temporarily) disabled visitors?

I appreciate any information you're able to provide.

Regards,

• REQUESTING ROUTE INFORMATION FROM TRAVEL CLUB •

Membership #88888888

Dear Acme Travel Club,

My wife and I are planning to drive from Roanoke, Virginia, to Taos, New Mexico, next month. We'd prefer to travel scenic state highways rather than interstates, but, because of health concerns, we also don't like to stray too far from the beaten path.

Could you provide us with maps and a recommended route based on the above considerations? We'd also like to avoid as many major construction zones as possible.

Sincerely,

• REQUESTING U.S. CUSTOMS INFORMATION ON FOREIGN TRAVEL •

Dear Director of Customs:

I'm planning to travel in Hong Kong, Singapore, and South Africa during the fall and would like copies of any publications or any information relative to customs restrictions for citizens returning to the United States from these locations.

Please send the information to my home address, listed above. Thank you.

Sincerely,

• REQUESTING VISA INFORMATION FROM FOREIGN COUNTRY •

Dear Visa Agent:

I plan to visit Sweden in the summer and need to have a current visa for that visit. I'll be staying in your country with relatives for approximately six weeks.

Would you please let me know what documents I must submit to apply for a visa and any other pertinent information such as applicable fees, forms, or restrictions? Will I be able to use the visa immediately, or is there some waiting period after issuance?

I'd welcome any other information you can include about health or medical regulations, customs, taxes, or procedures.

Thank you for your help, and I'll look forward to my stay in your country.

Sincerely,

• REQUESTING INFORMATION ABOUT FOREIGN COUNTRIES •

Dear Consul:

I plan to travel to the Far East (Bangkok, Japan, and Okinawa) in November and would like some information about this area.

Specifically, I'd like to know about areas of interest for tourists, any restrictions upon travel within each country, opportunities for temporary work there, and any immunization requirements or health-related restrictions in each country. Please provide any complimentary publications and an order form for any other helpful publications available for a fee.

Thank you for a prompt reply.

Sincerely,

• REQUESTING PASSPORT APPLICATION •

To U.S. Passport Office:

Please send me an application for a passport. Also please include any other information I'll need to complete the passport application, along with any time lines, restrictions, fee amounts, or required waiting periods.

I plan to travel to the Far East on March 3 and will appreciate your prompt response.

Sincerely,

• CHANGING PASSPORT INFORMATION •

Dear Passport Agent:

I've recently remarried and need to amend my passport. The original passport was issued on March 20, 2003, in the name Debra Jeltz. My current passport number is ABC1234.

Enclosed are my passport, a completed and signed change form, and a certified copy of my marriage certificate. After processing my amended passport, please return the passport and marriage certificate to me at the above address.

Thank you for your help with this change.

Sincerely,

MAKING ARRANGEMENTS

• REQUESTING TRAVEL AGENCY TO CONFIRM TRAVEL PLANS •

Dear Margie:

Thank you for researching the various vacation spots we discussed and putting together what sounds like a wonderful itinerary.

Would you please confirm the exact itinerary (including departure and arrival times), deposits and costs for each part of the vacation (the airfare for four, our resort accommodations, the rental car, and the three day tours we discussed), any regulations or restrictions, and any documentation that we need to travel? Also, please include any fees for changes or cancellations of any part of the plan.

Please send this complete confirmation of our itinerary and costs to me at the above address by April 1 so that we can finalize our plans and vacation schedules at work.

As soon as you provide this confirmation, we'd be happy to send you credit card information for any deposits required.

Sincerely,

• SUPPLYING MEDICAL CLEARANCE •

Example 1

Dear Medical Officer:

My father will be traveling on your cruise line aboard the *Princess,* May 6 to 18, on your trip from Miami to Acapulco. He is confined to a wheelchair and will require a stateroom with wheelchair access, located near the elevators, and with wheelchair ramps to the deck.

He will be traveling with a complete list of medical data and supplies of his necessary medications. Enclosed is a copy of Dr. Delroy Washington's statement certifying that he is medically able to travel aboard your ship as required by your guidelines.

If you have other questions about my father's medical condition or precautions, please phone me at (123) 456-7899. Otherwise, he'll be looking forward to a relaxing trip aboard your cruise line. Thank you for your kind attention to the medical details to ensure his safety.

Sincerely,

• SUPPLYING MEDICAL CLEARANCE •

Example 2

Dear Medical Officer:

I will be traveling on May 6 to Buenos Aires by way of your airline. I am confined to a battery-powered wheelchair as a result of the amputation of both legs.

If medical clearance is required by your airline, please send me all appropriate forms at your earliest convenience. Any other information that you can send regarding special assistance in boarding, equipment storage, or security processes will be very helpful to me as I make final plans in the next month.

Thank you for your help.

Sincerely,

• REQUESTING ROOM VIEW •

Dear Hotel Manager,

I'm writing in regard to my request for a room with an ocean view. My husband and I will be staying at your hotel later this month, from July 7 to July 9 (confirmation number 9999999). When I made the reservation, I was told that ocean-view rooms could be requested but were not guaranteed.

I thought you might be interested to know that my husband and I have stayed at your hotel once before, 20 years ago, on our honeymoon. I'll never forget waking to the sunrise over the water each morning; it was beautiful. It would mean so much to us if you're able to find us an ocean-view room for this, our second honeymoon.

Thanks for your kind attention and consideration.

Sincerely,

• REQUEST TO HOLD NEWSPAPER •

RE: Account #999999

Dear Circulation Department,

Please suspend daily delivery of my *Star & Ledger* from Saturday, June 11 through Sunday, June 19. Rather than credit my account for the missed days, please donate the newspapers to underprivileged youth through your Greenville Young Readers outreach program.

Sincerely,

• REQUESTING DISCOUNT FOR BEREAVEMENT TRAVEL •

Dear Customer Service Agent:

On September 6, I traveled from Las Vegas to Atlanta on Flight 498 to attend the funeral of my brother (Ernest Horner) and returned on Flight 567 on September 8. I understand that you have discount rates for bereavement travel, but neglected to ask for that rate during the emergency situation.

Would you please credit the difference between the fee I paid for the coach ticket ($652) and that discounted rate? My MasterCard account number is 4444-4444-4444-4444, with an expiration date of October 1, 20—.

Copies of my ticket receipt and the obituary notice are enclosed. Thank you for your prompt attention to this refund.

Sincerely,

• NEGOTIATING LOWER HOTEL RATE •

Dear Holiday Inn Manager,

Last week, I made a reservation to stay at your hotel for eight nights, beginning February 6, at a rate of $124 per night (confirmation number 9999999).

Since then, I've learned that comparable hotels in the area, including the Hyatt and Sheraton, are offering similar rooms at a rate of $112 per night during the same period. Would you be willing to match or beat their rates?

As a frequent guest at the Holiday Inn, I'd much prefer to stay with you, but I'm traveling on a tight budget and must take advantage of the most affordable lodging available.

I can be reached at the number above. Please contact me at your earliest convenience about the comparable pricing.

Thank you,

• GUARANTEEING RESERVATION BY PREPAYMENT •

Dear Resort Owner:

We have reservations with your resort for November 16 to 28 for a one-bedroom suite at a rate of $178 per night. Our confirmation number is 123456789.

Because the weather is so unpredictable at that time of the year, we may arrive later than expected. Therefore, we are providing credit card information so that the room will be guaranteed even if we are detained a day or so. My VISA account number is 4444-9999-8888-777, with an expiration date of May 20—. The account is in my wife's name: Leslie B. Swanson.

Please send us confirmation that you have received this letter and have guaranteed our accommodations by signing below and returning the letter for our files. We're looking forward to our stay with you.

Sincerely,

Requested Accommodations Guaranteed by Credit Card:

Signature _____ Date _____

• REQUESTING EXTENDED STAY •

Dear Marriott Manager,

I'm writing to request two additional nights for my existing reservation (confirmation #9999999).

Last week, I made the reservation for eight nights, beginning February 6. Since then, I've learned that I need to stay two more nights, but when I called your reservation line, I was told you're booked.

Comparable hotels in the area, including the Hyatt and Sheraton, can accommodate me for the entire ten-night stay at a competitive rate, but as a frequent guest at the Marriott, I'd much prefer to stay with you. That said, I'm unwilling to switch hotels during the course of my stay.

Please contact me at your earliest convenience to let me know if you can accommodate me on the two extra nights.

Regards,

• CANCELING RESERVATION •

Dear Resort Owner:

We must cancel our reservations with you for the week of February 2 to 8. Our confirmation number is 9999999.

Our change in plans has become necessary because of the unexpected serious illness of one of our children. If you make exceptions to your cancellation policy for such circumstances, we would appreciate your doing so in this case. If you cannot make an exception, you may deduct the $100 nonrefundable deposit on our credit card, with the credit card information we've already provided.

Please verify our cancellation as of this date with your own form or letter, or simply sign below and return this letter for our files.

Sincerely,

Authorization of Cancellation:

Signature _____ Date _____

APPRECIATION AND COMPLAINTS

• EXPRESSING APPRECIATION TO HOTEL •

Dear Manager:

Our family recently stayed in your hotel (May 10 to 14) while my husband attended a convention at the nearby convention center. The service we received from your concierge, Giles Thatcher, was exceptional.

My child became sick on the second day and Giles quickly arranged for the hotel van to drive us to a local clinic for medical care and then to pick us up at the clinic after we had seen the doctor. That may have been typical procedure; but what follows is very atypical.

The next day when my child had a sudden reaction to the medicine, Giles could not locate the van driver (it seems he was on some errand for another guest). Granted, it was not an emergency situation (just a rash), but Giles quickly volunteered to drive us again to the clinic for another visit. Then he waited with us and drove us to a nearby pharmacy to fill a prescription.

Later that day, he sent a bouquet of balloons and coloring books to the room to entertain my son. On each of the successive mornings, he phoned our room to ask about improvement in my son's condition. His calls showed genuine concern and provided a few minutes of entertainment for my son.

I travel frequently with my husband on business, and believe me, I recognize the difference between service provided because

(Continued)

"we must" and that provided from a genuine willingness to help and an attitude of serving the customer—no matter how young that customer may be. I hope you'll share my comments with Giles and reward him accordingly for his service to us. You're lucky to have such a fine young person on your staff.

We'll look forward to staying with you again when our plans call for travel to Baltimore.

Sincerely,

• COMPLAINING TO HOTEL •

Dear Manager:

I stayed in your hotel three nights (January 5 to 7) and experienced a traveler's nightmare during the visit: unsafe conditions, limited service in your restaurant and from the room-service menu, and inadequate maid service. Had I not been unable to find other accommodations on this convention-packed weekend, I would have left your hotel after the first night of inexcusable service. Because of unavailable accommodations elsewhere, I was forced to endure for the duration of the stay.

Considering the circumstances detailed below, I believe I'm justified in requesting at least a 50 percent refund of the final bill (enclosed). The clerk who checked me out on the morning of my departure had no authority to make any adjustment and suggested that I write this letter.

First the unsafe conditions: After I unpacked my bags and dressed for bed, another guest mistakenly barged in because he had been given a key to the same room. Upon retiring for the night, I discovered that the adjoining door to the next room was unlocked and broken. Then, after calling for repair, I had to wait two hours for someone to come to my room to repair the lock.

The following morning, I waited 50 minutes for room service for breakfast (the order was placed the evening before). The next morning, room service did not deliver my breakfast at all, claiming it never received the order. That evening, I tried to have dinner in your informal restaurant. It was 15 minutes before anyone approached my table to take my order. Then when I did order, the waitress returned to the table twice to tell me that the menu item was not in stock and asked me to make another selection.

(Continued)

As for maid service, I could tell only that my bed had been made and new towels delivered each day. No vacuuming. No bathroom cleanup.

It is clear that your hotel is badly understaffed. Had I chosen a less expensive hotel at cheaper rates, I might have excused such problems. But this type of environment and service is totally out of character for a hotel chain of your fame.

Please let me hear from you immediately about the adjustment to my bill.

Sincerely,

• APPRECIATION TO AIRLINE •

Dear President of Airline,

I'm writing to commend one of your flight attendants, Eunice McPhee, for her exemplary customer service aboard Flight 64 from New York to Los Angeles on June 4.

The morning of the flight, I contracted food poisoning, but I didn't realize how sick I was until the plane was already airborne. That's when I started throwing up. Fortunately, Ms. McPhee was there. She quickly found me a seat closer to the restroom, brought plenty of sickness bags, and made sure I had a steady supply of fluids. My condition wasn't pretty—pretty gross is more like it—but Ms. McPhee treated me with compassion and respect, never making me feel like a burden. She was as much a nurse as a flight attendant

I appreciate your employing flight attendants of Ms. McPhee's caliber, and I hope you'll see fit to recognize her superior service during Flight 64. Meanwhile, I look forward to patronizing your airline again soon.

Sincerely,

• COMPLAINING TO AIRLINE •

Dear Customer Service Representative:

I'm writing you regarding my dissatisfaction about the way in which your agent handled a situation involving a damaged piece of luggage during my trip from San Francisco to West Palm Beach on April 17, Flight 466.

At the conclusion of the incident, your representative told me to have the damaged bag repaired and enclose the receipt with my claim form and wait for reimbursement. I took the form and left the airport, but upon later reflection I decided that I did not want to handle the incident in that manner. Instead, I want reimbursement for the purchase of a new bag.

When the bag came off the plane, the hinges had become mangled, the sides were crushed, and clothes were hanging out on all sides. To make matters worse, the agent on duty showed no concern about the situation, preferring instead to "process us" quickly so that she could take her lunch break. Because there were seven other people waiting in line with damaged bags, I did not press her quick decision that I should be the one to do the work—take it for repair and fill out a claim form.

However, upon examining the bag more closely, I determined that any repair would be unacceptable with such damage. And because I had immediate need of a bag for a trip two days later, I purchased another one. Thus, I'm enclosing the receipt for that replacement bag rather than an estimate for the damage on my older bag.

Please send my reimbursement check immediately.

Sincerely,

• APPRECIATION TO RENTAL CAR AGENCY •

Dear President of Rental Car Company,

I'm writing to commend one of your agents, Jackson Coombs, for his exemplary customer service. On June 6, I rented a car from Mr. Coombs at the Greenville airport. Because of business obligations, I was an hour late returning the car, but when I explained the situation to Mr. Coombs, he didn't charge me a late fee.

Ten minutes later, I was approaching the security checkpoint when I realized I'd left my briefcase in the car. There simply wasn't time for me to retrieve it and still make my flight, so imagine my surprise and relief when I saw Mr. Coombs enter the terminal, carrying my briefcase, the lock and contents still intact.

I appreciate your employing agents of Mr. Coombs's caliber, and I hope you'll see fit to recognize his energetic commitment to customer service. I look forward to renting cars from your agency in the future.

Sincerely,

• COMPLAINT TO RENTAL CAR AGENCY •

Dear President of Rental Car Company,

I'm writing to complain about one of your agents, Jackson Coombs, for his exceedingly poor customer service.

On June 6, I rented a car from Mr. Coombs at the Greenville airport. Despite the fact that I had a confirmed reservation for a luxury car, Mr. Coombs told me he had nothing available but an economy model. I protested, and he told me I was lucky to be getting a car at all.

Furthermore, the rate he quoted me was much higher than I would expect to pay for an economy car. When I decided to try my luck at one of the other rental agencies in the terminal, Mr. Coombs informed me that, because I had a confirmed reservation, he'd be charging my credit card regardless of whether I actually rented one of your cars.

Needless to say, I won't be renting from your agency again unless I receive a full refund for both days of my rental. Also, I look forward to hearing how you'll address Mr. Coombs' short-comings in the area of customer relations and a positive, helpful attitude.

Sincerely,

OTHER RESOURCES BY DIANNA BOOHER

BOOKS

Clean Up Your Act

Communicate with Confidence: How to Say It Right the First Time and Every Time

The Complete Letterwriter's Almanac

The Esther Effect

E-Writing

Executive's Portfolio of Model Speeches for All Occasions

Freshcut Flowers for a Friend

Get a Life without Sacrificing Your Career

Good Grief, Good Grammar

Great Personal Letters for Busy People

Little Book of Big Questions

Love Notes

Mother's Gifts to Me

The New Secretary: How to Handle People as Well as You Handle Paper

Send Me a Memo

Speak with Confidence: Powerful Presentations that Inform, Inspire, and Persuade

Ten Smart Moves for Women

To the Letter: A Handbook of Model Letters for the Busy Executive

Well Connected: Power Your Own Soul by Plugging into Others

Winning Sales Letters

Worth of a Woman's Words

Writing for Technical Professionals

Your Signature Life

Your Signature Work

VIDEOTAPES

Basic Steps for Better Business Writing (series)

Business Writing: Quick, Clear, Concise

Closing the Gap: Gender Communications Skills

Cutting Paperwork: Management Strategies

Cutting Paperwork: Support Staff Strategies

AUDIOTAPE SERIES

Get Your Book Published

People Power

Write to the Point: Business Communications from Memos to Meetings

SOFTWARE (CDs and Web-Based e-Learning)

Effective Editing
Effective Writing
Good Grief, Good Grammar
Model Business Letters
Model Personal Letters
Model Sales Letters
Model Speeches and Toasts
More Good Grief, Good Grammar
Ready, Set, NeGOtiate

WORKSHOPS

Communicate with Confidence®
Developing Winning Proposals
eService™
Good Grief, Good Grammar
Listening Until You Really Hear
Meetings: Leading and Participating Productively
Negotiating So That Everyone Feels Like a Winner
Presentations That Work®
Resolving Conflict without Punching Someone Out
Strategic Writing™
Technical Writing

SPEECHES

Communicate with Confidence®

Communicating CARE to Customers

Communication: From Boardroom to Bedroom

Communication Cues and Clues for Rave Reviews

The Gender Communication Gap: "Did You Hear What I Think I Said?"

Get a Life without Sacrificing Your Career

Platform Tips for the Presenter

Putting Together the Puzzle of Personal Excellence

Write This Way to Success

You Are Your Future: Employable for a Lifetime

Your Signature Life®: The Plan and the Purpose—Despite the Pain and the Pace

FOR MORE INFORMATION

Booher Consultants, Inc.
2051 Hughes Road
Grapevine, TX 76051
817-318-6000
mailroom@booher.com
www.Booher.com

Dianna Booher and her staff travel internationally, speaking and presenting seminars and training workshops on communication and other personal development topics.

ABOUT THE AUTHOR

Dianna Booher is an internationally recognized business communications expert and the author of 42 books, including *Communicate with Confidence®, Speak with Confidence,* and *Get a Life Without Sacrificing Your Career,* all published by McGraw-Hill. She is founder and president of Dallas-based Booher Consultants. Among her clients are NASA, the Department of the Army, the U.S. Department of Veteran Affairs, and many Fortune 500 companies, including IBM, ExxonMobil, Frito-Lay, Bank of America, J. P. Morgan Chase, Caterpillar, Verizon, Siemens, Lockheed Martin, and Boeing, among numerous others.